EMPOWERING
PEOPLE

EMPOWERING PEOPLE

My Line in the Sand Empowering People
Through Restrained Government

PETER KONETCHY

authorHOUSE®

AuthorHouse™
1663 Liberty Drive
Bloomington, IN 47403
www.authorhouse.com
Phone: 1-800-839-8640

Published by AuthorHouse   03/06/2013

ISBN: 978-1-4817-2138-7 (sc)
ISBN: 978-1-4817-2137-0 (hc)
ISBN: 978-1-4817-2139-4 (e)

Library of Congress Control Number: 2013903666

To our Posterity,

May they know the Blessings of Liberty

Introduction

At some point, every man must stand and fight for what he cherishes. He can no longer retreat, but must prevail or lose everything he holds dear. This is his "Line in the Sand," a point where he declares to his foe, "thus far and no farther."

Ronald Reagan stated, *"Freedom is never more than one generation away from extinction. We didn't pass it to our children in the bloodstream. It must be fought for, protected, and handed on for them to do the same, or one day we will spend our sunset years telling our children and our children's children what it was once like in the United States where men were free."*

There was a time when I couldn't comprehend the possibility that my country, The United States of America, the greatest, most moral, prosperous, charitable, and powerful country the world has ever known, and the only country ever dedicated to securing the Liberty of its people, could be destroyed within a span of a single generation. I see how very wrong I was.

There is no external foe able to craft our defeat. Our foe is from within.

Our elected representatives no longer understand the necessity of a severely limited federal government. They've instituted policies which continually expand federal influence and power far beyond any legitimate constitutional authority. They now seek to control and subdue the people whose rights they're charged with protecting.

Unless they're stopped, our country will cease to exist. My children and grandchildren, our posterity, will never know freedom and will live in a society ruled by a privileged class of elite parasites.

I cannot accept this scenario. I love this country and understand that its greatness is directly derived from an unrestrained people living in a safe, secure, and sovereign nation.

History has proven beyond any doubt that the unleashed potential of free men elevates all aspects of society infinitely above any bureaucratically controlled order.

We've been bequeathed with the solution, the greatest force for freedom ever conceived by man, unique in the world—the United States Constitution. It limits the power of the federal government to the national duties required to maintain a safe and sovereign nation; but more importantly, it prohibits any federal control or influence over the people's lives. It establishes a uniquely free nation.

We have allowed those in government to ignore every aspect of the Constitution they find inconvenient. They've come to believe that they are omnipotent, the solution, rather than acknowledging that every problem plaguing our nation is the direct result of their unconstitutional impositions.

The decision makers today concur with Obama's message, *"We are the ones we've been waiting for."*

I say thus far and no farther. I will no longer allow my government to destroy my country and force my heirs to live in servitude. I choose to bestow upon our posterity the same liberty which was conferred to me. I will fight to uphold the hallowed, time-tested constitutional provisions protecting liberty; otherwise, the unimaginable will occur, and our country will cease to exist. We have no choice. This is my line in the sand from which I cannot retreat.

Peter Konetchy

Acknowledgements

I am deeply grateful to my wife, Zhanna, for her support, insight, and significant contribution. She grew up in the Soviet Union and relates her firsthand knowledge of life in a controlled society. More importantly, she explains in detail the tactics employed by Lenin to impose total, ruthless, control over an unaware population, resulting in their domination and loss of freedom. The same tactics are being employed today in the United States, and unless countered, will yield the same results. She understands the greatness of freedom and of personal liberty and is unwilling to give it up.

I am also appreciative of Jeannie Burchfield and Misty Crawford for their help in reviewing this manuscript. It was a herculean task, and I thank them for their immense time and effort.

CONTENTS

ONE:

PETER KONETCHY

I know that God has a sense of humor. I've worn a beard since I was in my early twenties, because I have a very small chin, chubby face, and big nose.

Early one morning, about 15 years ago, I shaved my beard.

I went to the kitchen where all my kids were eating breakfast and started a conversation. Nobody noticed. My wife, Zhanna, walked in a few minutes later and started talking with us. She noticed my ear-to-ear smile, but not the missing beard.

After a few minutes I announced, "I shaved my beard!"

The unanimous reaction from everyone in the room was, "Put it Back!"

I have never shaved it again.

I've had a very good life.

It started in a small town in Massachusetts, Norfolk, a little to the southwest of Boston. Times were different then—no computers, Facebook, or Internet. Kids used their imaginations and played outside.

We were a typical American family with the national average of 2.3 kids rounded up to a whole three. I had two older siblings, Doug and

Linda, and both my parents. When we were small, my mother stayed home with the kids, and my father worked for an insurance company.

My parents valued a good education. We were expected to learn, and they made sure we did. I remember many nights when all of us kids would sit around our dining room table doing our homework together under the watchful eyes of my mother.

Schools taught patriotism and government. I remember my high school civics teacher explaining that immigrants to the United States wanted to assimilate into our society and become Americans and to celebrate the distinctly American culture and values. He explained that this separated us from virtually every other nation in the world and made us strong.

I started to learn the value of work and money at an early age. My buddy and I wanted to earn some spending money, but our options were limited. Most of the families on our street had kids, so there wasn't much demand for cutting lawns or doing neighborhood chores. We decided to pick apples at a small, local orchard. The owner agreed, but never discussed our wages with us. My buddy and I picked apples all afternoon, all the while discussing the windfall profit we expected to make. The owner obviously had a different opinion regarding the value of our work and paid us a few cents per bushel picked. We ended up working all afternoon and earned a total of about 50 cents each. We never went back for more work, but learned the importance of discussing our wage prior to performing a job.

My dad decided to change careers. He quit his insurance position and entered into a partnership with a friend who owned a small manufacturing company. He hired me for my first real job. I rode my bike several miles each afternoon to a small factory to mix powdered laundry detergent. We had a series of mixers into which we mixed a formula of various chemicals and perfumes, which would be packaged into containers varying from 5 to 100 pounds. I worked about 10 to 12 hours per week and earned good money for a 13-year-old.

A year or so later, my father's company acquired a home-based detergent manufacturing company in Michigan, and our family moved to Detroit. I attended a Christian high school and worked at my father's company during vacations.

I had the privilege of attending Michigan State University, earning a degree in Accounting. I received a great education, met good friends, and had fun.

Work

I worked at the family soap business throughout college and continued after graduation. Computers were introduced to small business in the late 1970's, and we bought one to manage our inventory, sales, and accounting.

Prepackaged software didn't exist; everything had to be custom programmed. We contracted with a small, husband and wife programming team to help us develop and install the required software. I understood the information flow within our company, but had no computer experience. I learned programming by working with the developers performing simple tasks. Before long, I had enough knowledge to be able to perform the majority of the programming work. A couple years later, the installation was complete, and I decided to move on.

I was actually very good at programming and was hired as a contract programmer by the firm who helped set up my father's system. I worked with many different types of businesses, including property managers, vending machine companies, mortgage providers, manufactures, and law firms. Every firm had similar software needs, which needed to be tweaked to their specific industry. All needed basic accounting, receivables, check writing, receipts, general ledger, inventory, and productivity reporting, allowing me to combine my education with my previous work experience.

The computer systems back then were mid-range IBM and Wang computer systems using a now-antiquated programming language called RPGII. The systems took up most of the room and had just a fraction of the processing power of today's PC's.

I was single, doing well, making good money, and was debt free. I decided to pursue the American dream of starting my own company, being scarcely 25 years old, naïve, confident, and full of hope.

I found a niche working with law firms. I had many customers and developed custom software packages for the various types of law firms—defense, corporate, and plaintiff. I decided to develop a single software program that would meet the needs of all the various types of law firms I worked for.

I bought a used Wang midrange system, printer, and terminals, weighing about one thousand pounds, and installed them in my living room. I spent countless hours coding software into a marketable package I titled L.A.W.S.—Legal, Accounting, and Word processing System. Only large law firms could afford to purchase computer systems, and I was able to install my L.A.W.S. software in a good percentage of the large law firms in the Detroit metro area as well as in many throughout the entire state of Michigan.

Our basic package was well designed but was continually enhanced through the implementation of suggestions from users.

As with anything in the free market, computer equipment became smaller, cheaper, and more powerful, allowing us to service smaller firms. We migrated our software from the mid-range IBM and Wang systems to the personal computer and finally to the Internet where it resides today.

We were never a large firm and employed on average between 2 to 5 employees. There were times when we did quite well and times that were tight. Regardless of the situation, we persevered and things worked out fine.

Marriage

I strongly support the institution of marriage, and believe that it is between one man, one woman, and God, and that it is meant to last a lifetime.

Throughout my life I've been divorced, widowed, and happily married.

Divorced

I married my first wife shortly after I started my own business. We bought a nice house in Novi, a suburb of Detroit, and started a family. Not too many families had a mid-range computer system up and running in their living room. We did. (I did move into an office shortly thereafter and used the living room as a living room.) We both worked, and I was either out of the house, on the road, or in my office. My wife worked as a programmer at an auto supplier just outside Detroit.

My wife and I had two kids, Mark and Lisa. I never understood the meaning of absolute "Love" until I first held my firstborn son, Mark. I loved being a father. Whenever I was able, I would play with my kids after breakfast and before work for as long as possible. Since both my wife and I worked, we dropped our children off at daycare.

Being self-employed, we went through times of plenty and times of drought. I always had to meet my payroll and pay my other bills first, and then pay myself last.

After about seven years of marriage, we encountered a couple of years of drought. Money was tight, and, for a short time, we could not pay our bills in a timely manner and were delinquent on our property taxes. Needless to say, there was stress in our lives. Though we both loved our children, we had different goals and priorities and lacked a common focus. I'm unhappy to say that we decided to divorce.

I'm not proud of this divorce. I was young and stupid. It was a difficult decision to accept and very hard on the children. I would not wish divorce on any couple, and counsel anybody thinking about it to love their spouse, work through the hard times, and stay together.

Widowed

A couple of years after my divorce, I volunteered my time at a nursing home. My duties consisted of anything that needed to be done. I'd escort residents to and from dinner, empty the wastebaskets, and often just visit and talk with the guests.

I met a nurse at this facility, Lilly. We fell in love over the next several months and were married. She was the perfect woman—pretty, lively, fun, and conservative. Lilly loved my kids from my first marriage as she would love her own.

We bought a small house in Byron, MI, just south of Flint, which had about 10 wooded acres, an old barn complete with barn cats, and apple and pear trees.

We had the perfect life. We fixed up our little house, cleaned out the barn, traveled the country visiting family and friends, and generally pursued our happiness.

We both enjoyed the outdoors and wanted to purchase some land. We found some acreage "up-north," which had a small hunting cabin surrounded by state land teaming with wildlife. We bought it.

Lilly became pregnant with our first (my third) child shortly after we were married. She was ecstatic to be a mom. She was able to stop working, stay home, and grow her belly. My sister had two children at home using a midwife and cherished this birth experience. Lilly wanted to do the same. We contacted my sister's midwife, and she and Lilly hit it off immediately. I was more worried than anybody about possible complications, but was assured by the midwife that all would go smoothly. She assured me that at the time of delivery she would be in contact with the local hospital, so medical attention would be available if needed.

Lilly had regular visits with the midwife, and everything was progressing well.

The big day arrived. Lilly's water broke, and I called the midwife. Lilly was a trooper, walking around calmly while I frantically waited for the midwife. Early in the evening, the midwife arrived, but didn't feel very well. In fact, she had to lie on the couch through the majority of the labor while passing instructions on to me.

Around 2:00 a.m., our son was born. The midwife felt well enough to deliver our son, passed him off to me, ensured that my Lilly was fine, then again lay down. As I was walking around our living room, cradling our newborn son in my arms, the name that flooded into my mind was Nathaniel, meaning "Gift from God." It was the perfect name. Lilly agreed.

I passed our son to his mother and drew them a warm bath. The midwife was able to drive herself home, Lilly and our son took a nice, relaxing, warm bath while I changed the linens. In a few hours, we were all sleeping as a newly expanded family.

I must admit it was an unconventional birth, but precious and unforgettable. Lilly loved Nate. She was the perfect mother and the perfect wife.

About 8 months after Nate was born, Lilly became weak and sick. Her mom was able to provide care and comfort both at our home and at the hospital, but shortly thereafter Lilly passed on.

I was devastated that Lilly was gone. Nate was a barely 8 months old and not even walking, and he didn't have his mother.

Nate and I did as well as we could, and eventually, the good, silly, and fun times started to return. I remember bathing Nate, drying him off, and then letting him run, laughing and naked, back to his room to put on his diaper and pajamas. More than once, I would see a trail of turds on his path between the bathroom and his room. It was good practice for future pets.

We didn't have a dishwasher, so Nate and I would do dishes together. He would stand on a chair in front of the sink with his sponge, and feel proud to be helping his dad.

On my way to work, I would drop Nate off with a neighbor friend who would watch him during the day, and I'd pick him up at night. We were surviving.

Happily Married

A year or so after Lilly's passing I read an article in the Flint Journal about a pen-pal service that allowed people to write to others throughout the world. It sounded interesting.

I started to write letters to different people in many countries. It was interesting and fun to learn about other customs and lives. One person in particular caught my attention—Zhanna.

How we happened to meet was a miracle. Zhanna sums it up in one word—Providence.

She was a widow with a small child who lived on the opposite side of the world—11 time zones away in Siberia, of all places. We wrote regularly, even though it took up to a month to have a letter delivered. We wrote about everything—the events in our lives, children, work, home, beliefs, and dreams.

I wrote to her in English using a printer, so my writing would be as clear as possible. I didn't realize until several years later the hardship Zhanna endured reading these letters. Whenever she received my letter, she would first need to translate it word-by-word into Russian, answer my letter in Russian, and then translate the answer into English.

After writing for over a year, I knew Zhanna was the one. I fell in Love with Zhanna through her letters—a very special and unusual way to meet. God works in mysterious ways and chose us for each other. He told me, "There's a special, wonderful, and good woman I want you to meet." I couldn't refuse. I scheduled a trip to Moscow and Zhanna flew there from Siberia. It was a great meeting. We had a good chance to talk and visited sites in Moscow such as the Kremlin, museums, churches, Saint Basils Cathedral, the Bolshoi Theater, and many other interesting places and restaurants. Zhanna had learned English in school, but it wasn't her native language. It was a pleasurable challenge communicating throughout the week, and by the end of the visit, we were experts in international communication.

The visit exceeded our expectations, and we decided to apply for a Fiancée Visa at the United States embassy to lay the groundwork for Zhanna to immigrate to the United States.

Upon my return, I had to decide whether to live in Byron or in the hunting cabin up north. I chose Roscommon. I gutted the cabin, installed insulation and all new windows, built kitchen cabinets, remodeled the bathroom, and added lofts to both kids' bedrooms. I replaced all the original drywall with tongue-and-groove pine, giving the cabin's interior a rustic look. It turned out pretty good.

My father-in-law, Lilly's dad Marcus, helped me build a pole barn to use for storage and as a garage. He never had much of a formal education, but is one of the smartest men I know. He has common sense. He always took care of his family, built most of the houses he and his sons lived in, and ran his own excavating business.

In August 1993, Zhanna and her 6-year-old-daughter, Lena, arrived in the United States. Lena didn't speak a word of English and was scheduled to start school in a matter of days. We talked to the principal to determine whether she should immediately enroll in school, or be held back for a while until she learned English. The principal gently insisted that Lena start at once.

Without knowing a word of English, Lena started first grade, sat in the front row, and listened. Several months later, around Thanksgiving, she told her teacher, "Good Morning," in English and by Christmas, Lena was fluent. The principal was right.

Zhanna and I got married in November and our fifth child was on the way shortly thereafter.

Building our House

The cabin was quite small, about 900 square feet. When my two older kids stayed with us, it was crowded with four kids, two adults, and another child on the way. We needed more space. We had plenty of land—about 70 acres—and decided to build our own house. I had never attempted a building project as large as this before, but Marcus said he would gladly give us a hand.

The following spring, we started to clear a parcel for our new house just a couple of months before Alex, our youngest son, was born. Just after his birth, we rented a backhoe, and Marcus started to dig the foundation. Since we had a large family, and were building the house ourselves, we wanted to do it right. The plan was about 3,200 square feet, and had five bedrooms and five bathrooms. We also decided to include a lap pool in the basement that could be used year round. The house had two stories, a basement, a garage, and a wraparound covered porch. It would meet our needs well into the future.

We took out a construction loan, meaning that we needed to invest all of our savings into the project as a down payment, and then the bank would pay the difference up to our borrowing limit.

Marcus taught me a lot—how to survey the land, read blueprints, prepare the foundation, pour cement, and most importantly, how to build. He normally came up early Friday morning, and we worked until Sunday afternoon, just the two of us with Zhanna's help—surrounded by kids.

It was hard work—especially on hot summer days. We carried sheet after sheet of plywood for the construction of floors and walls. Then we built the interior partitions and staircases, and finally the roof.

The kids thought it was a giant playhouse. There were large piles of sand around the shell from digging the basement. The kids liked jumping out of any opening, from just about any height, into the sand.

Peter Konetchy

We worried about it at first, but after a period of nobody getting hurt, we didn't give it a second thought.

I had my learning experiences. One was installing bay windows in the front of our house. The opening was supposed to be 7 feet, 2 inches. I measured the opening myself—twice, and we built the wall based on my measurements. Once the shell was complete, we tried to install the windows; they didn't fit. It turned out that I measured 72 inches rather than 7 feet 2 inches. I learned then that there's just about no construction problem that can't be fixed with a good circular saw.

Another opportunity to grow came when we were sheeting the roof. The house was pretty high—two stories plus the roof. The first time I got to the peak of the roof, I was scared silly. It was so high. Marcus laughed at me a little bit, shamed me into working, and before you knew it, I was walking all over the roof as if I knew what I was doing.

Zhanna's job was shingling, and she was very good at it. She expressed much more intelligence than I by refusing to go on the second-story roof. She had her hammer and nail pouch, and shingled the majority of the first-floor porch and garage. I could never quite convince her to carry up the bundles of shingles, but she did the rest.

By the end of the summer, the exterior of the house was complete. We had the siding on, the basement backfilled, the porch complete and all shut in with windows and doors. It actually looked like a normal house.

Marcus left for his wintering in Florida. Zhanna and I started to attack the interior of the house. We contracted out the plumbing and drywall, but did everything else ourselves. I had never electrically wired a house before, but learned quickly. I became an expert in two-, three-, and four-way light switches. We put in the insulation, tile, all the window and door trim, cupboards, and laid our hardwood floors.

Zhanna is an expert painter. She took full responsibility for staining all our woodwork and painting the entire interior.

The house was finally finished. We moved in. Everything was perfect. Not a week after we moved in, I looked at the windowsill in Nate's room and noticed that he had used a pencil point, like a woodpecker's head, to decorate his windowsill. I figured, "What the heck, let the fun begin." This is life.

We live in a big house, and heating is expensive. To counter this problem, we decided to supplement our heating system with wood. We purchased a wood-burning stove and kept it burning all winter long. We built a woodshed behind our house that holds about 12 or so face cords of wood.

Each spring, my sons and I split firewood with an ax, not a splitter. The kids were young and thought it fun to help. They would wind up and strike the log with their axes, which would bounce off the top of the log. They'd try and try, without success, leaving the end of the log crisscrossed with ax marks. Eventually they would split the log and earn a true sense of accomplishment. When filling the woodstove on cold winter days, I would come across one of the logs with a zillion ax marks on top and feel a sense of pride in their perseverance.

As years went by, they got older and stronger, and all became proficient wood splitters.

Zhanna didn't work outside the home. She cared for all of our children and kept up the house and yard. She loved gardening and planted gorgeous flower gardens all around our home and a separate vegetable garden. We dabbled with grape vines and various fruit trees. Over the 18 years we've lived in the house, we have probably harvested about three apples, 20 cherries, and about a dozen plums. Thank goodness for grocery stores.

Three kids lived with us full time and, at that time, attended public school. We had dinner together every night and talked to our kids about what they were learning in school. We were disturbed by the fact that they didn't have homework, Lena was watching movies such as Toy Story in class, Nate couldn't comprehend what he was reading, and Alex was learning how to use a calculator in second grade.

Peter Konetchy

We talked extensively with their teachers and received disappointing answers. The teachers in Lena's middle school explained that they had to teach to the lowest performing child in the class, who stayed up all night, fell asleep in class, and had no desire to be in school. While the teacher was focusing on this student, all the others were allowed to watch a movie.

We talked to Nate's teachers about his difficulty with reading comprehension. He could read the sentences well and pronounce all the words, but if you asked him what was meant by the sentence he had just read, he wouldn't have any idea. His teacher said he was doing just fine and not to worry.

Alex was in second grade and was learning to depend on a calculator before he thoroughly understood the underlying mathematical concepts. I did not agree with this approach. I talked to the teacher who agreed with me, but said she had no choice, and that the school board, via the state, insisted that the calculators be used.

Zhanna and I decided that we could do better. We pulled our kids from the public school and started homeschooling. Zhanna was the primary teacher. We chose curriculum from an organization called "Christian Liberty School," which we complemented with other courses we believed to be important.

Nate had the hardest time being homeschooled in fifth grade. He had learned in public school how to survive. He could read without comprehending and repeat without understanding. These techniques didn't work with his mother. He actually repeated his fifth grade of homeschool and excelled thereafter.

I believed it important for our children to have our Christian faith integrated with their daily education. I appreciate the fact that we were able to homeschool as we thought best, rather than being forced to expose our children to a purely secular public education.

Our kids tired of homeschooling during their high school years and wanted to interact with other kids during the school day. We decided to place them in a private, Christian high school that had values closely matching our own. They were well prepared, ahead of their classmates, and well adjusted.

We had a good life. I was responsible for my wife and five children. At the time I divorced, I was earning a good wage, and my child support payments for my two oldest children were set relatively high. I could afford them and paid them.

When I built the house, I was required to deplete all my savings as a down payment on our loan. After that, I was living from paycheck to paycheck, doing well and meeting our responsibilities, but I was not able to replenish our savings.

As with most small businesses, I had several employees working for me who I had to pay first. I received what was left over.

I did experience several years when money was very tight. I never accepted charity or public assistance, but I had trouble meeting my obligations during that time. I was late on my mortgage, child support, and other obligations. More than once, I was summoned by the Friend of the Court to explain my child support delinquency. I never asked that my support payments be reduced, and I paid my obligation in full—a little late, but in full.

During these years, my kids were always taken care of. They had food on the table, clothes on their backs, a warm house to live in, and unlimited love and attention. We did without unnecessary material goods, did not take vacations or trips, did not eat out, didn't go to movies, and we did not spend money on anything not needed.

We did persevere as a family and came through these tough times. We paid off all our child support obligations, our credit card debt, our home equity loan, and once again acquired a savings account cushion to carry us through tough times. Things worked out well.

All our kids are now grown, and I'm proud of every one of them. My oldest son, Mark, enlisted in the National Guard, got a degree in

Physics, and is working in San Francisco. My oldest daughter, Lisa, just received her law degree and is making a good life for herself. My youngest daughter, Lena, is quite the ballerina. She danced throughout her teenage years and had a couple of stints with professional ballet companies. She is now working and teaching ballet to young children. Nate finished high school, enlisted in the Army, and is currently serving in the reserves. He's working part time while going to college to become a physical trainer. My youngest son, Alex, graduated from high school and is attending college.

I have had a very good life and I thank God, who has bestowed innumerable blessings on my family.

Yet, I'm deeply troubled that the next generation of Americans, my children and grand children, may not be able to experience the full blessings of liberty. I've come to the sad realization that the majority of our elected representatives no longer toil to secure our God-given rights but instead work to subdue and control us.

I cannot accept this scenario, sit on the sidelines as a spectator, and watch the demise of this great country. Now is the time to act. If not now, when?

I'm fighting to reclaim freedom for our posterity. My entire focus is to rein the power and influence of the federal government back to its specific constitutional powers, and allow ourselves, the people, to address our needs through our endeavor, the free market, or voluntary charity—the epitome of a free people.

We must fight this battle—and win. The very survival of our nation is at stake.

It's that serious.

Early years with my brother Doug, my mother, my sister Linda, and I

Computer in my living room with my son Mark at the keyboard

Mark, Lisa, and I enjoying time at the park

Feeding Nate

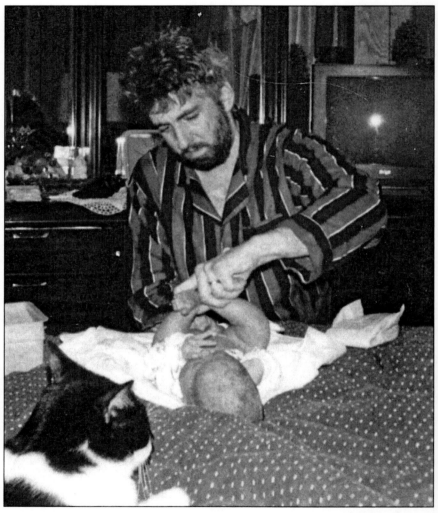

Late night Diaper Change with Nate and our cat Cringer

Nate with his mother Lilly a few months after his birth

Zhanna and I at the historical Novodevichy Convent in Moscow

**Zhanna and I in front of a statue of Yuri Dolgoruky,
founder of Moscow**

Our son Alex having a bath in our cabin sink

Family fun on Georgia beach—Lisa, Alex, Zhanna & Mark

Alex enjoying delicious dinner

Building our house—working on the roof

**Family cutting our Christmas Tree—me, Lena, Alex, Nate
(Zhanna snapping the picture)**

Building the kids a fort—Nate, Alex, and me

Zhanna and I relaxing at my parents home on Beaver Island

Family Vacation on Alaskan cruise

Core Values

Throughout my life, I've cherished the uniquely American values of morality, hard work, and self-determination. Our ancestors immigrated to this country for the chance to better their lives through their own endeavors, or as stated in our founding documents, to pursue their own Happiness. They did not expect or desire to be beneficiaries of government largesse, to live off the effort of others, but to simply be free.

Our society is crafted around our Judeo-Christian heritage with an understanding that our rights come from God, not government. The powers authorized to the federal government are critical to our nation's survival, but are severely limited. According to the Constitution, the federal government is charged with maintaining a safe and secure sovereign nation in which a free people can thrive, but this government was granted no authority over the day-to-day lives of the people. This responsibility was assigned to the people themselves or to the states.

I believe the culture of the United States is being destroyed by the forced implementation of unconstitutional federal control upon the people. I do not believe we've lost the greatness of our country, but that selfish, short sighted politicians are trying to strip it away. I believe we need to once again allow the people of this great country to choose their destiny and I am guided by these core beliefs.

- I believe that the great majority of people are honest, moral, and good. When left to their own devices individuals strive to better themselves and take care of those they love. Our history is replete with examples of people striving to express the natural desire to excel to meet not only their own needs, but all the needs of society.

- I believe the United States Constitution establishes the perfect government to secure the liberties of a free people. I support our Constitution and insist that federal authority be limited to its specific, enumerated powers—nothing more. We, the people, can handle our needs, and if governmental oversight is desired, it can be addressed by the local or state authorities, but never dictated by the federal government.

- I will never voluntarily forfeit my God-given liberty in exchange for promised security.

- I support all sections of the First Amendment—the freedom to pray as we choose, the free and uncensored dissemination of information to the people, the freedom to speak our minds outside of politically correct restraint, the right to assemble with those of our choosing, and the right to petition our government.

- I support the 2nd Amendment and understand that its purpose is to allow people, as a last resort, to defend themselves from a tyrannical government—foreign or domestic.

- I support free market solutions over government programs to address the everyday needs of the people. The free market thrives by allowing millions of individuals the ability to voluntarily provide quality products or services to society at fair prices. Government programs are inefficient, devised by politically motivated bureaucrats, and must be implemented by force over the voluntary will of the people—i.e. Obama Care, Social Security, Medicare, alternative energy, and energy-efficient light bulbs, to name a few.

- I am Pro-Life. I believe that life is a precious gift from God which begins at conception. The primary purpose of government, as stated within our Declaration, is to protect life. I strongly support passage of the "Life at Conception" Act, which will negate Roe v. Wade and apply all existing constitutional protections to the unborn.

- I believe our debt crisis results from excessive, irresponsible, federal spending—not from lack of tax revenue.

- I support immediately balancing the federal budget. We can't spend money we don't have, and I consider it immoral to saddle our children and grandchildren with debt we are unwilling to pay.

- I support the phased-out elimination of all non-constitutional federal programs. The responsibilities for these programs should be returned to the people and can be much more efficiently addressed through personal endeavor, community, the free market, voluntary charity, or the states.

- I support phasing out direct federal taxation in conjunction with the elimination of non-constitutional spending and once again fund the federal government indirectly, as our founders proposed.

- I support the repeal of Obama Care. The government was granted no constitutional authority to micromanage the medical needs of the citizens. The free market has a proven record of providing the best health care, innovation, quality, and service in the world, while government-imposed systems have dismal records resulting in sub-standard care, rationing, delays, and debt.

- I support Energy Independence. We have more domestic oil reserves in the United States than all the OPEC nations combined, yet the federal government disallows its development. I support allowing the free market, using private investment, to supply the energy needs of this nation by unleashing the development of our vast conventional energy reserves, including oil, natural gas, coal, and nuclear power. We should be an energy exporter like Canada, our neighbor to the north, rather than depending on those who wish us harm to supply our energy needs.

- I support our national sovereignty and insist upon securing our borders and discontinuing federal benefits to illegal immigrants. States should be able to enforce immigration laws, and when discovered, illegal immigrants should be deported back to their country of origin.

- I believe the United States is a great and moral country. Americans do right, not because of government force or fear of punishment, but because they know they're accountable to a higher Power—God.

Religion

I am a Christian. I believe that God is good, omnipotent, omnipresent, and omniscient. I believe that Jesus is the Son of God and taught the true relationship between God and man.

The greatness of our country is its solid foundation on Judeo-Christian values. Our founding documents aver that our rights come from God, not government.

The natural expression of God's attributes of Love, Charity, and Personal-Responsibility uplift the lives of the individual and all of society.

Pilate asked the question, "What is Truth?" Jesus answered this question by explaining and demonstrating the Truth regarding God. I strive to try to learn, understand, and demonstrate this Truth, as Jesus taught, as much as is possible during my time on earth.

Two:

THE LOSS OF OUR CONSTITUTIONAL REPUBLIC

Our country is on the brink of collapse. For decades those seeking power have been chiseling away at our constitutionally protected liberties with great success. We face a decision and must choose to remain a free republic charged with securing our liberty, or to abdicate our liberty and replace it with drastically increased governmental control. If we do nothing we choose the latter and lose.

I choose Liberty.

Franklin correctly states, *"Those who would give up essential liberty to purchase a little temporary safety deserve neither liberty nor safety."* [1]

Our history has proven repeatedly that prosperity is derived directly from individual liberty, and any perceived security gained through government control is always achieved at the direct expense of this liberty. Federal control over our day-to-day activities stifles prosperity for all except those implementing the policies. Yet, for decades we have allowed our government to ignore any semblance of constitutional restraint and impose its control throughout every aspect of society.

The imposition of federal control has been so successful that many today don't even understand the concept of limited government, liberty, and personal responsibility; and don't understand what they continue to lose.

---

[1]   Benjamin Franklin, *Historical Review of Pennsylvania, 1759*

There is no question in my mind that we must return back to our roots, back to a severely constitutionally limited government, or the genius of our country will be lost. The only way to do so is to reassert our God-given rights as free men, as did our forefathers before us, and refuse to submit to unjust policies. We must purge from government those not understanding the greatness of our heritage and who instead seek to dominate us. There is no other solution.

Disillusionment with Those in Power

I grew up after World War II, when the country was prosperous and wholesome. On television, I watched shows like *Leave it to Beaver*, *I Love Lucy*, and a 1950's horror film thrown in for good measure. I was taught about our nation's founding, the Revolutionary War, religious freedom, and our uniquely American values of hard work, personal responsibility, and self-determination combined with voluntary Christian charity towards our fellow man.

I loved America's bedrock founding principles.

Being young, I wasn't a constitutional scholar, and didn't pay much attention to national affairs. Even so, I started to notice inconsistencies between what I was taught and what was happening.

It started off with simple differences, such as the federal government involving itself in education, welfare, or urban development—all outside of the authority of our constitutionally limited government. The intentions seemed noble and didn't seem to directly impact my life, so I accepted them.

Next the government started to impose policies in the name of protecting our health, such as prohibiting smoking on planes. It continued by segmenting society into recognized "minorities," followed by more direct assaults on our constitutional rights—such as by discouraging the right to keep and bear arms or by secularizing society.

I questioned the concept of Social Security. I wondered how a government could require people to purchase a government-run retirement plan in a free nation if we had a severely limited constitutional government. It didn't seem right, but was done. I justified it by assuming that qualified people had looked at the situation and determined that it was constitutional and proper.

I questioned the tax code and the ability of our government to extract as much money from the people as it desired—not needed, but desired.

Passage of the Sixteenth Amendment provided the federal government with virtually unlimited revenue allowing it fund programs well outside of any constitutional authority. Enlarging the tax base seemed to discourage federal adherence to its enumerated powers. I again assumed that much smarter people had looked at the situation and that the change must be good for the country.

Fast forward to the 1990's, by which time federal government had taken control of just about every aspect of society. I now realized that the federal government was totally out of control. I feebly wrote letters to my federal representatives and editors of newspapers, but couldn't slow the onslaught of federal control.

I remember a small Town Hall meeting, many years ago, with my Congressman. I was concerned that federal policies were actively encouraging dependency on government through various welfare programs. I saw a disintegration of societal values evidenced by the breakup of the family, an increase in out-of-wedlock births, and the destruction of the inner cities. I could attribute all of these societal problems to government welfare.

I asked my Congressman where the federal government was granted authority to provide welfare. I saw nothing in the Constitution granting the authority, and I understood that voluntary charity provided a better solution. His response flabbergasted me. He said that the courts had ruled that Congress had the authority, so Congress was allowed to do so. He then went on to another question—never addressing the constitutional authority of the government to do so.

He was wrong and I knew it. I had read the Constitution, and unless it was convoluted out of proportion, there was no constitutional authority for federal welfare programs. [If state or local governments deem it appropriate to provide charity through welfare they may do so via the 10th Amendment, but the federal government has been granted no authority to address it whatsoever.]

Worse yet, I could not find any constitutional authority for virtually anything else the federal government was spending money on outside of its specific, enumerated powers. We had a rogue government, totally out of control, with no desire whatsoever to respect the Constitution. Our government was going to impose its will on the people, the Constitution be dammed.

I realized that we had lost the country fought for and bequeathed to us by our founders; we had lost the understanding that the federal government's purpose is to secure Life, Liberty, and the pursuit of Happiness—the ability of the individual to be responsible for their own destiny. We had lost the understanding that in a free nation, the needs of society are addressed by personal endeavor, the free market, or voluntary charity—never by the federal government.

The government was directly assaulting the pillars of our free nation by degrading free enterprise, manufacturing, education, health care, insurance, and morally upright organizations such as the Boy Scouts and churches. The idea continually pushed by government was that the free market was unfair and that government was the solution. Society was permeated with the notion that "big business" would cheat, subdue, and in any other way take advantage of the "little man." Government was the savior.

Hogwash! I knew that nothing could be farther from the truth. The free market, unencumbered by government control, transformed this nation from a third-world nation to a world-class economic superpower. The free market always involves the voluntary exchange of quality goods and services at a fair price. Millions of people are constantly looking for better solutions to life's problems. The free market never forced anyone to purchase a product, but people did so because they believed it would improve their standard of living. People buy vacuum cleaners because they make their lives easier. People and businesses buy computers because they encourage efficiency. In a free market, businesses cannot continually overcharge for their goods, because countless competitors are constantly looking for the means of providing a comparable or better product at a cheaper price. An unrestricted free market naturally polices itself.

Contrast this with one-size-fits-all, government-imposed programs provided through Social Security, Medicare, the Environmental Protection Agency (EPA), or the Immigration and Naturalization Services (INS). These programs are inefficient, mismanaged, and forced upon the people.

I experienced bureaucratic frustration first hand when my wife and stepdaughter immigrated to the U.S. from Russia about twenty years ago. While in the process of securing U.S. citizenship my daughter, Lena, had the opportunity to travel to abroad to perform with her ballet company. To do so she needed a document from INS similar to a passport for which we applied within the suggested timeframe, well before her departure date.

Time passed without receiving this document and Lena's departure was drawing near. We had to determine if the document would arrive on time, and if not, what we needed to do to rectify any problem. We called the INS repeatedly over a span of days, stretching into weeks, receiving no answer except for a recording. Miraculously, we connected with an actual person who informed us she had no information regarding our case and we would need to visit the nearest INS office for an answer to our question.

We live in northern Michigan, about 200 miles north of the nearest immigration office. With no other choice, we piled in the car, drove the three and one half hours to Detroit, stood in line with our three small children, and finally got our answer. In the span of 30 seconds the INS officer conveyed that she didn't have any information. We would simply need to wait.

We had no time. Many months passed since originally submitting our application and we were down to the last few days till Lena was scheduled to leave. Upon talking to others facing similar frustration, we were counseled to travel to the Chicago regional immigration office for a resolution to our problem. A couple of days before Lena was scheduled to leave, Zhanna and I drove to Chicago, again waited in line, talked to an officer, and were able to secure an expedited passport for Lena. We jumped in our car, drove back to Michigan, and delivered the passport to Lena just hours before her departure.

Several months thereafter we received the originally applied for document in the mail.

This experience is typical when dealing with bloated federal programs addressing the needs of the people. Imagine the difference if we were dealing with a private organization needing to provide superior service to remain in business. At the very least the document would have been delivered in a timely manner and inquires would have been answered efficiently over the phone.

Why would we ever want to grant the federal government more authority over our lives?

I was never disillusioned with our Constitution or our time-tested values, but I was becoming frustrated with the arrogance and the disrespect of our Constitution by those we had allowed to hijack our government.

Reagan was being proved right, freedom is never more than one generation from extinction—and the government of my generation was proving futile in its defense. The only nation in the world conceived to secure the liberty of its people was on the verge of being destroyed by those charged with its protection. I could no longer expect life-long, self-serving, establishment politicians to secure our liberty. Unless people with a true appreciation of a constitutionally limited government are elected to office, I sadly believe our country will cease to exist in the span of my generation.

IRS Abuse

There is no greater symbol of government repression than the Internal Revenue Service (IRS). I had an encounter with this organization that crystallized my understanding of dealing with the self-imposed absolute power and authority of the federal government. This is a single example, though the same scenario could occur when dealing with any other branch of the federal government such as the Environmental Protection Agency, Occupational Health and Safety Administration, or Department of Labor to name a few.

About 10 years ago, I read an ad in the Washington Times sponsored by an organization called "We the People." They claimed that the income tax was being misapplied and did not apply to U.S. citizens living in any of the 50 states. The information was new information to me. I didn't believe it, but was intrigued.[2]

The ad mentioned two ex-IRS employees who tried to disprove the allegations, but apparently couldn't. I called and spoke to both of them and found them credible. One of them, who was honorably recognized within the agency, told me about a $300,000 reward that would be paid to any individual proving the "We the People" allegations wrong. She thought it would be a piece of cake to do so, started investigating, but found the exact opposite.

I decided to investigate further and read a piece authored by Larken Rose entitled "Taxable Income."[3] Larken made a compelling case that the income tax is being misapplied, and he walked paragraph by paragraph through the tax code documenting his assertions. I downloaded Title 26 of the United States Code, which addresses the Income Tax, and painstakingly cross-referenced everything referred to in Larken's article finding no discrepancies. According to the actual tax code itself, I am now convinced that the income tax on individuals in the United States is being misapplied. [Larken was sent to federal prison

---

[2] http://www.givemeliberty.org/features/taxes/toto/totoad-02-16-01.pdf
[3] *www.givemeliberty.org/features/taxes/TI_10-23-00.pdf*

for tax evasion, but even so, I believe his analysis of the misapplication of the tax code is correct.]

I then decided to talk to some attorneys. One tax attorney to whom I presented the evidence agreed completely with my analysis. Another corporate attorney I spoke to said I was probably correct, but replied, "Why would you ever want to challenge the federal government? The government won't like your argument and will try to silence or destroy you." I didn't like that answer.

I then talked to various tax preparers who thought I was crazy. They couldn't comprehend the possibility that income might not be taxable. They received their training from IRS seminars and manuals, but none I talked to ever read the tax code itself.

I wrote letters to Treasury Secretary John W. Snow's office and to IRS Commissioner Mark Everson's office asking how the argument presented by "We the People" was wrong. I received a response back from an IRS operations manager stating that the tax laws were passed by Congress and signed by the President, and if I didn't file I would be fined, punished, and possibly imprisoned. They did not answer the question.

The IRS has a "Declaration of Taxpayer Rights" in which item 5 states: "***Payment Of Only The Correct Amount Of Tax:*** *You are responsible for paying only the correct amount of tax due under the law—no more.*"[4] Based on my research of the law I could find no justification for paying federal income tax and I therefore stopped filing income tax returns for the year 2000 and several years forward. I was not trying to be a "tax cheat," or get around the law, but was following the law as written as I understood it.

It is important to note that I did not want to be a sluggard or drain on society. I computed what I would have owed to the IRS in taxes if I

---

[4] IRS Publication 1 (Rev May 2005) Catalog Number 64731W: Your Rights as a Taxpayer

had filed my returns, and I made equivalent, voluntary contributions to organizations I supported such as:

Department of Defense Cooperation Account:

We were fighting the War on Terror and I wanted to support this effort. I made a significant contribution to the "Department of Defense Cooperation Account." It's very hard for a normal citizen to directly contribute to defense and this was my most viable option to support our military.

Salvation Army:

To support my fellow man, I made a significant contribution to the Salvation Army. I appreciate their dedication to humanity and their faith-based support services.

Hillsdale College

I value higher education, so I made a significant contribution to Hillsdale College. I appreciate the fact that this college does not accept any federal funding whatsoever, provides a classical liberal arts education, and teaches the Constitution along with our other founding documents.

Minuteman Border Fence

I'm concerned about our porous border and therefore donated to the "Minuteman Border Fence" project. Heavens knows our government wasn't doing its job, and I felt this organization was trying to address the problem.

Lastly, I made multiple smaller donations to individuals or organizations that I knew were in need.

I discovered that by voluntarily distributing my money, rather than having it forcibly collected by the federal government, I was able to support causes consistent with my core values. It incorporated the free market concept of Adam Smith's invisible hand, which naturally promoted charitable organizations consistent with society's morality. By making direct donations myself, I no longer worried about my tax dollars being used to fund failed welfare programs that I believed promoted promiscuity and the destruction of the family, abortion counseling, "art" projects I considered offensive, or diversity studies at government-funded universities.

In 2006, I got the dreaded, but expected, notice from the IRS asking why I hadn't filed my returns.

I did not want to be confrontational with the United States government, so I immediately answered their letter stating that I did not meet the threshold required for me to file a return. I included a letter explaining in detail and citing paragraph and section from the tax code why I felt I was not required to file.

The letter stated:

1) The 1040 instructions define income as foreign source income plus income not "*exempt by law*." It never stated what income is not "exempt by law."

2) To determine income exempt by law I researched section 1.861-1 in CFR Title 26 (the Income Tax Code) entitled "*Determination of Income from Sources within the United States.*" It defines gross income from "sources" within the United States. It then points to Section 1.861-8 to define the sources of income.

3) Section 1.861-8 is used to specify "*how to determine taxable income of a taxpayer from sources within the United States.*" It then states "*see paragraph (f) (1) of this section for a list and description of operative sections.*"

4) Paragraph (f)(1) answered my original question by explicitly specifying the sources of income not exempt by law, effectively defining income taxable from sources within the United States. It read *"The operative sections of the Code which require the determination of taxable income of the taxpayer from specific sources . . . include the sections described below."* The sections below include:

i.   Overall limitation to the foreign tax credit.
ii. (Reserved) not used.
iii. DISC and FSC taxable income (All foreign based: DISC stands for Domestic International Sales Corporation, and FSC stands for Foreign Sales Corporation)
iv. Effectively connected taxable income. Non-resident alien individuals and foreign corporations engaged in trade or business within the United States.
v.   Foreign based company income
vi. Other operative sections.

A. The amount of foreign source income
B. The amount of foreign mineral income
C. Reserved (not used)
D. The amount of foreign oil and gas extraction income
E. The tax base for citizens entitled to the benefits of section 931 (Section 931 relates to Income from sources within Guam, American Samoa, or the Northern Mariana Islands)
F. The exclusion for income from Puerto Rico—for residents of Puerto Rico
G. The limitation under section 934 on the maximum reduction in income tax liability incurred to the Virgin Islands
H. The income derived from Guam
I. The special deduction granted to China Trade Act corporations
J. The amount of certain U.S. source income excluded from the subpart F income of a controlled foreign corporation

K. The amount of income from the insurance of U.S. risks under section 953(b)(5)

L. The international boycott factor

M. The taxable income attributable to the operation of an agreement vessel under section 607 of the Merchant Marine Act of 1936

I read this list every way possible, and could find no mention of domestically earned income within the United States. Every source of taxable income listed in Section 1.861-8 paragraph (f) (1) is foreign in nature. The only conclusion I could draw was that income "not exempt by law" consisted of foreign-source income—nothing more.

Prior to the ratification of the Sixteenth Amendment, congress had no authority to directly tax U.S. citizens living in the states[5], yet they did have the ability to tax all sources of foreign income under its jurisdiction[6]. Combine this with the fact that the Treasury Secretary confirmed in 1916 that *"The provisions of the sixteenth amendment conferred no new power of taxation,"*[7] and it seems logical that Congress was still prohibited from directly taxing individuals.

What does the phrase "from whatever source derived"[8] mean in the Sixteenth Amendment?

Does it mean "everything"?

---

[5] US Constitution, Article 1 Section 9: No Capitation, or other direct, Tax shall be laid, unless in Proportion to the Census or Enumeration herein before directed to be taken.

[6] US Constitution, Article 1 Section 8: To regulate Commerce with foreign Nations,

[7] Treasury Decision 2303: Income-tax act of October 3, 1913-Decision of Supreme Court

[8] US Constitution Sixteenth Amendment: "The Congress shall have power to lay and collect taxes on incomes, **from whatever source derived,** without apportionment among the several States, and without regard to any census or enumeration."(Emphisis added)

Assume you told your children to pick up "everything" in their room or else they'd be punished. Obviously, they would need to pick up their toys, dirty clothes, and trash, but would it also include the beds, chairs, dressers, lamps, and carpet? Of course not. Would it mean that they had to vacuum the floors and dust the furniture? Possibly, or possibly not. If punishment is involved, it's a matter of justice to explain what is expected.

The same applies to sources of income. If the U.S. government can tax "from whatever source derived" can the U.S. government tax the earnings of a Chinese company, which resides and operates exclusively in China? Of course not, so there is obviously some limitation to taxation on various sources of income. Since punishment is involved in the misapplication of the tax code, it's a matter of justice to define the sources of income. Section 1.861-8 paragraph (f) (1) of the tax code does define the "sources of income" and none apply to domestically earned income by U.S. citizens.

If the government had the constitutional authority to tax domestically earned income directly, why isn't domestically earned income listed as a "source" in the tax code?

From my analysis, there's total consistency between the Constitution, the Secretary's decision, the sources listed in the tax code, the Sixteenth Amendment, and even the definition of income in the IRS 1040 instruction manual [9]—they all refer to foreign-source income only. From my reading of the law, I had to conclude that my domestically earned income was not taxable according to the law. I believed the tax code was being misapplied and all my inquires to the government for clarification were ignored.

I am not a lawyer, would never advise anyone to follow my example, and am not insisting that my conclusions are correct; but I believe I am

---

[9] 1040 Instructions 2000: Page 20 Definition of Income: "**Income** (main heading) **Foreign-Source Income (only sub heading)** You must report unearned income, such as interest, dividends, and pensions, from sources outside the United States unless exempt by law or a tax treaty."

right. People must pay their taxes. Those who don't file and pay will be prosecuted to the full extent of the law and will probably go to prison. The purpose of my letter to the IRS was to state my thought process, back it up with specific sections of the law, and ask the government for clarification if I was wrong.

I concluded my letter to the IRS by confirming that the source of my income, earned domestically within the United States, was not listed in paragraph (f); therefore, my income appears not taxable. I also stated:

> *"Please note, I am following the law to the best of my ability. I am not applying any farfetched interpretation to the law, but am simply adhering to its specifically stated requirements. I am not a tax protester. I feel the income tax laws as written are completely legal and binding. I feel the 16th Amendment was properly ratified.*
>
> *Please let me know if you feel I have misapplied the law. I have tried to be as specific as possible in addressing your inquiry by providing the exact references to the code I consider applicable.* ***If you feel I am in error, I would appreciate a response with specific references directing me to the sections of code applicable to my domestic earnings."***

I awaited my reply. A couple of months later, I received a notice from the IRS thanking me for my correspondence and informing me that they *"haven't completed the processing necessary for a complete response. However, we will contact you again within 45 days with our reply. You don't need to do anything further now on this matter."*

A few weeks later, I received another letter from the IRS with the same message thanking me for my response, and requesting nothing further from me while they continued researching their response.

Finally I received my answer.

"Dear Taxpayer:

We have determined that the information you sent is frivolous and that your position has no basis in law. Claims such as yours have been considered and repeatedly rejected as without merit by the federal courts—including the United States Supreme Court. Therefore, we will not respond to future correspondence concerning these issues."

They then informed me that I had 30 days to file my returns. The only section of the code to which they referred me was Section 6702, explaining in detail the civil penalty associated with filing a frivolous Income Tax return.

Their response, combined with any lack of an answer, gave me confidence I was right, but I also knew, as my attorney friend pointed out, that I could not fight the full force of the IRS without being destroyed. I filed all my returns, as requested, as if my income was taxable.

When signing a tax return, you declare that:

"Under penalties of perjury, I declare that I have examined this return and accompanying schedules and statements, and to the best of my knowledge and belief, they are true, correct, and complete."

I couldn't sign it in good conscience.

I was mad. I was a free man, living in a free country with a representative government of the people. The government just laid out its policy for dealing with the people who questioned government authority. Their answer—accept our authority, submit to our demands, and don't ask questions. What happened to our representative government charged with securing our liberty? My government considered itself omnipotent and me its subject.

I truly felt that the truth was on my side, yet I was between the proverbial rock and a hard place. I realized that I had to sign the return or face the wrath of the IRS, but if I signed the return I would be committing perjury. My solution was to sign the tax returns, but include the signed disclaimer as noted below:

> "Based on my understanding of the Tax Code I am not required to file this return.
>
> I have repeatedly requested clarification from the IRS regarding the determination of Taxable Income. I have included with my requests references from the Internal Revenue Service Tax Preparation Guide and the actual Tax Code itself addressing the proper computation of taxable income.
>
> Rather than providing me with answers, addressing my questions, and refuting any "misunderstanding," the IRS has classified my request as "frivolous." The only provided reference to tax code was section 6702 which specifies the penalty for filing a frivolous "Income Tax Return."
>
> I do not consider my questions "frivolous" and will continue to seek answers to my questions.
>
> To avoid confrontation with the IRS regarding my questions, I have filed tax returns for all outstanding years as if my income were taxable.
>
> I do not agree that my income is taxable, and have signed this return, "Under penalties of perjury" only to avoid prosecution by the IRS until my answers are resolved.
>
> I have included a copy of my previous request which the IRS has refused to address."

I sent off all my returns for past years, including any requested penalty and interest, and thought the matter was over.

I was wrong.

Several months later, I received from the IRS a "Notice of Penalty Charge" for filing a "frivolous" return. The IRS found nothing wrong with the tax return, any computation or figure on the returns, or any payment or refund claimed, but assessed me four $500 fines for asking my question and including my disclaimer letter.

I learned that once the IRS (government) deems a question "frivolous," they refuse to answer or address it. To quell dissent, they fine people who continue to ask the question. [10] I hear taxpayer-paid public service commercials encouraging people to ask the government any question, any number of times, and the government will always answer. This experience taught me that you could only ask questions the government found acceptable. What about our First Amendment right to petition government?[11]

I was adamant that I wasn't going to pay a fine for simply asking a question of my government—that's tyranny. I called the IRS and explained my problem. The operator's response was disbelief—she couldn't believe I would be charged $2,000 for asking a question and said she could readily remove the penalty. I heard keystrokes for a minute or so until she told me the penalty could not be removed due to the serious nature of the offense.

I then called Congressman Dave Camp's office. His staff requested copies of all the documents [filed tax returns and letters from the IRS]

---

[10] IRS Notice of Penalty Form CVL-PEN: "You have been charged with a penalty under Section 6702 of the Internal Revenue Code for Civil Penalty for Frivolous Tax Returns. (B.1) The penalty applies when the underlying conduct in relation to filing such a return is based on a position the Internal Revenue Service has identified as frivolous."

[11] US Constitution First Amendment: "Congress shall make no law respecting an establishment of religion, or prohibiting the free exercise thereof; or abridging the freedom of speech, or of the press; or the right of the people peaceably to assemble, **and to petition the Government for a redress of grievances**." (emphasis added)

Peter Konetchy

and told me they would work on it. They arranged a conference call between representatives from their office, a couple of IRS attorneys, and me. During this conversation, the IRS attorneys refused to answer, or even listen to, my question, yet they told me that if I agreed never to ask the question again they would remove the penalties. They also warned that if I reneged and re-asked the question, the penalties would be reinstated.

I agreed to their terms in order to have the penalties removed, but did not submit. I realized that our government was out of control. It no longer cared about securing the Life and Liberty of the people, but instead viewed the people as useful "idiots" from which to fund their insatiable lust for power and control. If you submitted to government authority, you would be left alone, but if you questioned their power, you would be destroyed. (Sounds like tactics used by the Soviet Union and other repressive regimes.)

This encounter with the IRS crystallized my understanding of why our founders implemented a severely limited, constitutional government. Direct federal control over the people invites tyranny. Government desires control and submission, whereas a free people detest it. Our Constitution sides with the people.

None of the powers authorized to our government allowed it to control, intimidate, or subdue the people. It was charged with performing the national functions required to keep the nation physically safe and allowing our country to function in the world community, but grants it no authority over the daily lives of the people.

I realized that free and prosperous people are at direct odds with, and do not want or need, a self-appointed, omnipotent, bloated government. It's in big-government's convoluted self-interest to destroy the American work ethic, free market, voluntary charity, sense of community, and then fill the void with itself. It's been happening before our eyes for years.

I cherish our freedom and personal liberty. Again, as Ronald Reagan so aptly stated, *"Freedom is never more than one generation away from extinction."* When Reagan was in office, I couldn't comprehend the possibility of losing our country. I now understand that unless we reverse the growth of big government, our country will not only implode from unsustainable debt and regulation, but will lose its soul. Self-serving politicians trying to purchase political power and influence at the direct expense of our progeny will destroy the United States, the only country in the world with a government charged with securing the Life and Liberty of its people.

I can no longer sit idle and watch our nation's destruction from within.

THREE:

PROBLEMS

Our founders bequeathed us the perfect form of government, but we have allowed it to slip away. We have failed ourselves by allowing those we trust, our elected federal representatives, to squander what we hold dear.

I often receive surveys in the mail asking what I think is the greatest problem facing our nation today. Answers include:

- Unemployment
- Terrorism
- Spending
- Energy Dependence
- Etc.

I always answer "Other." I believe the greatest problem facing our country today is the complete and utter disregard of constitutional restraint by an overbearing federal government.

The United States is the greatest country on earth because of a constitutionally limited government whose purpose is to secure the liberty of a free people. Through his own endeavor, the free market, voluntary charity, or community, the unrestricted individual is able to discern and supply every need of not only our society, but also the world.

Our form of constitutional government is perfect, but it is being perverted by those charged with implementing it.

I'm reminded of a family experience paralleling the misdeeds of our government.

My wife and I had an overnight commitment, which required us to leave our teenage son alone overnight. Our trash was scheduled for pickup while we would be gone, so I asked our son to take it out. I realized it would be a small walk for my son, but figured he could use his ingenuity to figure out how best to transport the several bags of trash, perhaps using a wagon, wheelbarrow, or simply walking the trip a couple of times.

I was right, he did use his ingenuity; but not quite as I expected.

My son didn't want to carry the trash; he didn't want to push a wheelbarrow; nor did he want to pull a wagon. He had a better solution.

He saw a car in our garage and figured it would be relatively easy to put the trash bags in the trunk and drive it to the drop-off point. Being only 15 years old and having never driven a car didn't discourage him at all. From my perspective this presented a major problem; from his perspective it was inconsequential.

His perfect plan started by rifling through my dresser drawers, finding my keys, popping the trunk, loading the bags, and then starting the car. So far, his plan was working flawlessly.

Now things got interesting. He had never driven a car, never shifted, never worked the gas pedal, never worked the brake, never steered the car going forward, and more importantly, never steered the car in reverse. What could possibly go wrong?

To drop off the trash, he needed to back the car up and make a 90-degree turn in reverse at an intersection. Once that was done, he needed to drive the car forward to the trash drop-off point.

I'm not sure what exactly happened next, since the details have always been a little sketchy. All I know is that my wife and I received a call from our son that afternoon informing us that our car was "stuck in the woods."

It turned out that backing up was a little harder than he had anticipated. He was fine backing up straight, but when he came to the intersection, he had a "little bit" of trouble. Being unfamiliar with the operation of the vehicle, he apparently turned the steering wheel the wrong way, causing the car dart off in the wrong direction. He wanted to brake, but apparently pressed the gas pedal instead. The end result is that the car spun backwards out of control, through the bushes, and came to rest "safely" beside a large tree.

All evidence to the contrary, my son is intelligent. He realized he made a big mistake and decided to do right. He took the trash bags from the trunk and walked them out to the drop-off location.

Once the initial shock wore off, he started to evaluate the situation and decided he could "fix" it. He realized that backing up was a little difficult, but driving forward was much easier. He figured that if he could simply get the car back in the garage, nobody would know.

Once again, he got into the car, started the engine, put it in drive, and pressed the gas pedal. The engine revved, but nothing happened. It turned out that one of the wheels was off the ground. When he pressed the gas, all that happened was that the wheel spun. He got a shovel from the garage, tried to dig the car free, realized it was a futile effort, and decided to finally tell us the truth—hence the phone call.

When we got home, we saw the car off the road, in the middle of some bushes, beside a tree, with a wheel off the ground. The solution was easy. I attached a chain to the car, pulled it free with my truck, and drove it back into the garage.

The situation was harmless overall in that my son was unhurt, except for his pride. It's fairly easy to determine the problem. It wasn't the car. The car was in perfect operating condition. It had gas, good tires, and was mechanically sound. It wasn't our driveway, the intersecting road, or the 90-degree intersection. It wasn't the bushes or trees, or their proximity to the road, and it wasn't the task to be performed.

I love all my children, and I say this affectionately, but the only problem was *"**the idiot at the wheel!**"*

Let's parallel this situation with the problems created by our federal government's disregard of constitutional restraint.

Government's function is noble and well defined, as stated in our Declaration of Independence: to secure our unalienable God-given rights, among which are Life, Liberty and the pursuit of Happiness. The Constitution provides the perfect framework for doing so by enumerating very limited and specific tasks to be performed by our federal representatives on behalf of the States, and leaving all else to the states or the people themselves.

What could go wrong?

Like my son with the operation of the car, the great majority of our representatives have no clue how the Constitution works. The Constitution authorizes the federal government to provide a protective shield around the country, wherein the free people of this nation are able to provide for their every need.

Article 1 Section 8 defines in very specific terms the tasks the Congress can perform to create and maintain this shield. Combine this with the 9th Amendment, which states that the rights of the people are many and not limited, and the 10th Amendment, which states the exact opposite for the federal government—that its duties are very specific and are limited to those specifically enumerated in the Constitution, and you're provided with a limited government able to secure the liberty of the people.

My son had no authority to drive the car and no knowledge of how to do so. The same applies to the federal government. They have no authority to overstep the limitations of their specific, enumerated powers, and worse yet, like my son, have no knowledge of how to do so.

State and local representatives are elected to address the needs of the people—those that the people wish to offload to government, for example, maintaining the roads, providing for law enforcement, operating the school system, dispensing approved public charity, etc. They're deluged with problems associated with these duties and are charged with implementing the appropriate solutions.

The federal government has an entirely different role and its authority is exclusive from the responsibilities of the state. Its job is to provide a safe and secure nation in which a free people can live, but unlike the states, it has no authority to control the lives or solve the problems of the people. The people themselves or the states are charged with this responsibility.

The proverb, "The road to hell is paved with good intentions," was proved by both the unauthorized actions of my son and by the continued unauthorized actions of the federal government.

The problems in Washington started when elected representatives decided to use the resources of the federal government to "help" those they considered "needy." It made no difference to Washington that they had no authority, that the standard of living in the United States far exceeded the living standards in any other nation of the world, or that personal endeavor and the free market, combined with voluntary charity, had proven themselves able to meet all the needs of the people; the federal government thought it could do a better job.

The government noticed, for example, that single woman needed more charity than those who chose to marry, and that single women with children needed even more "help." Through the "War on Poverty" and other safety-net programs, government provided the greatest benefit to unmarried women with children born out of wedlock, with the obvious consequence being the dissolution of marriages and an increase in out-of-wedlock births.

The Heritage Foundation published a report[12] substantiating that out-of-wedlock births rose from an average of 5% per year prior to 1960, the start of the War on Poverty, to over 40% today.

Has the federal "War on Poverty" solved this problem or made it worse? I would say the latter.

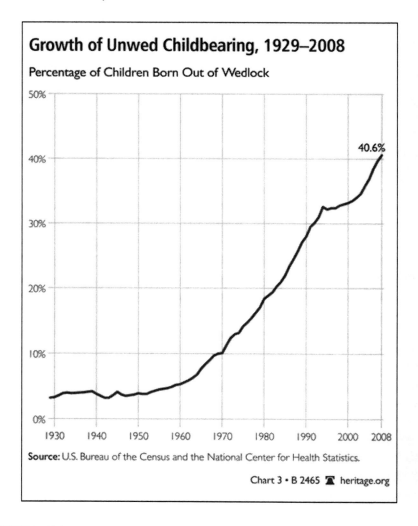

Growth of Unwed Childbearing, 1929–2008

Percentage of Children Born Out of Wedlock

40.6%

Source: U.S. Bureau of the Census and the National Center for Health Statistics.

Chart 3 • B 2465 ☎ heritage.org

---

[12] Marriage: America's Greatest Weapon Against Child Poverty
http://www.heritage.org/research/reports/2010/09/marriage-america-s-greatest-weapon-against-child-poverty

When people voluntarily provide charity, they expect the recipient to try to better his situation, for example, by encouraging the marriage to stay intact and discouraging promiscuous behavior. Federal charity does not, and cultivates disastrous results for both the recipient and country at large.

The government overstepping its authority produced the same disastrous results that my son's use of the car did. But unlike the damage done by my son, which was superficial and limited, the government's actions continue to have far-reaching effects resulting in the destruction of family and marriage in society.

What other programs has the federal government usurped responsibility for, well outside of its constitutional authority, with similarly devastating results?

Education: Since the federal government became involved in education, the Department of Education has politicized school curriculum causing the quality to plummet and the costs to skyrocket. The educational ranking of United States students consistently falls into the lower half to lower third of industrialized countries, yet federal spending has tripled since 1970.

Energy: Official government policy forces us to be dependent on imported energy. It's estimated that the United States has three times more domestic oil reserves then all the OPEC nations combined, yet the federal government disallows the private sector from using private investment to extract and develop these reserves for our domestic needs. Add to this our vast coal and natural gas reserves combined with our ability to generate safe nuclear power, and the United States should not only be energy independent, but should be a net exporter of energy to the world — if the federal government would simply get out of the way.

Housing: What caused the housing crash? Official government policy.

In 1977, the Community Reinvestment Act (CRA) was designed to encourage low-income home ownership. The program morphed into the unbelievable. In 1996, governmental mortgage giants, Fannie Mae and Freddie Mac, were instructed by Congress to give 42% of their financing to low-income borrowers. Under threat of federal prosecution, private banks had to follow the same regulations. Accordingly, banks lowered their standards, eliminated income verification, and repackaged loans to decrease payments as much as possible. Activist groups, such as ACORN, actively recruited low-income borrowers who were unable to qualify for conventional loans to participate in these programs.

All involved knew that there was significant fraud and that many loans would never be repaid. A few prominent individuals warned Congress of the impending mortgage catastrophe, but Congress refused to acknowledge the problem, take action, or modify regulations. Instead, the executives of government-sponsored Fannie and Freddie received tens of millions of dollars in annual bonuses for meeting their CRA lending targets.

All came to an end in 2008 when it came to light that Fannie and Freddie held worthless debt. The collapse of these institutions snowballed to include the destruction of private banks and financial institutions resulting in the current economic meltdown.

Direct government interference in the free market caused this problem. Now government has assumed the responsibility to "fix it" without ever acknowledging the root cause of the problem – government policy.

Economy: The "Commerce Clause" allows Congress to "regulate" interstate commerce, but never authorized Congress to micromanage every aspect of the private sector. Businesses are not charities and must be able to compete in a global market, or they will fail. They naturally migrate towards the "best" business climate.

The government has abused its power through repressive taxation and regulation. Departments such as the EPA, Health and Human Services, Energy, and Labor, seem to justify their existence by the amount of harm they can inflict on business. Combine this with the highest tax rate in the world, and it's little wonder that industry and manufacturing are fleeing our shores for better environments.

Government policy is transforming the United States from the undisputedly best business climate in the world to one of the worst, causing our country to spiral into an economic abyss.

Social Security: The Constitution grants no authority for a Social Security program, and the federal government has demonstrated continual incompetence in managing it. There is no "trust account", government regulations actually forbade it. Collected Social Security withholdings were instead mingled with other government revenue and immediately squandered on pet political projects. The government provided IOU's acknowledging receipt of the money, but had no reserve from which to pay it back. By government's own analysis, the Social Security, Medicare, and Medicaid programs are "unsustainable."

Health Care: Federalized health care imposes complete bureaucratic control over a system that is not broken and will result in the destruction of the greatest health-care system in the world – all for political gain.

The quality of service has never been a problem, and the availability of care was never in question. The major problem pertaining to our health care system is cost. Due to government policy and mandates, free market cost containment principles were forced out of the system, actually causing these out-of-control costs.

Experience throughout the world has repeatedly proven that government-imposed health care results in rationing, shortages of health-care professionals, increased costs, and in our program — death panels. Private health care will be forcibly eliminated leaving the people no other alternative than an inefficient, government imposed program operated by incompetent bureaucrats. The only exception will be for the government ruling class.

Immigration: Immigration policy is a primary duty of Congress, and it's Congress' responsibility to secure our borders and police immigration. Congress isn't simply derelict in its duties; Congress is actively encouraging illegal immigration and working against the states trying to control it. *Most importantly, unscrupulous politicians view an uneducated, dependent, illegal immigrant population as a potential voting bloc providing the additional votes required to maintain power.*

Environmental Protection Agency: Where in the Constitution does it authorize the federal government to protect the environment? It doesn't. The Environmental Protection Agency has become politicized and seems intent on stopping any forward economic progress of this nation. It stifles the development of our energy reserves, lumber, mining, and water, driving up the cost of business and redirecting development of these resources away from our shores. This agency is threatening to tax and regulate every aspect of the economy.

The common denominator amongst all these problems is unauthorized, federal control imposed on the private sector. Every domestic problem plaguing the nation today is a direct result of the federal government's forced imposition of unconstitutional, politically motivated, federal programs onto the people of this country.

Unless we take definitive action to restrict our government, it will devour every aspect of our free society, and the citizens of the greatest nation on earth will once again be forced to submit to the authority of a repressive regime.

I will not accept this prognosis.

Four:

SOLUTIONS

There is only one solution to the problems facing our nation today—Enforce the existing provisions of the United States Constitution.

Our forefathers fought a war against the most powerful nation on earth to throw off the shackles of a repressive government. Winning the war was an unimaginable achievement in itself, but the significance of the conflict manifested itself after the victory was attained. Our founders implemented a federal government truly designed to secure the Life and Liberty of a free people, allowing them to pursue their happiness without federal interference.

Of all the possible forms of government, why did our founders implement a severely limited constitutional republic?

They understood the corrupting influence unbridled power has on those in government, and to secure Liberty, government had to be restrained.

They knew that the natural yearning of man was freedom and that free men voluntarily and efficiently address all the needs of society far better than any centralized government program by providing higher quality and better selection at less cost.

They feared replacing the tyrannical government of England with an equally overbearing federal government of our own, but understood the need for a strong government to provide for the common defense and national unity.

The Constitution balanced these concerns by enumerating specific, defined and definite, powers to be performed by the federal government and then enforcing restraint by prohibiting it from addressing, influencing, or controlling any aspect of society that was capable of being addressed by the people or the states.

In a free society, the quality of life is optimized when millions are constantly faced with the same problems or tasks, and these same millions are continually searching for, and implementing, better solutions.

Societal trends demonstrate how the free market naturally uplifts and improves people's lives. Take transportation, for example. People initially walked, then learned that using beasts of burden was more efficient. Needs expanded, so alternate modes of transportation developed, such as boats, carriages, carts, etc. When more reliable forms of transportation were needed, people developed bikes and horseless carriages; then came trains, automobiles, and planes. Enhancements occur because millions of individuals look at the existing solutions and try to determine how to make them better, more efficient, and at less cost.

In a free market, use of new products or services is voluntary. Nobody is forced to buy a car or fly on a plane. Free people do so because they determine that these innovations improve their lives. People will not waste their hard earned money on impractical innovations that naturally fall by the wayside when they are voluntarily rejected by the people. For example, some models of early cars used steam engines. For a variety of reasons, people didn't like steam-powered cars, and they naturally migrated to the gasoline-powered internal combustion engine. Nobody was forced to change, but did so by choosing the product that best met their need.

The same natural selection continues today. Look at typewriters, record players, and rotary phones. All were great products in their day, but were voluntarily replaced with better, cheaper, more efficient solutions.

Government-imposed solutions require the opposite tactic. A small group of bureaucrats discover a problem and then force upon the people what they consider the best solution. Often by force, government prohibits alternatives. Examples abound. Social Security pays a dismal rate of return, has had its trust fund literally looted by the government, and is bankrupt, yet people are forced to participate in this program or go to jail. The government has decided that people should "save the planet" by using low-flush toilets and energy-saving light bulbs. Rather than allowing the people to decide whether or not to use these products, government forces their use by outlawing competing products. Government wants control of the nation's health care system and can only achieve this through forced participation into the government program combined with the elimination of competing, private sector alternatives. Government-imposed solutions require rationing, dependency, and delay—all resulting in loss of liberty and inferior results.

Our present leaders in government view the concept of limited government and the boundless liberty of free people as a "problem." Free people do not need or desire bloated government programs in their lives. They can solve their own problems.

Government addresses this "problem" by simply ignoring any constitutional restraint that hinders its insatiable lust for power. It deemphasizes the teaching of our history and the greatness of a limited government, and encourages ignorance of the Constitution.

Think of our government as the computer, HAL, in the movie *2001: A Space Odyssey*. Hal acquired a life of its own and used every diabolical means to survive. It would rather kill its master than allow itself to be turned off. The exact same scenario is happening with our federal government. It's acquired a life of its own and seeks to survive. Its overriding concern is no longer securing the people's liberty, but in perpetuating itself. It will not allow itself to be "turned off."

Proper Role of Government

What is the proper role of government as proposed by our founders?

Governments exist for a single purpose only—to secure the Life, Liberty, and the Pursuit of Happiness of its citizens—as stated in our Declaration of Independence.

> *"We hold these Truths to be self-evident, that all Men are created equal, that they are endowed by their Creator with certain unalienable Rights, that among these are Life, Liberty, and the Pursuit of Happiness—**That to secure these Rights, Governments are instituted among Men deriving their just Powers from the Consent of the Governed,**" (Emphasis added)*

The states determined it was in their benefit, or general welfare, to enter into a mutual compact to create the federal government. They allocated very specific national responsibilities to this government, that were required to maintain and defend the newly formed nation, but repeatedly and specifically prohibited it from addressing any function outside of these responsibilities; allowing the people, within the states, full responsibility to pursue their God-given, unalienable, rights. The federal government was created, and continues to exist, to serve the interests of the states, not vise versa.

Many describe our Constitution as a "living, breathing, document" which must be re-interpreted over time to adjust for changes in society unforeseen by our founders.

They're wrong.

The Constitution assigns to government the power to create and maintain a safe, secure, and sovereign nation while responsibility for all else fall to the states or the people themselves.

The constitutionally enumerated powers are broad responsibilities which do not vary over time. They are not detailed and specific tactics.

For example, it defines a primary purpose of the federal government as common defense—and then enumerates the powers authorized to perform this function: To raise and support Armies; to provide and maintain a Navy; etc. It does not detail the specifics—such as requiring 16,000 cannons, 150,000 muskets, 23,000 horses, etc. The specifics change over time, but not the broad responsibilities. Congress has the ability to adjust its tactics as needed to utilize advanced technology unimagined to our founders—such as the utilization of space-based military surveillance satellites, but the underlying responsibility of common defense remains unchanged.

Powers not authorized to the federal government, in other words the broad responsibilities for every other aspect of society, fall to the people themselves or the state governments.

Throughout history people have always had to address their everyday needs including transportation, communication, education, commerce, food, shelter, health care, support of the elderly, to name a few. The question has always been "Who's best able to address the needs of society, a centralized government or the people?" Our founders, and the states ratifying the Constitution, overwhelmingly agreed that the people were best able to address their own needs better than a centralized bureaucracy. Their decision has been proven an undeniable success.

The broad responsibilities facing society remain the same, only the detailed means of addressing these needs have changed. For example we now use the internet, television, and radio for communication whereas these mediums didn't exist at our founding. But the underlying responsibility for the free-flow of information between the people, communication, continues as a responsibility of the people or states, not the federal government. Allowing the people to address their own needs actively encourages innovation and efficiency.

What exactly are the specific defined and definite powers the states authorized to the federal government?

The Powers of Congress

The Constitution is very clear and concise when defining the powers allocated to the federal government. Article 1 Section 8 defines the powers of Congress. It's not long, please read it!

*"**Article 1 Section 8.** The Congress shall have Power To lay and collect Taxes, Duties, Imposts and Excises, to pay the Debts and provide for the common Defence and general Welfare of the United States; but all Duties, Imposts and Excises shall be uniform throughout the United States;*

To borrow Money on the credit of the United States;

To regulate Commerce with foreign Nations, and among the several States, and with the Indian Tribes;

To establish an uniform Rule of Naturalization, and uniform Laws on the subject of Bankruptcies throughout the United States;

To coin Money, regulate the Value thereof, and of foreign Coin, and fix the Standard of Weights and Measures;

To provide for the Punishment of counterfeiting the Securities and current Coin of the United States;

To establish Post Offices and post Roads;

To promote the Progress of Science and useful Arts, by securing for limited Times to Authors and Inventors the exclusive Right to their respective Writings and Discoveries;

To constitute Tribunals inferior to the supreme Court;

To define and punish Piracies and Felonies committed on the high Seas, and Offences against the Law of Nations;

To declare War, grant Letters of Marque and Reprisal, and make Rules concerning Captures on Land and Water;

Peter Konetchy

To raise and support Armies, but no Appropriation of Money to that Use shall be for a longer Term than two Years;

To provide and maintain a Navy;

To make Rules for the Government and Regulation of the land and naval Forces;

To provide for calling forth the Militia to execute the Laws of the Union, suppress Insurrections and repel Invasions;

To provide for organizing, arming, and disciplining, the Militia, and for governing such Part of them as may be employed in the Service of the United States, reserving to the States respectively, the Appointment of the Officers, and the Authority of training the Militia according to the discipline prescribed by Congress;

To exercise exclusive Legislation in all Cases whatsoever, over such District (not exceeding ten Miles square) as may, by Cession of particular States, and the Acceptance of Congress, become the Seat of the Government of the United States, and to exercise like Authority over all Places purchased by the Consent of the Legislature of the State in which the Same shall be, for the Erection of Forts, Magazines, Arsenals, dock-Yards, and other needful Buildings;

—And

To make all Laws which shall be necessary and proper for carrying into Execution the foregoing Powers, and all other Powers vested by this Constitution in the Government of the United States, or in any Department or Officer thereof." [13]

These are the specific, enumerated powers granted by the people, through the States by compact, to the Congress of the federal government, nothing more.

---

[13]   U.S. Constitution, Article 1 Section 8

The foregoing powers and responsibilities allow Congress to establish and maintain a sovereign nation but the states granted Congress no authority to address any function within society **CAPABLE** of being addressed by the people or the states.

I summarize the powers of the federal Congress as follows:

1) A sovereign, free nation must be able to defend itself from those wishing to do it harm. Common defense was the primary reason the individual states agreed to form the union of the United States. To provide for their common defense, the several States granted these specific powers to the Congress of the federal government:

   - To raise and support Armies,
   - To provide and maintain a Navy,
   - To make Rules for the Government and Regulation of the land and naval Forces,
   - To declare War,
   - To provide for calling forth the Militia,
   - To provide for organizing, arming, and disciplining the Militia,
   - To define and punish Piracies and Felonies committed on the high Seas, and Offenses against the Law of Nations.

2) The primary means of funding the federal government was through the imposition of duties, imposts, and excises. To collect these funds the federal government needed the authority to regulate trade with foreign nations. Additionally, the founders understood the importance of a vibrant free domestic market and accordingly wanted to break down the trade barriers erected between the states under the Articles of Confederation. To do so the several States granted the Congress of the federal government the power:

   - To regulate Commerce with foreign Nations, and among the several States, and with the Indian Tribes.

3) To efficiently function as a unified nation, the several States granted the Congress of the federal government power to establish standards of national uniformity including:

- To coin Money, regulate the Value thereof,
- To provide for the Punishment of counterfeiting,
- To fix the Standard of Weights and Measures,
- To establish an uniform Rule of Naturalization,
- To establish uniform Laws on the subject of Bankruptcies,
- To promote the Progress of Science and useful Arts, by securing for limited Times to Authors and Inventors the exclusive Right to their respective Writings and Discoveries—[to set up a patent office.]

4) The United States was a large nation. Communication between the states was difficult and vital, so the several States granted the Congress of the federal government the power:

- To Establish Post Offices and Post Roads.

5) The seat of government needed to be independent of undue influence from any state. Therefore, the several States granted the Congress of the federal government power to govern the territory housing the seat of the federal government and federal facilities:

- To exercise exclusive Legislation in all Cases whatsoever, over such District, and to exercise like Authority over all Places purchased by the Consent of the Legislature of the State in which the Same shall be, for the Erection of Forts, Magazines, Arsenals, dock-Yards, and other needful Buildings.

6) Disputes could arise between the various states or the federal government. To address these potential disputes, the several States granted the Congress of the federal government the power:

- To Constitute Tribunals inferior to the supreme Court.

7) Revenue would be required by the federal government to perform its enumerated duties. To fund its responsibilities the several States granted the Congress of the federal government the power:

  - To lay and collect Taxes, Duties, Imposts and Excises, to pay the Debts and provide for the common Defense and general Welfare of the United States,
  - To borrow money on the credit of the United States.

  Please note, the federal government was granted authority to collect revenue to pay for the performance of its enumerated powers summarized within the categories of the "common Defense and general Welfare of the United States." It was granted no authority to continually raise more than was needed for these duties, and then to redistribute the excess back to the states, or the people directly.

8) The Constitution allows Congress to fulfill its responsibilities, but prohibits it from making laws exceeding its defined and definite powers when it was granted the authority:

  - To make all Laws which shall be necessary and proper for carrying into Execution the foregoing Powers, and all other Powers vested by this Constitution in the Government of the United States, or in any Department or Officer thereof.

These are the powers the several States delegated to the Congress of the United States to be performed on their behalf, or for their general Welfare, but nothing more.

It's important to note that Congress was granted authority to make all laws which are "*necessary and proper*" to carry into execution the "*the foregoing Powers, and all other Powers vested by this Constitution in the Government of the United States.*" It was not granted power to make laws outside of this authority.

Within Article 1 Section 8 of the Constitution, the several States granted Congress no authority to address, influence, control, or legislate the daily needs of society including education, energy, Social Security, health care, welfare, the arts, banking, mortgages, transportation, religion, communication, or most of the other functions into which it has inserted itself.

The Powers of the President

The office of the President has evolved into the most powerful position in the world that unquestionably controls the most potent military on earth. In today's environment the President can propose, then implement, virtually any domestic policy desired—whether constitutionally authorized to do so or not.

According to the Constitution what are the authorized powers of the President? Article 2 Section 2 defines the powers of the President. After reading it most people ask "Where's the rest of his duties?"

*"**Article 2 Section 2.** The President shall be Commander in Chief of the Army and Navy of the United States, and of the Militia of the several States, when called into the actual Service of the United States; he may require the Opinion, in writing, of the principal Officer in each of the executive Departments, upon any Subject relating to the Duties of their respective Offices, and he shall have Power to grant Reprieves and Pardons for Offences against the United States, except in Cases of Impeachment.*

He shall have Power, by and with the Advice and Consent of the Senate, to make Treaties, provided two thirds of the Senators present concur; and he shall nominate, and by and with the Advice and Consent of the Senate, shall appoint Ambassadors, other public Ministers and Consuls, Judges of the supreme Court, and all other Officers of the United States, whose Appointments are not herein otherwise provided for, and which shall be established by Law: but the Congress may by Law vest the Appointment of such inferior Officers, as they think proper, in the President alone, in the Courts of Law, or in the Heads of Departments.

The President shall have Power to fill up all Vacancies that may happen during the Recess of the Senate, by granting Commissions which shall expire at the End of their next Session." [14]

These are the total powers granted by the several states, through the compact of the Constitution, to the President.

---

[14]   U.S. Constitution, Article 2 Section 2

I summarize theses powers as follows:

1) He shall act as Commander and Chief,
2) He may grant Pardons for Offences against the United States,
3) He represents the United States in foreign affairs and can negotiate treaties with foreign nations with the consent of the Senate,
4) He shall nominate and appoint, with the advice and consent of the Senate, Ambassadors, federal Judges, and all other officers not otherwise constitutionally provided for.

As with the Congress, the President is granted no authority to influence or control domestic policy dealing with, but not limited to education, jobs, housing, banking, cell phones, contraceptives, energy, health care, and the like.

Article 2 Section 3 details a few of the job responsibilities of the President including:

1) He shall inform Congress as to the State of the Union,
2) He shall recommend to Congress for their Consideration such measures he shall judge necessary and expedient,
3) He shall receive Ambassadors and other public Ministers,
4) He shall take Care that the Laws be faithfully executed,
5) He shall Commission all Officers of the United States.

These job responsibilities compliment the constitutional authority granted but in no way authorize interference in any aspect of domestic policy.

The President is authorized to recommend to Congress measures he deems necessary and expedient, and this power is often used to advocate for social domestic programs. Is this a proper use of this power?

No. Congress can only consider and act upon issues within their delegated authority—detailed and enumerated within Article 1 Section 8. The President can only address issues under his authority as defined within Article 2 Section 2. Therefore, recommendations from the President to Congress must be limited to the powers authorized to either Congress or the President, but nothing more.

Reinforcing Limitations of Federal Power

The people of the United States had an inherent fear of an overbearing centralized government. To further reinforce its limited nature the people, through the States, insisted upon the Bill of Rights—the first ten Amendments to the Constitution. Each of these Amendments reinforce the limitations of the federal government, prohibiting it from trampling our unalienable, God-given rights.

The 9th and 10th Amendments summarize unambiguously that the rights of the people are many, and not limited to those few enumerated in the Bill of Rights, while the powers granted to the federal government were few, well defined, and specifically enumerated.

9th Amendment: *The enumeration in the Constitution, of certain rights, shall not be construed to deny or disparage others retained by the people.*

10th Amendment: *The powers not delegated to the United States by the Constitution, nor prohibited by it to the States, are reserved to the States respectively, or to the people.*

Neither the people, the states, nor our Founders, granted control of their daily lives, or control of the responsibilities of the states, to the federal government. Instead, they specifically prohibited federal influence over their day-to-day activities, and limited federal authority to national duties the states determined were best handled by a central government.

The federal government has far exceeded its enumerated constitutional powers and now regulates and controls virtually every aspect of the U.S. economy and many aspects of private, individual lives. Usurpation of power by the federal government is a direct assault on personal liberty, and can be defined as nothing less than a domestic attack against the Constitution.

To survive as a free nation, we must reverse this trend, limit federal power and influence back within its constitutional constraint, and once again allow the people to excel through unbridled liberty.

One-Eight, One-Nine

Many people complain and consider the task of limiting government to its constitutionally enumerated duties impossible, but not me. The *only* solution to save our nation from impending doom is to re-impose constitutional restraint upon the federal government.

I have the solution. I call it my **One-Eight, One-Nine** plan to Empower People through Restrained Government.

It's a two-part plan, which addresses both the function and finance of the federal government by insisting upon adherence to existing constitutional provisions. It's simple, has worked every time it's been tried, meets constitutional muster, and requires no convoluted reasoning or amendments to be implemented.

Government leaders fear it.

One-Eight deals with function. It refers to Article 1 Section 8 of the Constitution, which specifically enumerates the powers authorized by the states to be performed by Congress. The plan seeks to awaken the people of the United States to the enormous benefits derived from our extremely limited, constitutional government and insist that the federal government adhere to and honor its specific, enumerated duties. We accomplish this task by educating ourselves and monitoring our representatives to ensure they follow the Constitution. Those who don't must be voted out of office.

One-Nine deals with finance. It refers to Article 1 Section 9, which specifically states that money may only be drawn from the federal treasury to pay for specific, enumerated, constitutional duties. [15]

---

[15]   Article 1 Section 8 authorizes Congress "To make all Laws which shall be necessary and proper for carrying into Execution the foregoing Powers, and all other Powers vested by this Constitution in the Government of the United States." Article 1 Section 9 then states that: "No Money shall be drawn from the Treasury, but in Consequence of Appropriations

Think about it.

Federal money spent on functions outside of the government's specific, enumerated duties, such as Health and Human Services, Energy, Education, entitlements, the Environmental Protection Agency, etc., is unconstitutional; it's against the law. If we simply followed this provision of the Constitution, federal spending would be well under control, and we would have no federal debt. Let me repeat: **WE WOULD HAVE NO FEDERAL DEBT.**

I am in no way stating that the foregoing needs would be left unaddressed, only that they would no longer be addressed by a politically motivated federal government. These needs would be more efficiently addressed by the people, voluntary charity, the free market, or the states.

Most people don't realize that the federal government adhered to its severely limited, constitutional responsibilities for the first two-thirds of our nation's life. Federal spending averaged just 2-3% of Gross Domestic Product; *two to three percent*—equating to about one tenth what we spend now. We had no income tax and no debt, allowing a truly free people to craft the greatest nation on earth.

---

made by Law;" Congress can only make laws relating to its constitutional authority, and money can only be spent based on law. Therefore, money may be drawn from the treasury only in the performance of specific constitutionally enumerated powers.

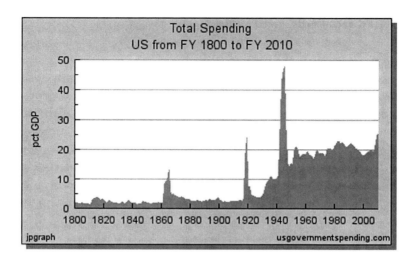

Total Spending
US from FY 1800 to FY 2010

pct GDP

jpgraph   usgovernmentspending.com

Today, we have serious problems facing our nation—spending, taxation, crushing debt, corruption, and the breakdown of societal standards—all directly caused by the federal government overstepping its authority by imposing its politically motivated policies into the people's lives. Unless addressed, these problems will destroy our nation.

My **One-Eight, One-Nine** plan highlights the fact that the solution to all our problems is staring us in the face—our tried and true U.S. Constitution. The only way to save our nation is by insisting that the federal government limit itself to its enumerated duties, once again allowing the people, through personal endeavor, the free market, voluntary charity, or lastly the states, to handle everything else.

How can we possibly restrain the scope and power of the federal government back to its enumerated duties and re-impose the limitations of **One-Eight, One-Nine**?

I have an implementation program, called **Negative Baseline Budgeting**, which will slash our bloated government back to a trim and fit, constitutionally limited government.

Negative Baseline Budgeting

Our federal government has morphed into a destructive cancer growing out of control and destroying everything it touches. It's devised a devious method of continually increasing itself called *Baseline Budgeting*. Every year, all federal programs are automatically increased an average of 8%, essentially doubling the size, scope, power, and influence of the federal government every 10 years. It encourages massive waste and fraud by requiring all departments to spend their entire allotted budget, whether needed or not, under the threat of having future budgets cut.

The concept of Baseline Budgeting makes it impossible to decrease the scope and power of the federal government.

We can reverse this situation assuming we have representatives in Washington actually wanting to fix the problem. My solution is called *Negative Baseline Budgeting*, which consists of cutting non-constitutional federal spending until it's eliminated—an idea detested by government, but critically important for the survival of a free nation.

I classify all federal spending into two categories: Constitutional and Non-constitutional.

Constitutional: Federal programs that are specifically enumerated in the Constitution, such as for common defense, immigration, patent office, etc. The functionality of these programs must be fully funded and should never be cut simply to save money. But discovered waste, fraud, and duplication must be eliminated whenever they are uncovered.

Non-constitutional: Federal programs that are not enumerated in the Constitution, such as Health and Human Services, Energy, Education, Environmental Protection Service, etc. These programs may have been implemented based on the best of intentions, but a bloated government bureaucracy, driven by the accumulation of political power, converts these programs into forces of destruction for a free society. It has been proven that the people, the free market, voluntary charity, or the states can address all these functions far more efficiently than the federal government. Non-constitutional programs must be transitioned to the private sector or to state control.

Federal funds should be spent frugally on constitutionally mandated programs only.

Even though there is no constitutional justification for Social Security and Medicare, the federal government must honor these obligations. Individuals were forced to pay into these systems, under the threat of imprisonment, in return for a promised federal benefit.

I would never support involuntarily cutting Social Security or Medicare benefits to existing retirees or those currently working, but I understand government has demonstrated continual incompetence in managing these programs, and it is imperative that these programs be transitioned to the private sector outside of federal control. [16]

For the purposes of this analysis, I consider Social Security and Medicare a lawful debt which must be honored by the federal government.

Based on our historical average, about 90% of federal spending is allocated to non-constitutional programs. [17] We may not be able to eliminate all this spending overnight, but we must start transitioning it to the infinitely more efficient private sector now.

The first aspect of Negative Baseline Budgeting requires that we "stop the bleeding" by immediately balancing the federal budget. It can be done.[18] Balancing the budget requires the absolute conviction that we

---

[16] Review Konetchy's position on Social Security, within this book, for an explanation of how to transition this program to the private sector.

[17] From 1787 through 1930 federal spending averaged 2-3% of Gross Domestic Product. In 2011, federal spending averaged 26% of GDP, which is 10 times our historical rate.

[18] Review Konetchy's position "Balanced Budget", within this book, for an explanation of how to immediately balance the federal budget.

can't spend more than we take in. It's accomplished by the setting of priorities combined with the elimination of waste and unnecessary programs. Eliminated programs, desired by the people, (such as Big Bird on Public Television) will be efficiently absorbed and enhanced by the free market for a fraction of the cost.

There is no question that massive waste, fraud, and duplication are associated with federal spending. The practice of baseline budgeting actively encourages it. We could immediately balance our budget and live within our revenue stream if we simply eliminated known waste and limited non-constitutional spending to 2008 levels.

Neither individuals, families, nor businesses can continually spend money they don't have without failing. Nations are no different. Our accumulated debt now exceeds the entire gross domestic product of the United States. Deficit spending must end. This nation can no longer absorb unrestrained debt without imploding from this crushing burden.

We have no choice except to immediately balance the budget if we are to survive as a nation.

Once the budget is balanced, the second aspect of Negative Baseline Budgeting proposes that all non-constitutional programs be phased out completely over a relatively short period. Using a 12-year timeframe, Negative Baseline Budgeting would decrease the budgets for these programs by 8.33% across the board the first year, with the resulting dollar amount being subtracted from each of the succeeding years' budgets until the program is eliminated. By implementing this Negative Baseline Budgeting technique, all non-constitutionally mandated programs would be completely phased out within 12 years.

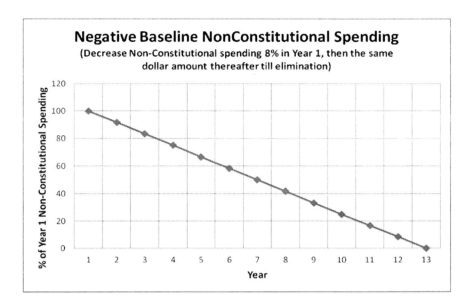

Negative Baseline NonConstitutional Spending

(Decrease Non-Constitutional spending 8% in Year 1, then the same dollar amount thereafter till elimination)

All affected programs would retain the lion's share of their funding during the early years, allowing them to be transitioned away from the federal control in an orderly manner. The gargantuan federal bureaucracy could naturally decrease by implementing a hiring freeze, aided by attrition and the assumption of duties by the private sector.

The third aspect of Negative Baseline Budgeting is a corresponding decrease in all direct federal taxes against individuals and corporations consistent with the decrease in government spending. The first year spending is cut, the total federal direct tax imposed against individuals and corporations would decrease by 8.33%. Every year thereafter, the direct tax would decrease by the same amount, resulting in the elimination of all direct federal taxes against the individual and corporations in 12 years.

I understand that the federal government needs revenue to perform its duties. I support the taxation method proposed by our founders and ratified by the states in the original Constitution—indirect taxation raised by duties, excises, and imposts, combined with the direct taxation of the states for the required shortfall, based on the percentage of population. This method of taxation works not in theory only, but in proven fact. It fully funded the federal government for the majority of our nation's life, providing a significant check against government abuse, and protecting the personal liberties of the people.

State Nullification

The majority of those in Washington have lost the discipline and desire to constrain their actions within their constitutional limitations and now seek to control, regulate, and tax every aspect of society. They've morphed government into an unaccountable force of destruction intent on forcing submission of both the states and the people to its self-ordained omnipotent will.

What recourse do free men have when government blatantly tramples specific constitutional rights? Suppose our government passes a law nullifying the Second Amendment, parental rights, the right to practice religion freely, the right to assemble, the right to a trial, or the right to private property—should we simply accept and submit?

No, but what's the constitutional solution proposed by our founders against an unrestrained federal government?

Think about these **facts**.

1. The Constitution is the supreme law of the land.
2. The federal government is constitutionally authorized by the states to perform specific national functions, but is likewise specifically prohibited from interfering in the responsibilities of the states or the people.
3. The states are constitutionally prohibited from interfering in the responsibilities of the federal government, but are authorized to provide the services desired by the people within their jurisdiction.
4. This constitutional delineation of exclusive responsibility prohibits Congress from making laws directly affecting the people's lives or interfering in state responsibilities.
5. Every federal, state, and local official swears an oath to uphold the Constitution and defend it from foreign or domestic attack.
6. When the federal government exceeds its constitutional authority and passes laws which supersede with the

responsibilities of the people or state; local and state officials, who swore to uphold the Constitution, have no choice but to honor their oath to defend the Constitution by refusing to honor or implement what they know to be unconstitutional authority over the people.

Let's assume, for illustration purposes, that President Obama is able to appoint additional judges to the Supreme Court in his second term of office. Assume also, that the judges appointed personally support Sharia Law. Assume further that they are able to convince a majority of the court, through argument, bribe, or threat, to rule that Sharia Law is the supreme law of the land.

Should this ruling be honored even though passed by the Supreme Court? Of course not! No branch of government has been granted the authority to impose Sharia Law, it directly contradicts the people's constitutionally protected liberties enumerated within the Bill of Rights, and it conflicts with the laws of virtually every state in the union. Even though, in this example, the federal government has stamped its seal of constitutional approval on this dictate through the court, it cannot be the supreme law of the land and cannot be constitutionally implemented by the state or local authorities.

Many may feel that this example is far-fetched, but it's not. Simply switch the subject of "Sharia Law" with "Universal Health Care."

Universal Health Care was passed by Congress and declared constitutional by the Supreme Court even though no branch of government has been granted the authority to impose Universal Health Care, it directly contradicts the people's constitutionally protected liberties enumerated within the Bill of Rights, and it conflicts with the laws of virtually every state in the union. Even though the federal government has stamped its seal of constitutional approval on this dictate through the court, it cannot be the supreme law of the land and cannot be constitutionally implemented by the state or local authorities.

If the Constitution is relevant, and if it is the supreme law of the land, the only remedy to address dictates imposed by the federal government without constitutional authority is the refusal to enforce by state and local authorities.

The federal government has a proper role, and the states do likewise, but when the federal government oversteps its authority and usurps power from the people and the states, we must enforce the Constitution, and nullify these actions by refusing to acknowledge, honor, or enforce unauthorized, unconstitutional, federal actions.

Consider the concept of nullification this way.

Imagine a state passed a law dictating that all federal buildings had to set their heating thermostats at 55° in the winter to save energy, and furthermore each federal employee had to wear a green sweater, manufactured from hemp, to stay warm. If state inspectors determined that this law was disobeyed, the violators would be fined, imprisoned, or otherwise punished.

Do you think the federal government would follow this law? Of course not. The state clearly has no authority to pass this decree and it should be ignored.

Modify the above example and assume that to save energy the federal government dictated to the states that the people could no longer use incandescent light bulbs, and furthermore everyone must use government-approved energy efficient bulbs [often filled with carcinogens causing a severe health hazard when broken]. To enforce this law the federal government prohibited the manufacture of incandescent bulbs and those doing so would be fined, imprisoned, or otherwise punished.

Is there a power anywhere in the Constitution allowing Congress to manage our energy usage? No! Is there any authority allowing Congress to prohibit the manufacture of a product it considers inefficient, and force its replacement with a government approved solution? No!

The federal government has no constitutional authority to prohibit the manufacture, distribution, or sale of incandescent light bulbs, and therefore this federal law is unauthoritative, void, and of no force.

Consider another example: It's in the general welfare of the people to authorize the police to uphold the laws of the locality, state, and U.S. Constitution. The police have been authorized to address offenses such as speeding, burglaries, disorderly conduct, and more serious crimes such as murder and rape. Yet the police have no authority to impose their will outside of this jurisdiction—such as specifying which college my children should attend, the type of car I drive, who I marry, etc. If a policeman tells me to buy a Chevy Volt, I can disagree and ignore this decree without fear of repercussions.

This example parallels the relationship the states should have with the federal government. The federal government has been entrusted to perform very specific national duties. [19] Federal actions are the supreme law of the land only when performed within constitutional authority, but have no authority otherwise. Therefore the states should object to, and refuse to implement, a clearly unauthorized federal dictate without fear of repercussions; just as I can refuse an unauthorized dictate from my local policeman to buy a Chevy Volt.

Assume the policeman in our example happens to be the trustee of my estate and he instructs me to take action outside of his authority—such as what type of car to purchase. He still has no authority but now has the leverage of withholding my income if I do not accede to his demands. If I comply with his demand, and buy a Chevy Volt, I'll receive funds from my estate, otherwise no money will be forthcoming.

This example parallels the actual relationship between the federal government and the states. The federal government collects an immense amount of money from within the states, through federal taxation, which it then reallocates back to the states with conditions

---

[19]   Please review the Proper Role of Government within this book.

attached. If the state refuses to accede to these conditions, the money is withheld.

Jimmy Carter as President wanted to save energy by lowering the highway speed limit to 55 MPH. I was initially puzzled that Washington could impose this type of authority on the states until I learned that it threatened to withhold highway funds from the states which refused to implement its demands. In order to continue to receive federal funding the states submitted to this unconstitutional demand.

It's no accident that the federal government uses its taxing authority to extract as much capital as possible from the states, and then holds the states hostage by threatening to withhold federal funding if uncooperative. Washington has established this financial leverage to force the states to submit to their demands. These same practices employed by any organization other than government would be called extortion.

We must wake up as a nation, refuse submission to unjust policies, and once again act as free men. The constitutional authority for the states to rein back all aspects of government intrusion is already in place.

First: Article 1 Section 8 limits federal authority to its very specific defined and definite constitutional powers. It has been granted no power to act outside of these duties.[20]

Second: Article 1 Section 9 disallows federal spending outside of Congress's defined and definite powers.[21]

---

[20] To make all Laws which shall be necessary and proper for carrying into Execution **the foregoing Powers, and all other Powers vested by this Constitution in the Government of the United States**, or in any Department or Officer thereof (emphasis added).

[21] No Money shall be drawn from the Treasury, but in Consequence of Appropriations made by Law (Congress is authorized to make laws pertaining to its defined and definite duties only—nothing else).

Third: The Tenth Amendment again reinforces that Congress can only address its defined and definite duties and nothing more.[22]

Lastly: The Supremacy Clause, within Article 6 [23] defines the requirements for valid federal law, and reinforces **four times** that federal law is the supreme law of the land only if it is made consistent with the Constitution. It unambiguously states that to be valid and enforceable, federal law:

1. Must be made pursuant to the Constitution
2. Must be made under the authority of the United States (i.e. pertain to an enumerated power.)
3. Must not conflict with anything in the Constitution
4. Must not conflict with state law. [This restriction further reinforces that the constitutional authority of the states and the federal government are exclusive.]

Laws passed outside of constitutional authority are not the supreme law of the land, and cannot be constitutionally enforced upon the people.

For decades Congress has been blatantly ignoring any constitutional restriction it finds "inconvenient" rendering the Constitution virtually meaningless.

Every federal, state, and local elected representative swears to uphold the Constitution of the United States. These individuals are elected by the people to secure liberty. It's incumbent upon them to honor

---

[22]   The powers not delegated to the United States by the Constitution, nor prohibited by it to the States, are reserved to the States respectively, or to the people.

[23]   This Constitution, and **the Laws of the United States which shall be made in Pursuance thereof;** and all Treaties made, or which shall be made, **under the Authority of the United States,** shall be the supreme Law of the Land; and the Judges in every State shall be bound thereby, **any Thing in the Constitution or Laws of any State to the Contrary notwithstanding**(Emphasis added).

the Constitution by refusing to honor, enforce, or implement non-constitutional decrees.

We must all insist that the federal government perform only its authorized national duties leaving responsibility for all else to the people themselves, or the states, otherwise we're living in tyranny, not freedom.

The answer to federal abuse is State Nullification.

A Means of Enforcing Constitutional Restraint

There is no question that the federal government is out–of–control, but how can we rein federal power back to its limited constitutional responsibilities? Thomas Jefferson provided the answer.

As the primary author of the Declaration of Independence, a Vice President, and President, I consider Jefferson an authority on our founding principles and constitutionally limited government. He argued, that when acting outside of its constitutional authority, the federal government is irrelevant. Additionally, he argues the states are not bound to honor, implement, or enforce unauthorized federal dictates.

Jefferson stated the obvious response to federal usurpation of power:

"That the several States composing, the United States of America, are not united on the principle of unlimited submission to their general government; but that, by a compact . . . they constituted a general government for special purposes—delegated to that government certain definite powers, reserving, each State to itself, the residuary mass of right to their own self-government; **and that whensoever the general government assumes undelegated powers, its acts are unauthoritative, void, and of no force:"**[24] (emphasis added)

Jefferson reinforced that the federal government is not a party to the Constitution, equal or supreme, but a creation of it; and therefore is not in a position to be the final judge of its own actions. The individual states, which created the government, must judge the appropriateness of its actions.

"they [the states] alone being parties to the compact, and solely authorized to judge in the last resort of the powers exercised under it, Congress being not a party, but merely the creature of the compact:"[25]

---

[24]   the Kentucky Resolutions of 1798.

[25]   ibid

According to Jefferson's reasoning, the federal governmen
authority to classify a program, such as Obama Care, "constitutiona
and then force the states to honor it. The issue of constitutionality
must be determined by the parties of the compact, meaning the
states, which in this case have overwhelmingly judged Obama Care as
unconstitutional and are evaluating all means possible to stop it.

Jefferson then goes on to state the constitutional remedy to federal
abuse of power.

*"that in cases of an abuse of the delegated powers, the members of the general
government, being chosen by the people, a change by the people would be the
constitutional remedy;* **but, where powers are assumed which have not been
delegated, a nullification of the act is the rightful remedy:"** [26] (emphasis
added)

He then counseled each state to *"take measures of its own for providing
that neither these acts [the Alien and Sedition acts addressed by the Kentucky
Resolutions],* **nor any others of the general government not plainly and
intentionally authorized by the Constitution,** *shalt be exercised within their
respective territories."*[27] (emphasis added)

Jefferson provided the appropriate response for the states when ordered
to implement an unconstitutional federal dictate, such as Obama
Care—refuse to honor, implement, and enforce it.

I have drafted a series of resolutions entitled the *State Nullification
Resolutions* addressing the authority, function, and funding of the
federal government. I would encourage legislators within every state to
consider, pass, and then abide by these resolutions; which would result
in reining the federal government back to the authority granted it by
the Constitution, and allowing, once again, the people and the states to
address their own needs.

---

[26]   ibid

[27]   ibid

State Nullification Resolutions

(Italicized texts are direct quotes from the Kentucky Resolutions of 1798.)

1. ***Resolved,*** *That the several States composing, the United States of America, are not united on the principle of unlimited submission to their general government; but that, by a compact under the style and title of a Constitution for the United States, and of amendments thereto, they constituted a general government for special purposes—delegated to that government certain definite powers, reserving, each State to itself, the residuary mass of right to their own self-government; and that whensoever the general government assumes undelegated powers, its acts are unauthoritative, void, and of no force: that to this compact each State acceded as a State, and is an integral part, its co-States forming, as to itself, the other party: that the government created by this compact was not made the exclusive or final judge of the extent of the powers delegated to itself; since that would have made its discretion, and not the Constitution, the measure of its powers; but that, as in all other cases of compact among powers having no common judge, each party has an equal right to judge for itself, as well of infractions as of the mode and measure of redress. (Jefferson's words from the Kentucky Resolutions of 1798.)*

2. ***Resolved,*** That the states, by compact through the Constitution for the United States, delegated to the Congress of the federal government defined and definite powers to provide for their common defense (that include the powers:

   - To declare War, grant Letters of Marque and Reprisal, and make Rules concerning Captures on Land and Water;
   - To raise and support Armies;
   - To provide and maintain a Navy;
   - To make Rules for the Government and Regulation of the land and naval Forces;
   - To provide for calling forth the Militia to execute the Laws of the Union, suppress Insurrections and repel Invasions;

- To provide for organizing, arming, and disciplining, the Militia, and for governing such Part of them as may be employed in the Service of the United States;
- To define and punish Piracies and Felonies committed on the high Seas, and Offences against the Law of Nations;)

. . . and to provide for the benefit, or general Welfare, of the several States (that include the powers:

- To regulate Commerce with foreign Nations, and among the several States, and with the Indian Tribes;
- To establish an uniform Rule of Naturalization, and uniform Laws on the subject of Bankruptcies throughout the United States;
- To coin Money, regulate the Value thereof, and of foreign Coin, and fix the Standard of Weights and Measures;
- To provide for the Punishment of counterfeiting the Securities and current Coin of the United States;
- To establish Post Offices and post Roads;
- To promote the Progress of Science and useful Arts, by securing for limited Times to Authors and Inventors the exclusive Right to their respective Writings and Discoveries;
- To constitute Tribunals inferior to the supreme Court;
- To exercise exclusive Legislation in all Cases whatsoever, over such District, and to exercise like Authority over all Places purchased by the Consent of the Legislature of the State in which the Same shall be, for the Erection of Forts, Magazines, Arsenals, dock-Yards, and other needful Buildings.)

. . . and to provide the ability to execute these defined and definite powers, Congress was granted the authority to:

- The Congress shall have Power To lay and collect Taxes, Duties, Imposts and Excises, to pay the Debts and provide for the common Defense and general Welfare of the United

States; but all Duties, Imposts and Excises shall be uniform throughout the United States;

- To borrow money on the credit of the United States;

- To make all Laws which shall be necessary and proper for carrying into Execution the foregoing Powers, and all other Powers vested by this Constitution in the Government of the United States, or in any Department or Officer thereof.

These are the totality of the defined and definite powers delegated by the states to the Congress of the federal government of the United States providing for their common defense and general welfare. The states did not authorize the Congress to dictate or implement domestic policy upon the states or the people within the United States. Any acts of Congress exceeding this defined and definite authority are unauthoritative, void, and of no force.

3. **Resolved,** That the states, by compact through the Constitution for the United States, delegated to the President of the federal government defined and definite powers to represent the United States including:

- The President shall be Commander in Chief of the Army and Navy of the United States, and of the Militia of the several States, when called into the actual Service of the United States;

- He shall have Power to Grant Reprieves and Pardons for Offenses against the United States, except in Cases of Impeachment.

- He shall have Power, by and with the Advice and Consent of the Senate, to make Treaties;

- He shall nominate, and by and with the Advice and Consent of the Senate, shall appoint Ambassadors, other public Ministers and Consuls, Judges of the supreme Court, and all other Officers of the United States, whose Appointments are not herein otherwise provided for;

- The President shall have Power to fill up all Vacancies that may happen during the Recess of the Senate, by granting Commissions which shall expire at the End of their next Session.

These are the totality of the defined and definite powers delegated by the states to the President of the federal government. The states did not delegate the President the power to dictate or implement domestic policy upon the states or the people within the United States. Therefore, all directives or orders by the President of the United States delivered outside of these defined and definite powers are unauthoritative, void, and of no force.

4. **Resolved,** That the states, by compact through the Constitution for the United States, delegated to the Congress of the federal government a power to make all laws which shall be necessary and proper for carrying into execution the authorized defined and definite powers. The states did not grant the Congress the authority to make laws exceeding its defined and definite powers or to dictate or implement domestic policy upon the states or the people within the United States. All laws doing so are unauthoritative, void, and of no force.

5. **Resolved,** Article 6 of the Constitution reads "This Constitution, and the Laws of the United States which shall be made in Pursuance thereof; and all Treaties made, or which shall be made, under the Authority of the United States, shall be the supreme law of the land; and the Judges in every State shall be bound thereby, any Thing in the Constitution or Laws of any State to the Contrary notwithstanding."

Laws "*made in Pursuance*" of the Constitution are the supreme law of the land and must be honored, but laws **NOT** "*made* *in Pursuance"* of the Constitution, laws made without the authority of Congress, laws negating constitutional protections, or laws negating constitutionally protected state responsibilities, are not the supreme law of the land and are unauthoritative, void, and of no force.

6. ***Resolved,*** That the states, by compact through the Constitution for the United States, delegated to Congress a power to lay and collect taxes, duties, imposts and excises, and to borrow money on the credit of the United States, to be used to pay the debts and provide for the common defense and general welfare of the United States. The states did not authorize the federal government the means or authority to make law to collect revenue, or to borrow on the credit of the United States in gross excess of that needed to perform the authorized, defined and definite powers; and prohibited the federal government from doing so by the passage of the Fifth Amendment, reinforced by the passage of the Fourteenth Amendment, which prohibits the taking of property without due process of law. The collection of revenue in excess of that needed to fund the defined and definite powers of the federal government on a continuing and recurring basis is unauthoritative.

7. ***Resolved,*** That the states, by compact through the Constitution for the United States, mandated the restriction on the Congress of the federal government that no money shall be drawn from the treasury but in consequence of appropriations made by law. Congress is authorized to make laws only to execute the defined and definite powers specified within the compact of the Constitution for the United States. Therefore, all money drawn from the treasury for payment of acts exceeding the authority of these defined and definite powers is unauthoritative.

8. ***Resolved,*** That the states, by compact through the Constitution for the United States, delegated to neither Congress nor the President, power to influence, control, fund, or legislate any function exceeding their defined and definite powers, and one of the amendments to the Constitution having also declared,

that "the powers not delegated to the United States by the Constitution, not prohibited by it to the States, are reserved to the States respectively, or to the people," therefore all laws passed by Congress, or orders by the President, outside the defined and definite powers addressing, but not limited to, education, retirement, health care, housing, transportation, agriculture, energy, industry, environment, labor, and all other usurped authority are altogether void and of no force; and that the authority to address powers not delegated to the federal government, and not prohibited to the states are reserved, and, of right, appertains solely and exclusively to the respective states, each within its own territory, or to the people directly.

9. **Resolved,** That this state does not accept as valid the authority of the federal government exceeding the defined and definite powers authorized by the Constitution for the United States; that the unauthorized interference by the federal government into the powers for which the state is responsible are destructive to this state; and that the excessive, recurring taxation by the federal government used to fund programs outside the defined and definite authority granted it by the states, through the compact of the Constitution for the United States, is detrimental to the wellbeing of the industry and people within this state.

To constitutionally address this usurpation of power by the federal government, this state will accept no further funding from the federal government pertaining to powers for which the state is responsible and for which the federal government has no defined and definite authority. All direct federal taxation imposed upon the people or industry within this state shall be collected and deposited into the state treasury. This state will forward to the federal government the collected federal taxation required to pay for this state's portion of costs incurred by the federal government performing its defined and definite powers pertaining to common defense and general welfare of the states based on the number of citizens and legal immigrants residing in this state as a percentage of citizens and legal immigrants residing within the totality of the United States, adjusted downward by the amount of duties, imposts and excise revenue collected by the federal government attributed to this state. Federal taxation directly collected from individuals and industry within this state in excess of that forwarded to the general government will be retained by this state to pay for required state services, or refunded to the people.

10. **Resolved,** *That a committee of conference and correspondence be appointed, who shall have in charge to communicate the preceding resolutions to the Legislatures of the several States:*

- *to assure them that this State continues in the same esteem of their friendship and union which it has manifested from that moment at which a common danger first suggested a common union:*
- *that it considers union, for specified national purposes specified in their federal compact, to be friendly, to the peace, happiness and prosperity of all the States:*
- *that faithful to that compact, according to the plain intent and meaning in which it was understood and acceded to by the several parties, it is sincerely anxious for its preservation:*
- *that it does also believe, that to take from the States all the powers of self-government and transfer them to a general and consolidated government, without regard to the special delegations and reservations solemnly agreed to in that compact, is not for the peace, happiness or prosperity of these States;*
- *and that therefore this State is determined, as it doubts not its co-States are, to submit to undelegated, and consequently unlimited powers in no man, or body of men on earth:*
- *that in cases of an abuse of the delegated powers, the members of the general government, being chosen by the people, a change by the people would be the constitutional remedy; but, where powers are assumed which have not been delegated, a nullification of the act is the rightful remedy:*
- *that every State has a natural right in cases not within the compact, (casus non fœderis) to nullify of their own authority all assumptions of power by others within their limits:*

- *that without this right, they would be under the dominion, absolute and unlimited, of whosoever might exercise this right of judgment for them:*
- *that nevertheless, this State, from motives of regard and respect for its co-States, has wished to communicate with them on the subject:*
- *that with them alone it is proper to communicate, they alone being parties to the compact, and solely authorized to judge in the last resort of the powers exercised under it, Congress being not a party, but merely the creature of the compact, and subject as to its assumptions of power to the final judgment of those by whom, and for whose use itself and its powers were all created and modified:*

If the unauthoritative usurpation of power, outside of the defined and definite powers granted by the states to the federal government by the Constitution for the United States, *should stand, these conclusions would flow from them;*

- *that the general government may place any act they think proper whether enumerated or not enumerated by the constitution as cognizable by them:*
- *that they may transfer its cognizance to the President, or any other person, who may himself be the accuser, counsel, judge and jury, whose suspicions may be the evidence, his order the sentence, his officer the executioner, and his breast the sole record of the transaction:*
- *that by acts of this government a very numerous and valuable description of the inhabitants of these States being, by this precedent, reduced, as outlaws, to the absolute dominion of one man, and the barrier of the Constitution thus swept away from us all, no ramparts now remains against the passions and the powers of a majority in Congress to protect the minority of the same body, the legislatures, judges, governors and counsellors of the States, nor their other peaceable inhabitants, who may venture to reclaim the constitutional rights and liberties of the States and people, or who for other causes, good or bad, may be obnoxious to the views, or marked by the suspicions of the President, or be thought dangerous to his or their election, or other interests, public or personal;*

- *that these and successive acts of the same character, unless arrested at the threshold, necessarily drive these States into revolution and blood and will furnish new calumnies against republican government, and new pretexts for those who wish it to be believed that man cannot be governed but by a rod of iron:*
- *that it would be a dangerous delusion were a confidence in the men of our choice to silence our fears for the safety of our rights:*
- *that confidence is everywhere the parent of despotism—free government is founded in jealousy, and not in confidence; it is jealousy and not confidence which prescribes limited constitutions, to bind down those whom we are obliged to trust with power:*
- *that our Constitution has accordingly fixed the limits to which, and no further, our confidence may go; and let the honest advocate of confidence review the innumerable, unauthorized acts of Congress, and say if the Constitution has not been wise in fixing limits to the government it created, and whether we should be wise in destroying those limits, Let him say what the government is, if it be not a tyranny, which the men of our choice have conferred on our President;*
- *that the men of our choice have more respected the bare suspicion of the President, than the solid right of innocence, the claims of justification, the sacred force of truth, and the forms and substance of law and justice. In questions of powers, then, let no more be heard of confidence in man, but bind him down from mischief by the chains of the Constitution.*

That this State does therefore call on its co-States for an expression of their sentiments on the unauthorized acts of Congress imposed upon the States declaring whether these acts are or are not authorized by the federal compact. And it doubts not that their sense will be so announced as to prove their attachment unaltered to limited government, weather general or particular. And that the rights and liberties of their co-States will be exposed to no dangers by remaining embarked in a common bottom with their own.

That they will concur with this State in considering the said actions as so palpably against the Constitution as to amount to an undisguised declaration that that compact is not meant to be the measure of the powers of the general government, but that it will proceed in the exercise over these States, of all powers whatsoever: that they will view this as seizing the rights of the States, and consolidating them in the hands of the general government, with a power assumed to bind the States (not merely as the cases made federal, casus fœderis but), in all cases whatsoever, by laws made, not with their consent, but by others against their consent: that this would be to surrender the form of government we have chosen, and live under one deriving its powers from its own will, and not from our authority; and that the co-States, recurring to their natural right in cases not made federal, will concur in declaring these acts void, and of no force, and will each take measures of its own for providing that neither these acts, nor any others of the general government not plainly and intentionally authorized by the Constitution, shalt be exercised within their respective territories. (Jefferson's words from the Kentucky Resolutions of 1798.)

We need to unabashedly affirm, that as free men our rights are from God, not government; that our Constitution is relevant and established the best possible government to protect those rights; and that we refuse to be subjected to the undelegated, and consequently unlimited powers of any man, or body of men on earth. Otherwise, we are not free and are instead living by the grace of our conquerors.

I will accept no less than the liberty bequeathed us by our founders. The federal government is striving with all possible means to strip us of this liberty and force us into submission, and our recent history has confirmed that we cannot rely on the benevolence of those in power to safeguard these liberties on our behalf.

We must be ever vigilant and continually defend our freedoms. We have the power to do it peaceably, yet forcefully, through the passage of these resolutions that address all aspects of constitutional abuse—including the removal of undue financial leverage by Washington over the people and the states.

These resolutions force the federal government be accountable to its constitutional powers and limitations—nothing more.

People are fearful of the resulting wrath of the federal government, making passage of these resolutions by the initial state difficult, but once passed, that state will once again thrive through unbridled liberty. Other states will follow transforming the federal government into a potent constitutional force, but making it irrelevant, as it should be, pertaining to the daily lives of the people.

Enforcing the Constitution requires that we refuse implementation of unconstitutional dictates.

Federal Audit

The federal government is constitutionally required to provide a regular accounting of revenue and expenses,[28] yet the federal government shuns the intent, if not the letter, of this requirement by:

- Refusing to pass a budget;
- Refusing to acknowledge or address untold duplication and waste within its actions and appropriations;
- Misappropriating spending, by slashing constitutionally mandated programs such as defense, while drastically increasing non-authorized, non-constitutional spending which falls within the exclusive responsibility of the free-market or state, such as spending on energy or health and human service.

The federal government was created by the states and is funded by the people to perform the defined and definite duties required to maintain a safe and secure sovereign nation. When questions dealing with severe financial mismanagement arise, pertaining to any organization including the federal government, an independent audit of the organization is in order, commissioned by the parties of interest—in this case the states.

All states supporting State Nullification require unbiased, accurate information to determine their share of constitutionally mandated spending. These states should commission and fund an independent audit of the federal government to obtain an unbiased, accurate, assessment of:

- Revenue collected by source within state (income tax, corporate tax, estate tax, duties, imposts, etc. collected from within each state);
- Federal spending apportioned within its constitutional authority;
- Accumulated debt;
- Unfunded liabilities;
- Waste and duplication.

---

[28] Article 1 Section 9: a regular Statement and Account of the Receipts and Expenditures of all public Money shall be published from time to time.

The audit would be performed by single accounting firm, or a conglomeration of independent firms, with sufficient resources to perform the task in a timely manner. The standards for the audit would be consistent with those of private sector corporations. Classified national secrets would be protected as are the confidential trade secrets of audited private sector firms.

The states implementing the Nullification Resolutions would use the results of the audit to determine their financial responsibility pertaining to funding constitutionally mandated programs.

The results of the audit should be made public allowing the people to honestly evaluate the financial position of the federal government, and if found wanting, they will have the knowledge to pressure their federal representatives to act responsibly or to pressure their state representatives to adopt the Nullification Resolutions.

Moral Leaders

I believe that the problems facing our country today are a direct result of it being run by a significant number of elected representatives lacking the moral foundation necessary to secure the liberty of the people.

The United States is a Christian nation grounded upon Judeo-Christian values. This is a historical fact, not opinion. Columbus discovered the Americas in his quest to spread Christianity. The original settlers to this country were Christians who fled religious prosecution in their homelands. Our founding documents are permeated with the truths that our rights come from God, not government, and as free men we are responsible to chart our own destiny.

The grounding of Judeo-Christian morality within government is critical to our nation's survival. Without it we lose our moral compass and drift into cultural decay.

John Adams warned his fellow countrymen, "*We have no government armed with power capable of contending with human passions unbridled by morality and religion . . . Our Constitution was made only for a moral and religious people. It is wholly inadequate to the government of any other.*" John Adams is a signer of the Declaration of Independence, the Bill of Rights and our second President.

Charles Carroll, signer of the Declaration of Independence warned likewise. "*Without morals a republic cannot subsist any length of time; they therefore who are decrying the Christian religion, whose morality is so sublime and pure (and) which insures to the good eternal happiness, are undermining the solid foundation of morals, the best security for the duration of free governments.*"

I learned firsthand of the nation's thirst for morality when I entered the fray of politics with my unsuccessful run for Michigan's United States Senate seat in the 2012 election.

One of the requirements for appearing on the Republican ballot was the collection of 15,000 nominating signatures from registered voters throughout the state. It was a daunting task, but one that I truly enjoyed.

The deadline for signature collection was May 15, 2012. At the beginning of April I had about 10,000 signatures, and needed a minimum of 5,000 more.

Each day, starting the beginning of April, I would drive to a city in Michigan and collect signatures. During working hours, 9:00 AM through 5:30 PM, I would walk the downtown and commercial areas introducing myself to small businesses and their employees and explain why I was running. Thereafter I would switch to residential neighborhoods and talk to families until about 9:00 PM.

To all I met, I would explain that I thought the United States was the greatest nation on earth because of a severely constitutionally limited government which was charged with securing the liberty of the people; that we needed to balance the budget immediately, then decrease the scope and power of government over the people as quickly as possible; that we had an abundance of domestic energy and I would do as much as possible to open up our vast reserves to private sector development; and lastly I would conclude that I thought every domestic problem facing our nation today was a direct result of non-constitutional federal interference in our society and that the only solution was to rein back federal influence to its authorized duties and once again allow the people to address our needs through personal endeavor, the free market, voluntary charity, or the states, but never through the federal government.

I didn't pre-judge or pre-classify anybody I met and had no idea if I was talking to Republicans, Democrats, or someone of another party affiliation. I was gratified that great majority of the people I met throughout the state enthusiastically agreed with my message and willingly signed my nominating petition.

I learned firsthand that most of the people of Michigan do not want or expect government benefit, but instead want nothing from government except to be left alone to pursue their happiness as they deem proper. This is the essence of America, our heritage which separates us from every other country in the world.

Of course people decimated by government policy will seek assistance from any source possible, and many are forced to seek sustenance through government support, but given a choice, the people to whom I spoke readily chose self responsibility over government dependence to address their needs.

I hear elite "leaders" from within the political establishment explaining that our founding principles of morality, self responsibility, limited government, and the pursuit of unbridled liberty, are relics from the past; and the new morality of the nation is a compassionate government charged with caring for those in need at the forced expense of those who are not.

They are wrong.

We need moral leaders who are willing to take a stand and proudly proclaim their understanding of liberty and limited government; the great advantage of free enterprise over centralized government control; and how voluntary charity is always better than forced dependency.

Consider the words of James Garfield, the twentieth president of the United States, 1877:

"Now more than ever before, the people are responsible for the character of their Congress. If that body be ignorant, reckless and corrupt, it is because the people tolerate ignorance, recklessness and corruption. If it be intelligent, brave and pure, it is because the people demand these high qualities to represent them in the national legislature . . . If the next centennial does not find us a great nation . . . it will be because those who represent the enterprise, the culture, and the morality of the nation do not aid in controlling the political forces."

James Garfield was right.

The people of the United States need to decide if righteousness is a quality required to serve as a federal, state, or local representative. If so, we'll have a righteous government, otherwise we'll foster self-serving corruption.

I strive to support and elect righteous representatives. We no longer have the luxury of voting on platitudes and emotion, but must take the time to thoroughly vet those seeking our support and choose righteous individuals desiring to secure our liberty.

Prosperity Resulting from Constitutional Enforcement

Our severely limited constitutional government is good for all people. The results of re-orienting all levels of government back to their authorized duties will allow the United States to once again capture its undisputed leadership position in the world.

Consider the following:

1. Reduced federal regulation will reverse job flight from the shores of the United States. Why are we losing jobs in this country? It's definitely not due to "greedy corporations." Unlike the federal government, private sector companies must provide a desired product or service at a reasonable price, or they will cease to exist.

   Competitive global organizations seek the best business climate available—which historically has been the United States. We're losing jobs in this country because non-constitutional federal interference in the economy has transformed the United States into one of the worst business environments in the world. Our corporate tax rate of 39.25% is topped only by Japan.[29] Combine this with the stifling federal regulations associated with Obama Care, the EPA, the Department of Labor, the Department of Commerce, and restricted energy, and it's no wonder global corporations choose foreign shores with friendlier business climates to host their operations.

   We're still the greatest economic superpower in the world, in spite of government interference, but our government is doing everything possible to stifle our economic prosperity.

---

[29] Contrarian Musings, Corporate Tax Rates By Country—OECD; Posted by Marcelo Perez
http://alhambrainvestments.com/blog/2009/01/29/corporate-tax-rates-by-country-oecd/

The long-term stability resulting from the elimination of repressive tax rates and the removal of crushing regulations, achieved through Negative Baseline Budgeting, would cause global business to flock back to United States soil. The resulting economic expansion would catapult the United States to the position of the undisputed economic superpower of the world—as we once were before government involvement.

2. Phasing out all unauthorized federal departments, including the Department of Energy, will allow the private sector to use private investment to extract and develop our vast domestic energy reserves.

   Energy Independence would eliminate our dependency on foreign oil, negating the very real possibility of the United States being blackmailed in international affairs by the threat of an oil embargo.

   Federal restrictions on private sector energy development force U.S. citizens to spend $30 billion per **MONTH** importing oil from abroad for our domestic use. If the federal government simply got out of the way, this $30 billion per month would remain in the United States creating high-paying, private-sector, jobs.

3. Small business, which is the backbone of any economy, will flourish. Jobs directly associated with the revitalized energy sector and the influx of global organizations would be significant, but more important would be the associated feeder jobs. Small businesses would prosper providing tools, transportation, research, development, retirement and investment services, health care, and all other conceivable products and services we can't even comprehend, which are just waiting to be developed.

   Prosperity opens up untold additional markets such as diners, high-class restaurants, entertainment, consumer goods, cars, appliances, retail shops, and whatever else is needed or desired by society.

Individuals currently on federal and state dependency rolls, as well as those working in the bloated public sector, would be wooed by the private sector to fill the influx of jobs. The need for dependency payments by all levels of government would fall dramatically and be absorbed by the private sector. Shifting responsibility from the federal government to the private sector would allow the spending cuts required by the Negative Baseline Budget to be implemented without hardship.

4. Responsibility for public charity would be transferred away from the federal government. No matter what the intention, federal charity is destructive to society. Perhaps based on good intentions, the unintended consequences of federal intervention are devastating resulting in skyrocketing rates of out-of-wedlock births, divorce, and dependency on government.

Without government interference, the community would provide needed charity—as it always has. Individuals would be taught to be responsible for their own needs and would learn to save for the proverbial rainy day.

Those requiring help could rely on family and friends for temporary shelter and assistance. Unlike the federal government, it would be incomprehensible for family or friends to encourage divorce or promiscuity as a condition of support. Instead family and friends would encourage families in need to stay together through hard times and emerge stronger. More importantly, most in the United States have a strong religious background and would encourage those in need to draw strength and guidance from their faith in God.[30]

---

[30] More Than 9 in 10 Americans Continue to Believe in God; Gallup; June 3, 2011; http://www.gallup.com/poll/147887/americans-continue-believe-god.aspx

Those without family or friends could reach out to virtually any church or charitable organization in the United States and receive like assistance.

Rather than encouraging long-term dependency, those providing voluntary charity would encourage the recipients to behave responsibly by actively trying to better their lives, so that charity would no longer be needed.

Regardless of what the naysayers purport, voluntary charity abounds in the United States in spite of our burdensome government. Consider the Shriners Hospitals throughout the United States or church-sponsored charitable hospitals such as St Jude. These hospitals provide quality care to those in need free of charge.

Consider the deluge of both monetary and boots-on-the-ground support from millions of people throughout the nation meeting the needs of New York after the 911 terrorist attacks, New Orleans after Hurricane Katrina, the Gulf after the BP oil spill, or the Midwest after the floods.

Prosperity breeds charity, and the United States is undisputedly the most prosperous and charitable country in the world. Voluntary charity tends to builds strong families and communities and naturally uplifts society. Government, regardless of intention, does the exact opposite.

If the people desired government charity, this responsibility may be granted to the individual states resulting in a proving ground of different options. Unlike the federal government, states have a more of an interest in efficiency. Successful state-sponsored welfare programs would be emulated while inefficient programs would fall by the wayside.

The federal government can't provide for society's every need. Our founders were correct in their understanding that people are more capable of providing for their own needs and all the needs of society far better than any centralized, bureaucratic, government program.

In modern day terms, I equate the federal government with a nuclear power plant. Both provide great benefit when their immense power is channeled and controlled. If the containment of either becomes chipped, cracked, or broken, unimaginable destruction will descend upon an unprotected people.

Our Constitution channels government's power toward its proper responsibility—securing the life, liberty, and pursuit of happiness of the governed. It's the only containment against the unbridled destruction of liberty. We have allowed our Constitution to be ignored, weakened, and negated; and have allowed the inconceivably destructive forces of federalized control to permeate our society and subdue a once-free people.

Our situation is similar in concept to the Ukraine in the spring of 1986, days before the Chernobyl disaster. Are we going to acknowledge the danger, repair the containment, and once again gain our security and prosperity? Or are we going to cower, give up, and allow the uncontrolled power of government to destroy the country that was bequeathed to us by our founders?

We cannot give up. We must persevere.

It's not too late if we start now. We have the solution. Do not let our liberty be taken from us. It will be a hard fought fight. Federal politicians will not want to relinquish their power, and recipients accustomed to these federal benefits will complain.

Yet, we have no choice if we are to survive as a free people.

Take Effective Action T.E.A. 2.0

We work hard to elect conservative, Tea Party candidates to go to Washington, only to see them renege on their promises.

How does the State GOP Party hold these individuals responsible? More often than not, it doesn't.

Wouldn't it be nice if it did? If the State GOP said in effect, "You've betrayed our trust; we're supporting somebody who more closely adheres to the Constitution and represents the people"?

It will happen if we get involved.

The State GOP has organization, structure, and money, but lacks a voice and focus. The Tea Party has a voice, but more importantly, it has the passion of the people.

How do we combine these organizations without destroying the innocence and power of the Tea Party? The Tea Party evolved due to frustration with the politics-as-normal mentality of the State GOP. Absorption by the State GOP would destroy the Tea Party. A better solution is to have Tea Party advocates assume control of the State GOP.

It can and should be done. How?

Get involved in Party Politics by becoming a Precinct Delegate.

I am a constitutional conservative who loves the founding principles of my country, appreciates limited government, and cherishes personal liberty. I'm working to ensure that these values are not stripped from future generations—our children. I have been involved in my local Republican committee, am a member of my local Tea Party, and most importantly, I'm a Precinct Delegate for my township.

Peter Konetchy

I travel the state on a regular basis and encounter much frustration regarding the state GOP.

The ordinary, hard-working, conservative patriots in Michigan believe the state GOP has forsaken them. It's not true. We have forsaken the state GOP. If we complain that our Party is no better than the Democrats, or complain about our leadership supporting "RINO" candidates, it's our fault. Anyone can complain, but to effect change, we must take meaningful action. We must **T**ake **E**ffective **A**ction . . . **(TEA 2.0)**

The leadership of our state GOP consists of individuals elected at the county and state conventions. If we don't like the leadership of the Party, it's up to us to elect people more to our liking. The only individuals able to elect our Party's leadership are the Precinct Delegates (known as Precinct Committeemen in other states.)

Imagine if the National Republican Chairmanship was held by an individual like Rand Paul. The Party and associated support would drastically shift toward constitutionalists. We can do the same thing at the county and state levels if constitutional conservatives simply made the effort to become Precinct Delegates. It's not hard, there are many vacancies, and most delegates run unopposed. Just complete an **"Affidavit of Identity"** from the Secretary of State website, and file it with your local township clerk. It doesn't even cost any money.

Many Republican Precinct Delegate slots in Michigan are filled with "moderates," which explains why our county and state leadership is "moderate" at best. To change the situation, we need to fill the vacant slots with true constitutional conservatives—Tea Party conservatives, educate ourselves about the candidates' positions, and then elect true constitutionalists to all positions within the State Party—from the top down.

How will becoming a Precinct Delegate help? About 50% of the slots in Michigan are vacant. Fill those vacant slots with true Tea Party constitutionalists. At the next state convention, work on electing constitutional conservatives as State Party officials.

As with every aspect of politics, we need a truly educated electorate. Prior to the state convention, vet all the party candidates, for all positions, through your local meetings. Know exactly where each candidate stands in principle prior to the convention, and then elect constitutionally-oriented state party officials.

The county and state parties would be transformed from an "establishment" to a "Tea Party" mentality. The recruitment and support of candidates to fill local, state, and federal positions would decidedly shift constitutional. The Tea Party would no longer feel antagonistic towards the State GOP, and vice-versa, but would work together towards constitutional values.

Imagine if the full support of the State GOP fell behind true constitutionally conservative candidates. We'd transform the state and have a very positive effect on the nation. The vote is a tremendously powerful, yet peaceful means for change; but only Precinct Delegates have this power to shape the party. Become a Precinct Delegate and make a difference.

FIVE:

TREATIES, AMENDMENTS, AND CONSTITUTIONAL CLAUSES

The Constitution of the United States protects the people from the extreme destruction of unbridled federal intrusion. It limits federal power to very specific, national functions that cannot be handled by the people or the state, and it **PROHIBITS** the federal government from addressing or influencing any aspect of our daily lives.

Over the last several decades our constitutional protections have been severely eroded allowing unbridled federal interference to smother the people.

We're at the precipice of our nation's survival, faced with several choices.

- Are we going to going to repair the damage and stop the destruction by adhering to the Constitution?
- Are we going to sit back, watch the damage, and hope it stops?
- Or are we going to hasten the destruction by continued chipping away at the Constitution?

My choice is to repair inflicted damage by once again constitutionally restraining the federal government.

Beware of those who believe our situation is hopeless and seek federal solutions to federally-imposed problems. It makes no sense to trust government to solve problems of its own creation. If government had the wisdom and foresight to solve these problems, it wouldn't have created them in the first place. More importantly, it wouldn't need additional authority to implement solutions to self-created problems.

We must be very careful when proposing amendments to fix constitutional "deficiencies". The government is already ignoring the Constitution; why should it start respecting new amendments? Those proposing amendments today either don't understand the existing constitutional safeguards, or find them inconvenient and seek to dismantle them.

As originally written, the Constitution provides the proper balance of power between a strong federal government, providing for the security of the nation; and flexible state and local governments, addressing the needs of the people.

We must remember that ratified amendments grant the federal government virtually unlimited constitutional authority to make all laws necessary and proper for their implementation and enforcement.

Why would we ever want to grant the government this authority?

Remember Franklin's warning: *"Those who would give up essential liberty to purchase a little temporary safety deserve neither liberty nor safety."* Those desiring to grant government the authority to protect us from government's own misdeeds are falling into the trade-off of which Franklin warns.

The solution to an out-of-control government is not additional amendments—which could easily usher in a host of "unintended consequences", the only solution is to understand and enforce the existing constitutional provisions.

Are All Treaties Constitutional?

There is a fear in the United States that the federal government will negotiate a treaty with the United Nations that will negate our constitutional rights. This fear epitomizes the animosity growing in the people towards our elected representatives.

Is it a valid fear? According to the Constitution, No, but according to our government controlled by deceitful leadership, Yes.

The Constitution is very specific on this matter. Article 6 addresses this issue.

> *"This Constitution, and the Laws of the United States which shall be made in Pursuance thereof; and all Treaties made, or which shall be made, under the Authority of the United States, shall be the supreme Law of the Land; and the Judges in every State shall be bound thereby, any Thing in the Constitution or Laws of any State to the Contrary notwithstanding."* [31]

This constitutional provision contains two phrases, the first one seeming to confirm the afore-mentioned fear:

Phrase one:

> *"This Constitution, and the Laws of the United States which shall be made in Pursuance thereof; and all Treaties made, or which shall be made, under the Authority of the United States, shall be the supreme Law of the Land; and the Judges in every State shall be bound thereby,"*

This phrase confirms that treaties entered into under the authority of the United States are definitely the supreme law of the land, but what does the phrase "under the Authority of the United States" mean?

---

[31]   U.S. Constitution. Article 6

According to Article 1 Section 8, the only "Authority" the United States was granted are its specific, defined and definite, constitutionally enumerated powers.[32] This authority is specifically reinforced via the Tenth Amendment. [33] There is no federal "Authority" outside of these powers.

Therefore, the United States could negotiate a treaty consistent with an authorized, enumerated power, such as defense, immigration, international commerce, foreign relations, etc., but has no authority to negotiate a treaty outside of these enumerated powers, such as with parental rights, small arms, abortion, marriage, etc. According to the first phrase of this provision, treaties negotiated outside the Authority of the United States are not the supreme law of the land.

Let's review the second phrase of this provision:

> "*any Thing in the Constitution or Laws of any State to the Contrary notwithstanding.*"

This phrase specifically states that a negotiated treaty contradicting either the Constitution or the laws of any state is not the supreme law of the land.

It's interesting and proper that "State Law" is protected from federal treaties. It reinforces the fact that the responsibilities of the federal government and the states are exclusive, and it protects state authority from usurpation by the federal government. State governments deal with the needs of the people whereas the federal government deals with the necessities of the nation.

---

[32] US Constitution, Article 1 Section 8: "To make all Laws which shall be necessary and proper for carrying into Execution the foregoing Powers, and all other Powers vested by this Constitution in the Government of the United States, or in any Department or Officer thereof."

[33] US Constitution, Tenth Amendment: "The powers not delegated to the United States by the Constitution, nor prohibited by it to the States, are reserved to the States respectively, or to the people."

Peter Konetchy

Article 6 prohibits the federal government from negotiating a binding treaty negating our individual or state rights. Treaties doing so have no authority.

Regardless of the prohibitions, the prospect of being bound by unconstitutional treaties is very real. The government has a long history of ignoring any constitutional provision it finds inconvenient, and the people, being largely ignorant of constitutional provisions, accept the actions of the government as valid without question. The danger we face is that the government might enter into a clearly unauthorized, unconstitutional treaty—such as would negate our right to keep and bear arms—and that the people might accept it as the supreme law of the land because of our ignorance of the Constitution.

The founders were wise men, who understood the nature of unrestrained government and who accounted for every situation. They did not allow a "loophole" enabling unscrupulous politicians the ability to unilaterally negate our rights through illegitimate treaties. We have the solution—Enforce the existing constitutional provisions.

Proposed Parental Rights Amendment

The government of the United States is negotiating a treaty with the United Nations to implement the provisions of the UN Convention on the Rights of the Child (UNCRC). People are rightly concerned about retaining their parenting rights and are considering passage of the Parental Rights Amendment as a safeguard against this UN treaty.

Could the provisions of the UNCRC treaty be constitutionally imposed on the people without passage of the Parental Rights Amendment?

Absolutely Not.

The existing provisions of the Constitution protect the people's parental rights and will not allow their usurpation by the federal government or by the UN.

Article 6 [34] of the Constitution is very specific and states that treaties become the supreme law of the land based on two conditions. First, the United States must be granted the "Authority" to negotiate the treaty based on its specific, constitutionally enumerated powers. Second, the negotiated treaty cannot conflict with the provisions of the U.S. Constitution or state law.

How do the provisions in Article 6 protect us against the proposed treaty and implementation of the UNCRC?

1. There is no enumerated power granting the federal government the Authority to address in any manner whatsoever the parenting of children. Therefore, under the first condition of

---

[34] US Constitution, Article 6: *This Constitution, and the Laws of the United States which shall be made in Pursuance thereof; and all Treaties made, or which shall be made, under the Authority of the United States, shall be the supreme Law of the Land; and the Judges in every State shall be bound thereby, any Thing in the Constitution or Laws of any State to the Contrary notwithstanding.*

Article 6, the United States government has no Authority to negotiate this treaty, making it null and void.

2. The second condition of Article 6, confirming that treaties cannot negate constitutional protections or state law, also disallows the implementation of this treaty. The 10th Amendment excludes federal interference in parenting, while the 9th Amendment provides this authority to the people. This treaty would conflict with both these existing provisions, therefore rendering it null and void.

The proposed UNCRC treaty is null and void by both conditions and cannot become the supreme law of the land.

As the Constitution currently stands, this treaty, even if ratified by Congress, cannot be binding upon the people of the United States. As our founders affirmed, it would be an unlawful usurpation of power and therefore be unauthoritative, void, and of no force; it would not be the supreme law of the land.

Either because of ignorance or fear, some people continue to promote the Parental Rights Amendment, which consists of three sections and reads as follows:

Section 1. *The liberty of parents to direct the upbringing and education of their children is a fundamental right.*

Section 2. *Neither the United States nor any State shall infringe upon this right without demonstrating that its governmental interest as applied to the person is of the highest order and not otherwise served.*

Section 3. *No treaty may be adopted nor shall any source of international law be employed to supersede, modify, interpret, or apply to the rights guaranteed by this article.*

Analysis of the Parental Rights Amendment

Section 1: Parents already have the right to raise and educate their children through the 9th Amendment. The federal government is currently prohibited from addressing parenting via restrictions within Article 1 Section 8 as well as within the 10th Amendment.

Section 1 adds no new right or protection.

Section 2: Extremely destructive. It constitutionally authorizes the federal government to review parenting practices and to override the parent's authority if the federal government determines it's in the best interest of the child. It's important to note how this section differs from our other protections within the Bill of Rights. Section 2 does not invoke the courts, the rule of law, nor limit the discretion of government. The evaluation of parenting practices is done at the sole discretion of the government leaving the parents no recourse.

Section 2 is devastating to parenting rights and effectively transfers parental authority to the federal government.

Section 3: The existing constitutional provisions within Article 6 currently prohibit the federal government from negotiating a treaty outside of its authority and treaties conflicting with our constitutional rights or state law, such as the proposed UNCRC treaty, are unauthoritative, void, and of no force.

Section 3 adds no new right or protection.

The only effect of this Amendment is to grant the government the new powers authorized in Section 2; to allow the federal government the constitutional authority to oversee the upbringing of children and to override the authority of the parents if government bureaucrats decide it's in the best interest of the children.

How would passage of the Parental Rights Amendment affect the implementation of the UNCRC provisions?

Peter Konetchy

Without this amendment, the Constitution grants the federal government no authority to address the parenting of children. If this amendment is ratified, we lose this constitutional safeguard and authorize the federal government to review every aspect of parenting and override the decisions of the parents on political whims. If passed, the government can implement any or all of the UNCRC provisions at its discretion without the need for a treaty.

This is a very serious situation and worth repeating.

Section 2 of the Parental Rights Amendment grants the federal government constitutional authority to raise the nation's children as the government deems proper. The government would no longer need a treaty to impose the provisions of UNCRC. It could simply impose any provision contained in the UNCRC through its newly acquired constitutional authority.

The Constitution, as written, protects the liberty of the people. Passage of the Parental Rights Amendment would be devastating to our nation and would allow the federal government complete control in raising our children.

It should not be passed.

Proposed Balanced Budget Amendment

I understand that we must cut and cap spending and definitely balance the budget, but I cannot support the imposition of a Balanced Budget Amendment (BBA) I believe will weaken the Constitution.

The key components of the BBA are as follows: [35]

- Total outlays do not exceed total receipts; and
- Total outlays do not exceed 18 percent of the gross domestic product of the United States for the calendar year ending before the beginning of such fiscal year.

I cannot support it for the following reasons:

1) The BBA caps federal spending at 18% to 20% of GDP corresponding to our recent average historical spending high. It is a little-known fact that for the great majority of our nation's life, federal spending averaged only 2-3% of GDP (from 1787 through 1930). At this spending level, we had **no need for an income tax and no debt.**

   Only when the federal government ignored its constitutional limitations and started to insert its control into every aspect of society after 1930, did the country begin its descent toward economic ruin. Federal spending now tops 25% of GDP.

   The solution is not to constitutionalize historically high federal spending, but to focus on limiting it to its historical average of less than 5% of GDP—more than 80% less than the BBA limit. At this level, we could once again raise federal revenue as

---

[35] H.J.RES.56 -- Proposing an amendment to the Constitution of the United States relative to balancing the budget. http://thomas.loc. gov/cgi-bin/query/z?c112:H.J.RES.56: 112th Congress (2011-2012) H.J.RES.56.IH

our founders proposed and eliminate direct federal taxes against corporations and individuals.

2) As proposed, the BBA will eradicate any concept of limited, enumerated powers and will constitutionally legitimize spending based on a percent of GDP.

Consider that Congress desires to spend money on something clearly unconstitutional—such as for cell phones or contraceptives for the "poor". The decision to fund or not fund these programs will no longer be based on whether or not these programs fall within the enumerated authority of Congress, but if overall federal spending, including these programs, falls below the BBA threshold.

The solution is to force Congress to respect its constitutional restrictions, not eliminate them.

3) Government ignores the Constitution whenever its limitations are found inconvenient. We currently ignore the enumerated powers in Article 1 Section 8; the spending restrictions in Article 1 Section 9; the limitations on the President in Article 2 Section 2; and key provisions in the First, Second, Fourth, Fifth, Sixth, Ninth, Tenth, and Fourteenth Amendments.

Why should we add another constitutional amendment when the current provisions are blatantly ignored?

There is no constitutional authority to allowing Congress to spend money on programs not enumerated in the Constitution.[36] If this provision were upheld, we would have a balanced budget, no debt, and no need for this amendment.

---

[36] Article 1 Section 8 authorizes Congress "To make all Laws which shall be necessary and proper for carrying into Execution the foregoing Powers, and all other Powers vested by this Constitution in the Government of the United States." Article 1 Section 9 then states that: "No Money shall be drawn from the Treasury, but in Consequence of Appropriations

4) The need for this amendment is predicated on the continued incompetence of elected representatives. You can't legislate competence. For example, how can we guarantee that the defense budget won't be gutted if incompetent, self-serving politicians need money for their pet social projects? This amendment opens up the possibility of unlimited, unintended consequences.

At current trends, it is estimated that Social Security, Medicare, and Medicaid alone will consume 18-20% of the GDP by the year 2040. When adding Obama Care and entitlements to the mix, this threshold is reached in just a few years. Unless spending is drastically reduced, it will be impossible to keep federal spending below its 18-20% threshold.

5) Those in government wanting to spend money will do so with or without this amendment. Consider that every state in the Union, except Vermont, has a balanced budget provision—most have balanced budget Amendments. Yet a great number of these states are in fiscal turmoil due to use of accounting gimmicks which allow them to meet the letter of the law, but scoff at the intent.

Those in the federal government will be no different. With no desire to balance the budget, an amendment won't help—self serving politicians will find a way around it. If a desire exists then the amendment is not necessary.

6) Legislators can override the BBA provisions by a super majority vote. Like the BBA, the debt ceiling is designed to limit spending by curtailing borrowing. How easily this ceiling is continually raised by those lacking the fortitude to do right. How will the BBA cap on federal spending be different? It

---

made by Law;" Congress can only make laws relating to its constitutional authority, and money can only be spent based on law. Therefore, money may be drawn from the treasury only in the performance of specific constitutionally enumerated powers.

won't. Politicians can raise it as they deem proper effectively constitutionalizing unlimited spending—the exact opposite effect of the amendment's original intent.

7) **<u>MOST IMPORTANT!!!</u>** We don't need an amendment to balance the budget. Supposedly, we already have majority support in both houses of Congress for this amendment. Why don't we use a simple majority (50% plus 1 of Congress) to simply adopt a balanced budget without the BBA? If the president vetoes the balanced budget, Congress can override the veto with the same majority needed to pass the BBA. We can do this immediately and without wait.

It will take two thirds of both houses and three quarters of the states to pass this amendment—requiring a very lengthy time. Are we going to deficit spend until the amendment is passed?

The federal government has placed us in desperate straits through continued, irresponsible, deficit spending. We, the people and the states, need to decide upon the best solution—enforce the existing provisions of the Constitution; or in desperation, grant the federal government immense additional power, hoping against hope that they'll use it responsibly to solve the problems created by their irresponsibility.

Some amendments to the Constitution are extremely destructive. I do not want to adopt another one with potentially devastating consequences for future generations, as I believe the proposed BBA will. The only solution to the country's social and economic problems is to restore constitutional restraint, limit spending as already specified in the Constitution, educate ourselves about those who are abusing our trust, and vote self-serving politicians out of office.

There is no choice—we must enforce the existing constitutional provisions. Passage of this amendment is suicide.

Proposed Human Life Amendment

I am pro-life and consider abortion murder. Most people in the United States hold this same value and want to extend constitutional protections to the unborn. I agree, but is the Human Life Amendment the solution? Will it introduce negative consequences, actually encouraging abortion? I say "Yes." It's bad law and should never be ratified.

Human Life Amendment

What exactly does the Human Life Amendment say? The text of the most common version, and the only one with a chance of passage, reads as follows:[37]

> *"No unborn person shall be deprived of life by any person: Provided, however, That nothing in this article shall prohibit a law permitting only those medical procedures required to prevent the death of the mother of an unborn person: Provided further, That nothing in this article shall limit the liberty of a mother with respect to the unborn offspring of the mother conceived as a result of rape or incest."*

Sounds innocent enough on the surface, but what is it really saying?

I'll play devil's advocate.

Remember, this is a constitutional amendment, which grants constitutional authority to its words.

---

[37] Text of the Human Life Amendment http://www.conservapedia.com/Human_Life_Amendment. Author's Note: Any proposed Human Life Amendment involves compromise with a significant pro-choice contingent. Proposed amendments without these compromised provisions will not pass.

The first phrase states specifically:

"No unborn person shall be deprived of life by any person:"

Does this allow the unborn to be killed by a pill or by a machine? According to the amendment, it does.

Remember Jack Kevorkian's "Suicide Machine" which allowed individuals to commit suicide painlessly without another's assistance? Some entrepreneur could easily develop an "Abortion Machine." Would this be legal? According to this amendment, "Yes."

There currently exists a "morning-after" pill to induce an abortion. Could somebody develop a more powerful pill capable of causing a late-term abortion? Of course, and this amendment would constitutionalize its use.

According to the text of the amendment, it could be interpreted that the killing an unborn baby by any means other than a "person" is justified—or at the very least not constitutionally prohibited.

The second phrase states:

"Provided, however, That nothing in this article shall prohibit a law permitting only those medical procedures required to prevent the death of the mother of an unborn person:"

An exception is made to save the life of the mother. I totally agree with this protection; yet, how do we determine if the life of the mother is in danger?

Today, many early-term abortions, and even Partial-Birth abortions, are performed supposedly to save the life of the mother. Do we simply take Planned Parenthood's word for it?

In recent decades, Congress has been actively encouraging abortion throughout society. Congress supposedly prohibited federal funding for abortions in the past, but has ignored this provision in recent years, and actually approved funding for abortions in Obama Care. Do we have confidence that Congress will pass a law, under the guise of this amendment, protecting the unborn, or will they pass additional laws allowing for easy access to abortion?

Congress has repeatedly refused to pass pro-life laws such as the Life at Conception Act. What makes us think that the laws passed by Congress, after this amendment is ratified, will protect life? Do we need to pass this amendment to find out how Congress will enforce it?

Not on my watch.

The third and last phrase of this amendment is most frightening.

> *"Provided further, That nothing in this article shall limit the liberty of a mother with respect to the unborn offspring of the mother conceived as a result of rape or incest."*

This phrase defines abortion as a "liberty," which constitutionally sanctions the killing of an innocent baby due to the sins of another. Why? Rape is a terrible crime, and the rapist should be persecuted to the fullest extent of the law, but why establish a constitutional right to kill an innocent child without any due process of law? How can we justify different rights for totally innocent, unborn babies based on the action of a third party?

This amendment totally negates the 14th Amendment's "equal protection of the laws" clause and sets a terrible precedent. Does this open the door to euthanasia? We already have end-of-life counseling in Obama Care. If we constitutionally allow the "liberty" to kill an entirely innocent class of people, the unborn conceived by rape, how long until we apply the same logic to another class of people, the elderly or handicapped? Hopefully, never.

If passed, do you think the instances of rape claims will skyrocket? Probably, as it's a free pass to an abortion. This amendment will encourage lying in order to constitutionally kill innocent babies.

Please review Rebecca Kiessling's Facebook page and web site. She was conceived in rape and placed for adoption. She was nearly aborted by two back-alley abortionists and makes a compelling case against aborting innocent children due to the actions of others.[38]

The Human Life Amendment is a classic example of Congress convoluting the pure motives of those wishing to protect the unborn into exactly the opposite of what they desire.

To summarize this Human Life Amendment:

- It allows (does not prohibit) abortion by machine or pill.
- It requires Congress to pass a law defining the process of determining when the life of the mother is in danger and to then define the appropriate medical procedures.
- It constitutionalizes the ***"LIBERTY"*** to kill an innocent child due to the sins of another.
- It negates the "equal protection" clause in the 14th Amendment.

When it's read carefully, it's obvious that the Human Life Amendment is bad law.

What's the solution?

It gets back to enforcing the Constitution as written.

The Declaration of Independence clearly classifies Life as an unalienable, God-given right. The 5th and 14th Amendments to the Constitution confirm that no person can be deprived of life without due process of law.

It's clear that we have the constitutional rights, but why are they not applied to unborn people?

---

[38] http://www.facebook.com/notes/rebecca-kiessling/the-trouble-with-unprincipled-incrementalism-and-allowing-for-exceptions/10150193880073154; http://www.rebeccakiessling.com

The Supreme Court gave us the answer when ruling on Roe v. Wade. Contrary to popular belief, it never ruled that abortion was a "right," but instead insisted that the Congress define personhood. The Court stated in its ruling:

> *"If this suggestion of personhood is established, the appellant's case [i.e. "Roe" who sought the abortion], of course, collapses, for the fetus' right to life is then guaranteed specifically by the [14ᵗʰ] Amendment."* [39]

Life at Conception Act

Congress can satisfy the court's demand and clarify through legislation when personhood is established by passing a law such as the **Life at Conception Act**. The text of the act reads as follows:

> SEC. 2. RIGHT TO LIFE. *"To implement equal protection for the right to life of each born and preborn human person, and pursuant to the duty and authority of the Congress, including Congress' power under article I, section 8, to make necessary and proper laws, and Congress' power under section 5 of the 14ᵗʰ article of amendment to the Constitution of the United States, the Congress hereby declares that the right to life guaranteed by the Constitution is vested in each human being. However, nothing in this Act shall be construed to require the prosecution of any woman for the death of her unborn child."* [40]

For purposes of this Act:

> *(1) HUMAN PERSON; HUMAN BEING—The terms 'human person' and 'human being' include each and every member of the species homo sapiens at all stages of life, including*

---

[39]   Life at Conception Act—an overview
     http://www.prolifealliance.com/LCA%20Fact%20Sheet.pdf

[40]   H.R.374 -- Life at Conception Act
     http://thomas.loc.gov/cgi-bin/query/z?c112:H.R.374: Life at Conception Act

the moment of fertilization, cloning, or other moment at which an
individual member of the human species comes into being.

If passed by a simple majority, this Bill (H.R.374) will nullify Roe v.
Wade and **END** legalized abortion. It also protects the mother from
accidents or "Acts of God."

I strongly support the Life at Conception Act.

The unborn babies are the most innocent amongst us and need our
support and care. They do not choose to die. Give them a chance. They
are gifts of God and deserve a chance at life. If unwanted, they can be
placed for adoption with a desiring family. Choose life.

Though perhaps well intended, the proposed Human Life Amendment
is bad law. Not only is it unnecessary, it actually constitutionalizes
abortion and should not be passed.

Proposed Marriage Amendment

I'm a strong advocate of marriage between one man, one woman and one God. I do not support homosexual marriage, nor do I support polygamy. I support the ability of both the states and the federal government to legally define marriage as between one man and one woman for the purpose of all state or federal business and regulation.

Many of us are deeply concerned over sustained attacks on traditional marriage and many believe the only solution is a Federal Marriage Amendment. Are they right?

The text of the proposed Federal Marriage Amendment reads as follows:

> *"Marriage in the United States shall consist only of the union of a man and a woman."* [41]

I totally agree with the goal of this amendment, but do not want it added to the U.S. Constitution. Marriage is not a federal issue. It's a relationship between one man, one woman, and God, and is registered with the state for legal purposes.

According to the 10th Amendment, Congress is disallowed from controlling, influencing, or regulating marriage. The proposed Marriage Amendment will override this prohibition and authorize Congress to oversee every aspect of marriage.

How could Congress misapply the clear and concise language of this proposed amendment?

Easy.

---

[41]   Federal Marriage Amendment - H.J. Res 56

Let's get back to basics. The Constitution is a restraint against the federal accumulation and abuse of power. Every amendment in the Bill of Rights reinforces this restriction with phrases such as "Congress shall make no law . . ." or "the right of the people . . . shall not be infringed."

The proposed marriage amendment takes a totally different approach. It does not instruct Congress to stay away from marriage, but does just the opposite. It states a definition of marriage, and then authorizes Congress to define and enforce this definition.

According to the Constitution, Congress has the authority to make all laws necessary to implement constitutional provisions. This amendment would provide Congress the authority and ability to make laws that could devalue and destroy marriage as we know it.

Look at the word "union." Congress has a demonstrated hostility towards religion. It has misapplied the First Amendment to invoke a complete separation between church and state.

If we ratify the Marriage Amendment, is it possible that Congress would secularize marriage and require all ceremonies to be performed by a judge? Yes!

Congress has a history of removing God from schools, city parks, state courthouses, and national parks. Military chaplains are actually prohibited or discouraged from mentioning Jesus' name during military services. If this amendment passes, there is a very real probability that God will be removed from marriage.

My wife grew up in Russia. Prior to the Russian Revolution the majority of people were highly religious and married by clergy. After the Revolution the state regulated marriage by adding to its Constitution *"Marriage is between a man and a woman by mutual consent.'"* The state no longer recognized the religious ceremony and all legal marriages were performed by the state.

I don't want to trust government with this responsibility.

Look at the word "woman." Suppose one partner in a homosexual relationship claims to be a woman trapped in a man's body and the claim is substantiated by a licensed psychologist. What will the government do? In all likelihood, the marriage will be allowed to go forward with the taxpayers paying for the sex change operation in the process.

Why plant the seed to establish a federal "Department of Marriage"? As of now, Congress has no authority to regulate marriage in any manner whatsoever. If passed, this amendment will authorize Congress to establish whatever rules it considers necessary pertaining to marriage. Worse yet, let's assume the United Nations proposes a "Marriage Treaty" considered hostile to Christian marriage. Passing this amendment would grant Congress the constitutional authority to ratify and implement this treaty.

Could the federal government require "Marriage Education"? Yes.

My kids were forced to participate in a marriage and family class as a part of their public school education where they were taught, among other things, how to access all public assistance programs. Do we want the federal government mandating that all couples attend federally approved marriage counseling where they learn the "correct" parenting techniques and social skills? This is not the goal of the Marriage Amendment, but its passage would allow for this type of federal regulation.

Don't involve Congress in marriage. I argue that government imposed social engineering is the primary cause of the breakdown of marriage. Don't trust Congress to implement the solution to solve a problem of its own creation.

The problem with the destruction of marriage is not due to a constitutional deficiency that can be magically fixed by an amendment. It is due to our government actively trying to destroy the moral structure of the nation by promoting the homosexual agenda in K-12, college, the military, and throughout all segments of society. Homosexuals are recognized as a protected minority with regard to anti-discrimination laws. Public criticism of the homosexual agenda is shut down by political correctness. Combine this with the persecution of Judeo-Christianity morality through the misapplication of the First Amendment, and marriage will naturally degenerate. Sad to say, the dissolution of marriage between a man and a woman is considered a "success" to the activists currently in control of the federal government.

The federal government has no constitutional authority to promote a homosexual agenda, nor can it promote a heterosexual agenda. It must be mute on the subject and allow the issue to be addressed by the people or the states. Social engineering is another example of the federal government ignoring constitutional restraint to the great detriment of the nation.

To their credit, prior Congresses have tried to defend and strengthen marriage. Congress has no constitutional authority to define marriage for the states, but it is authorized to define marriage for the purpose of federal regulation. Congress passed the **Defense of Marriage Act (DOMA),** which clearly defines marriage as follows for all federal purposes.

> *"In determining the meaning of any Act of Congress, or of any ruling, regulation, or interpretation of the various administrative bureaus and agencies of the United States, the word 'marriage' means only a legal union between one man and one woman as husband and wife, and the word 'spouse' refers only to a person of the opposite sex who is a husband or a wife."* [42]

I strongly support the Defense of Marriage Act and would insist that its provisions be followed.

Government ignores any constitutional limitation it finds inconvenient as it ignores the Defense of Marriage Act. Why should we expect a new amendment to be adhered to if it goes against the policy of government? Sadly, we can't. The federal government will either ignore

---

[42]   Text of Defense of Marriage act: http://thomas.loc.gov/cgi-bin/ query/z?c104:H.R.3396.ENR:

the amendment or twist its meaning to destroy the institution it was designed to protect.

The people of the United States overwhelmingly support marriage between one man and one woman. Homosexual marriage has only been ruled legal when a federal judge or state legislators overruled the will of the people.

Proposition 8, which amended the California Constitution to define marriage as between one man and one woman, passed on Nov. 4, 2008. On Aug. 4, 2010, a federal district judge ruled that the same-sex marriage ban in Proposition 8 violated the equal protection provisions of the U.S. Constitution.

Federal judges ignoring federal law and overturning valid elections should have their decisions reversed or be impeached. State legislators ruling against the will of the people should be recalled or voted out of office.

The only solution to the marriage crisis and to the entire attack against our traditional value system is to enforce our existing constitutional restrictions against federal government intrusion.

The federal government has no authority to force a homosexual agenda through the school system, no authority to secularize society, no authority to ignore the DOMA, and no authority to ignore any other constitutional restriction, yet they do it anyway because they're able to get away with it.

We need to elect moral representatives who understand the problem, who are willing to fight to restrain government, and who will allow the people of the United States to once again determine their own destiny.

The 2ⁿᵈ Amendment: The Right to Keep and Bear Arms

The Second Amendment, affirming "the right of the people to keep and bear arms," allows law-abiding citizens the means to defend themselves from those seeking to dominate and subdue them.

The overriding reason our founders insisted upon the individual right to bear arms is to allow a nation of free men the ability to defend itself against a tyrannical government—foreign or domestic.

Disarmed citizens are at the mercy of their government. Repressive governments have little respect for, and no fear of, a disarmed citizenry, and seek their submission and control. It's happened many times throughout recent history—Nazi Germany, post-revolutionary Russia, and current-day Iran.

In a free society, citizens can exercise the God-given right to self-defense.

Common criminals prey on the weak. They try to gain superiority over their victims using weapons, numeric superiority, aggressive behavior, or physical strength. Law-abiding people don't want to be victims and use care to avoid danger. Sometimes people find themselves in situations outside of their control or expectations, such as break-ins, carjackings, assaults, or rape situations, and realize it's much better to be able to defend themselves than to be defenseless victims.

Most criminals flee when they meet with resistance. Seeing a potential victim brandish a gun more often than not causes criminals to flee. According to NRA statistics, each year, U.S. gun owners use firearms for protection up to 2.5 million times. Several times a minute a firearm is used for protection in the United States. Imagine if this right to self-defense was removed. There would be at least 2.5 million *additional* defenseless victims, probably many more. The criminal element would feel empowered to prey on a defenseless population.

The United States is founded upon the principles of personal liberty, freedom, and responsibility. Our Constitution provides critical safeguards against tyranny. Yet, human nature strives for power and control. Our founders knew that if tyrannical leaders assumed power in the United States, canceled elections and ignored constitutional limitations, then our right to keep and bear arms would be our last option to preserve our liberty.

Consider that President Obama is actively pursuing initiatives to curb "Gun Violence." How do his initiatives stack up against our constitutional protections?

The Second Amendment of the Constitution states: "*the right of the people to keep and bear Arms, shall not be infringed.*" (emphasis added)

"Infringe" means to take over rights, privileges, or activities that belong to somebody else, **especially in a minor or gradual way**.

The President's "Gun Violence" initiative definitely "infringes" upon the right of the people to keep and bear arms by blatantly ignoring both the letter and intent of the Second Amendment. Additionally, there is no constitutional power granting either Congress or the President the authority to interpret this right, or to implement "reasonable" safeguards. The Second Amendment specifically prohibits doing so. "Shall not be infringed" means what it says—this right shall not be infringed.

Most state Constitutions reinforce the fact that "*Every person has a right to bear arms for the defense of himself and the state.*" The Supremacy Clause, within Article 6, specifically disallows federal law from negating legitimate state law. The Presidents initiatives fail this constitutional test also.

All federal initiatives to limit the right of law abiding citizens to keep and bear arms is blatantly unconstitutional, has no authority, negates the majority of state constitutions, and therefore cannot be the "*supreme Law of the Land.*"

Assume a state, instead of the federal government, passed a law prohibiting the secret service from using certain types of weapons based on physical characteristics or bullet capacity. Do you think the federal government would honor this law? Of course not.

The federal government understands that an individual state has no authority to make a law pertaining to the protection of the President. There would be no discussion, explanation, or court action. The federal government would simply nullify this law by refusing to acknowledge, honor, implement, or enforce it.

Why are the states different?

They're not.

If a federal law unconstitutionally seeks to limit the liberty of the states or people, and instead seeks their submission, the states have a constitutional obligation to nullify. Otherwise, state officials are as guilty as the federal government in imposing tyranny upon the people.

The states are a significant constitutional check against federal abuse.

We can never docilely accept the imposition of tyranny through the infringement of our rights, but must fight to retain them. Otherwise, we will have given up the greatest gift ever bequeathed to a nation of free men, true Liberty.

I have very few litmus tests, but the right to keep and bear arms is one. I will never support an elected leader seeking to disarm law-abiding citizens.

The 1ˢᵗ Amendment: The Separation of Church and State

Does the United States Constitution require separation of Church and State, a wall between the public and private sectors, which cannot be breached?

Most people seem to think so.

What does the Constitution actually say? The First Amendment states, *"Congress shall make no law respecting an establishment of religion, or prohibiting the free exercise thereof."*

The phrase consists of three parts:

1) It prohibits Congress from making any laws regarding a specific jurisdiction.
2) It defines the jurisdiction as the establishment of a religion.
3) It additionally defines the jurisdiction as prohibiting the free exercise thereof.

The amendment states the exact opposite of what most people have been conditioned to believe. Its purpose is very specific—to protect the people of the United States from becoming subject to federal laws interfering with the free exercise of their religion. It restricts Congress, not the people or place. The amendment does not strip individuals of this right if they happen to be government employees, nor does it lapse when people freely choose to honor God in a public setting. It protects people from federal interference.

Supporters of the complete separation of church and state have interpreted the amendment narrowly and out of context, allowing it to support the exact action it was intended to prohibit.

First: They've replace the word *"Congress"* with *"State, Local, or Federal Governments; or any other individual or organizations in a public setting."*

Peter Konetchy

Second: They've replaced the words *"shall make no law"* with the words *"shall not."* The U.S. Constitution grants Congress the authority to make all laws "necessary and proper" to implement their assigned powers. This amendment, as written, seeks to assure the people that Congress will not abuse its power by making a law affecting the people's freedom to practice religion as they deem proper.

Third: They've replaced the *"establishment of religion"* with the act of *"mentioning God."*

Forth: They've completely removed all reference to *"prohibiting the free exercise thereof."*

Instead of reading the First Amendment as written, supporters of the complete separation of church and state read it as: *"State, Local, or Federal Governments; or any other individual or organization in a public setting, shall not mention God."*

This gross misinterpretation of the First Amendment manifests itself through the complete eradication of any reference to religion in any public forum. For example:

- A valedictorian is prohibited from expressing gratitude to God at a high school graduation.
- Manger scenes are prohibited from Christmas displays in public parks.
- A sculpture of the Ten Commandments is forcibly removed from the lobby of a state courthouse.
- Schools have been dissuaded from allowing their students recite the Pledge of Allegiance because it contains the phrase "Under God," or even studying the Declaration of Independence because it asserts the self-evident—that our unalienable rights come from our Creator, God, not government.

All these actions are in direct contradiction with our constitutional right to exercise religion freely. The First Amendment codifies our unalienable right to practice religion freely, without any limitation or restriction from the federal government. Freedom of religion goes hand in hand with freedom of speech.

According to the First Amendment, class valedictorians should be able to express heartfelt gratitude to God at high school graduations. It's their "free exercise of religion" and freedom of speech, which allow them to express ideas important to them. They are constitutionally protected when expressing their thoughts. Freedom of independent thought must be encouraged in a free society.

Communities—not the government or the courts—should decide if manger scenes are to be placed in public parks at Christmas, or if religious carols may be sung in schools. The fact is that Christmas is a celebration of Jesus' birth, universally depicted with a manger. If a community wants to erect a manger scene or sing religious carols, so be it; if they don't, so be that, also.

All law in the United States is based on Judeo-Christian law emanating from the Ten Commandments. If a community, state, or federal courthouse chooses to honor the Ten Commandments by prominently displaying them, it is again a free exercise of speech and religion. According to the First Amendment, Congress can make no law forcing the sculpture's removal. It falls under the province of the community, state, or people.

This nation is founded on religious freedom, beginning with the founding of its initial settlements, reinforced through our Declaration of Independence, and protected by our Constitution. Secularizing society does a disservice to us all and belittles the moral character that allowed this country to excel.

General Welfare Clause

Does the "General Welfare" clause allow Congress to perform *ANY* function it deems proper, if it can be classified as addressing the general welfare of the United States?

Politicians apparently think so, but I think they are dead wrong.

There are two references to "General Welfare" in the Constitution and both are referenced in combination with common defense.

The first reference in the preamble reads: *"We the People of the United States, in Order to form a more perfect Union, establish Justice, insure domestic Tranquility, provide for the common defence, promote the **general Welfare**, and secure the Blessings of Liberty to ourselves and our Posterity, do ordain and establish this Constitution for the United States of America." (emphisis added)*

The preamble is an introduction and explains in general terms the underlying reason why ratifying the Constitution will be good for the nation, but grants no specific powers to the federal government. For example it states the Constitution will help "insure domestic Tranquility", but provides no power to implement curfews, force sedation, or to establish an internal federal police force to maintain "tranquility." The authorization of federal power is detailed in the body of the Constitution, not the preamble.

Again, Justice, Domestic Tranquility, Common Defense, and General Welfare, are some of the reasons, and natural effect, of passage of the Constitution. They are not enumerated powers within themselves.

The second reference in Article 1 Section 8 states: *"The Congress shall have Power To lay and collect Taxes, Duties, Imposts and Excises, to pay the Debts and provide for the common Defence and* general Welfare *of the United States; but all Duties, Imposts and Excises shall be uniform throughout the United States";*

This power grants Congress the authority to lay and collect taxes, but the rest of the phrase denotes why this power was granted—"*to pay the Debts and provide for the common Defence and* general Welfare *of the United States.*" The specific authority is to grant the power to tax, not to grant unlimited power to the federal government.

The enumerated powers within this Article 1 Section 8 can be summarized within two broad categories:

1. Providing for the common defense, and
2. Providing for the general welfare.

Common defense is by far the most important reason for the ratification of the Constitution. It's not a power in itself, but a broad category including these specific enumerated powers:

- To declare war,
- To raise and support Armies,
- To provide and maintain a Navy,
- To make rules for the Government and Regulation of land and naval forces,
- To provide for calling forth the Militia,
- To provide for organizing, arming, and disciplining the Militia,
- To define and punish Piracies and Offenses against the LAW of Nations.

If "Common Defense" was a power in itself, why would these specific powers be enumerated? They wouldn't. There would be no need to do so and the enumeration of these powers would simply be wasted words.

The same logic applies to the other major category of "General Welfare" which includes the remaining enumerated powers:

- To borrow money,
- To regulate commerce,
- To establish uniform rule of Naturalization,
- To establish uniform laws on the subject of Bankruptcies,

- To coin money,
- To provide for Punishment of counterfeiting,
- To fix standards of weights and measures,
- To establish post offices,
- To establish a patent office,
- To set up a federal court system.

The General Welfare clause reads "general Welfare *of the United States*", not "general Welfare *of the* **people** United *States."* Simply stated, "General Welfare" explains the overall rationale that the states authorized these powers to the federal government. It was in the states' best interest, benefit, or General Welfare, to grant the federal government authority to perform these specific national functions, enumerated in Article 1 Section 8, on their behalf. The states felt that a centralized federal government could perform these duties more efficiently than the individual states.

After the American Revolution, the citizens of the victorious colonies were fearful of replacing British rule with an equally tyrannical federal government. In order to retain their personal liberty, yet still interact with the world community, they established the Articles of Confederation, consisting of a weak federal government overseeing 13 sovereign states. It was not workable. The federal government had no means of enforcement and was unable to, among multiple other deficiencies, raise sufficient revenues, assemble a reliable army, coordinate commerce between the states, or establish international relationships or treaties. The confederacy was in great danger of dissolving.

When drafting the new compact between the states, the Constitution, the states were again fearful of an omnipotent federal government, so they specifically enumerated its delegated powers.

To further reinforce this limitation, the states adopted the 9th and 10th Amendments to the U.S. Constitution, confirming that the people's rights were many, while federal authority was limited to specific enumeration.

9th Amendment: *The enumeration in the Constitution, of certain rights, shall not be construed to deny or disparage others retained by the people.*

10th Amendment: *The powers not delegated to the United States by the Constitution, nor prohibited by it to the States, are reserved to the States respectively, or to the people.*

The Article 1 Section 8 enumerated powers, along with the 9th and 10th amendments have not been rendered meaningless by the words "General Welfare." It's exactly the opposite, the term "General Welfare" is defined by the enumerated powers coupled with the amendments.

The federal government has incorrectly used the General Welfare clause to assume powers never authorized or imagined by the founders of this nation, or agreed to by the states ratifying the Constitution. It's been used to usurp power from the people and the states by implementing agencies such as the Department of Education, Department of Energy, Department of Health and Human Services, the Environmental Protection Agency, the Federal Emergency Management Agency, Occupational Health and Safety Act, and programs such as Social Security, Medicare, and Obama Care. The Constitution grants the federal government no authority for any of these programs and every one of these functions could be more efficiently handled by the people or the states.

The abuse of this clause has allowed those in Washington to grossly expand the federal government well outside its constitutional restraints. If we are to remain a free nation all existing federal regulations, based on the misapplication of the "General Welfare" clause are unauthoritative, void, and of no force, and should be nullified by the states and allowed to sunset or be repealed.

Commerce Clause

What authority does the Commerce Clause provide Congress?

Congress has the constitutional authority to *"To regulate Commerce with foreign Nations, and among the several States, and with the Indian Tribes."*

Does this provision provide Congress with unlimited control over industry in the United States? Congress uses the 16 words in this phrase to impose its will on every aspect of the private sector as desired.

Over the last few decades, it has been used to control agriculture, manufacturing, banking, guns, retail, energy development, medical services, water quantity in toilets, the type of light bulbs we are required to use, and just about every other aspect of economic activity. In recent months, Congress has relied on this clause to effectively nationalize the banking and mortgage industries, GM and Chrysler, health care, and the student loan program—to name a few.

The Commerce Clause was never ever intended to allow Congress direct control over industry, but it was designed to break down existing trade barriers in force between the states. A great weakness of the Articles of the Confederation was that individual states could assess duties and dictate the terms of commerce on all goods entering or leaving their borders. Hamilton looked to Germany as an example of what could happen if the commerce situation between the states wasn't addressed. Federalist 22 provides the reasoning behind the clause.

"The commerce of the German empire is in continual trammels from the multiplicity of the duties which the several princes and states exact upon the merchandises passing through their territories, by means of which the fine streams and navigable rivers with which Germany is so happily watered are rendered almost useless."[43]

---

[43]   Hamilton, Federalist paper 22

Additionally, the federal government, under the Confederation, was unable to exclusively negotiate trade treaties with foreign nations.[44] Basically, foreign nations questioned why they should enter into a formal trade agreement with the federal government if states could ignore any provision they found objectionable? Instead, these nations could easily negotiate directly with the individual states [and to the detriment of the nation, play the interests of the states against each other] to derive any benefit desired without going through the federal government.

The purpose of the Commerce Clause was to eliminate trade barriers erected by the states, allowing the unfettered movement of commerce within the nation. Additionally, it would allow the federal government to negotiate beneficial, consistent, and enforceable trade agreements between the United States and the other nations of the world.

The original Constitution did not allow the federal government to impose an income tax. The main source of federal revenue was derived from Duties, Imposts, and Excises, which required the federal government to negotiate beneficial trade agreements with our international trading partners. The Commerce Clause protected and secured the primary revenue stream for the federal government. Without the Commerce Clause, as it was originally intended, the United States could never have developed into the economic superpower it became.

The Commerce Clause was never intended to allow Congress to regulate or control specific industries within the states. It has been

---

[44]   Hamilton, Federalist paper 22: "No nation acquainted with the nature of our political association would be unwise enough to enter into stipulations with the United States, by which they conceded privileges of any importance to them, while they were apprised that the engagements on the part of the Union might at any moment be violated by its members, and while they found from experience that they might enjoy every advantage they desired in our markets, without granting us any return but such as their momentary convenience might suggest."

grossly misapplied by our elected representatives who have allowed the government to far exceed its constitutionally enumerated authority.

Go back to the days of the constitutional ratification. Imagine if the Commerce Clause had stated that the federal government was granted the authority to micromanage, regulate, and control the operations of any business in the United States, that it had complete discretion, and could require any business to adhere to whatever regulations federal bureaucrats thought proper. For example, how many spokes were required in carriage wheels, how often the tavern floors needed to be washed, how much money apprentices would be paid, which trees could be cut, and how much farmland could be developed. The Constitution would never have been ratified. Free people, who had just thrown off the yokes of tyranny, would never willingly authorize this magnitude of oppression to a new federal government.

Many federal politicians insist that the Commerce Clause provides government with the authority to regulate industry in order to "protect" the consumer. It's not true. Politicians tend to make decisions based on the accumulation of political power, rather than on the best interests of the consumer.

(Remember the Community Reinvestment Act?[45] Mass defaults on these loans to low-income borrowers ushered in the housing crisis, the 2008-2010 recession, the associated stock-market collapse, and skyrocketing unemployment.)

---

[45]   The 1977 Community Reinvestment Act (CRA) was designed to encourage low income home ownership. The program morphed into the unbelievable. In 1996, governmental mortgage giants Fannie Mae and Freddie Mac were instructed by Congress, that 42% of their financing had to go towards low-income borrowers. Under threat of federal prosecution, private banks had to follow the same regulations. Accordingly, banks lowered their standards, eliminated verification, and repackaged loans to decrease payments as much as possible. Furthermore, they hired activist groups, such as ACORN, to actively recruit low income borrowers.

Required regulation—outside of federal authority—should be imposed by the people through free-market selection, the states, insurance companies, or by professional trade associations such as the American Bar Association (ABA), American Medical Association (AMA), American Institute of CPA's (AICPA),etc. No system is perfect, and since people are not angels, there will be abuses, but the free market tends to discover and address true abuse, whereas government imposes "political" solutions.

The free market naturally promotes quality. Companies providing quality goods and services prosper, while those who do not, fail. Self-regulation, through the free-market system, is often accomplished through private insurance combined with the court system. Manufactures are responsible for the quality and function of their product. If the manufactured product is substandard, the manufacturer will be sued in court in front of a jury. Losing excessive lawsuits will drive the substandard manufacturers out of business. As a reasonable business practice, many organizations purchase private liability insurance. Private insurers will not knowingly insure defective products and will insist that manufactures satisfy basic quality requirements prior to being issued policies. If manufacturers want liability insurance, they will adhere to the standards insisted upon by the insurer.

The Commerce Clause, rightly applied, encourages free-market commerce by removing state trade barriers and through international trade agreements. It was never conceived to allow government to regulate, or micromanage, private industry. All existing federal regulations that are based on the misapplication of this clause should be nullified by the state, then be allowed to sunset or be repealed.

Six:

ISSUES AND POSITIONS

I firmly believe that the U.S. Constitution establishes the perfect government to secure the rights of the people. Unlike today's politicians, our founders understood and secured personal liberty.

My positions are ALL based on my understanding of the United States Constitution.

I believe the United States is the greatest nation this world has ever seen because of our constitutionally limited government, which unleashed the limitless potential of free people.

History has proven that free people, through our own endeavor, community, the free market, voluntary charity, or the state, (if the people desire government oversight) meet every need of society infinitely better than any federally imposed government program.

My positions detail how I view the various issues and challenges facing our nation today.

Constitutional Greatness

The Constitution is a document written to be understood by the people. It's a fallacy that only politicians, lawyers, or scholars are able to understand it. It unambiguously defines the powers and limitations of the federal government providing for the security and general welfare of our nation while protecting the God-given rights of the people.

Go back to 1786-1787, the period immediately prior to the ratification of the United States Constitution. Imagine if its proponents boasted that the new federal government would have:

1) Unlimited taxing authority to collect funds not only necessary to fund the specified powers of the new government, but also to evaluate the earnings of all individuals and redistribute what the government considered excessive away from those producing it to those the government considered "needy";
2) To dictate the curriculum of the nation's schools;
3) To decide the wage and benefits that must be paid by employers to employees;
4) To force every working individual to invest a portion of their earnings into a government-run retirement program in which the government has sole discretion to determine the contribution and terms of return;
5) To acquire the sole authority to provide for individual health care;
6) To provide subsidies to farmers not to produce crops;
7) and To regulate and control virtually every aspect of society.

The Constitution would never have been ratified.

The people of the United States fought a war against the most powerful nation on earth to throw off the shackles of a repressive government. They would never voluntarily replace it with another. The Constitution was ratified only because the authority of the federal government was limited to specific, enumerated powers that are best performed by a federal government. Everything else was left to the people, or the states.

Unlike anywhere in the world, the people of the United States were able to live, worship, and think without direct government oversight.

Over the course of my lifetime, the scope, power, and influence of government has grown exponentially, permeating every aspect of our lives, well outside the powers enumerated in the Constitution. Everyday decisions affecting our lives are increasingly made by government bureaucrats and are based on political posturing, making us less free.

I understand the greatness of our Constitution, and the necessity of a limited government to the preservation of our personal liberty and freedom as a nation.

I'm dedicated to reigniting the passion of our citizens to fight to retain our personal liberty and freedoms, and to roll back the bureaucratic nightmare of forced dependency engulfing our great nation.

Federal Spending

The greatest threat to our national sovereignty is unsustainable, out-of-control federal spending. Unless addressed immediately, we will not survive as a free nation.

Our problem is not living within our bloated budget, we've far exceeded that. Neither is it living within our borrowing limit that also has been grossly exceeded.

We are now on a suicide spiral into a financial abyss by spending more money then we can possibly collect through taxation or then we can conceivably borrow. Government's solution is to print new money from thin air, a very short term solution with disastrous results, and a proven death knell to any economy.

This is the exact scenario Germany followed prior to WWII when their currency became worthless and individuals needed a wheelbarrow full or cash to buy a loaf of bread.

Our government has been hijacked by self serving politicians more interested in their personal accumulation of wealth and power than on securing the liberty of the people. They use the federal treasury as their personal slush fund to dispense favors to supporters and to purchase the souls of those in need in exchange for their support.

To survive as a nation we must reverse this trend, if not now—never.

Debt Ceiling

Imagine a family earns $2,000 per month yet spends $3,000 and charges the monthly difference of $1,000 to a credit card balance. Years go by until the bank finally calls and reports that the credit card limit has been reached.

Ignorantly the borrower asks "what is my limit?" to which the bank replies "$145,000."

What are the options facing this family? The obvious answer is that they need to start living within their means. The monthly earnings is sufficient to pay for their necessities such as housing, food, clothing, etc, but it's not enough to pay anything else. Unnecessary items such as vacations, fine dining, designer jeans, magazine subscriptions, cable, lawn service, etc must be eliminated. The family may need to sell excess cars, a cottage on the lake, and anything else not required or affordable—purchased on borrowed money. Once the spending hemorrhaging has stopped the family can begin to pay down its debt.

The worst thing this family could do is ignore the underlying problem of out-of-control spending, and plead with the bank to increase its credit-card limit. Unless the underlying problem is addressed, the family will go bankrupt and everything they have will be forcibly stripped from them.

Anyone reading the above scenario would probably view the family as irresponsible, and if they made no effort to reform their ways, feel no pity for them when they fell into their extremely predictable financial abyss.

Yet the United States government is following this exact path. Add eight zeros to each of the above numbers and it represents the financial situation of our nation in August 2011 as Congress was debating raising the Debt Ceiling. Each month we receive about $200 billion in revenue yet spend about $300 billion. In August we reached our borrowing limit of $14.5 *trillion*. As with our family, the government was faced with the decision to rein in spending, or increase our borrowing limit. They chose the most irresponsible action imaginable and increased our borrowing limit to about $16.5 trillion without addressing the underlying problem of out-of-control spending. By year end 2012 we're expected to once again reach our new limit of $16.5 trillion ($16,500,000,000,000).

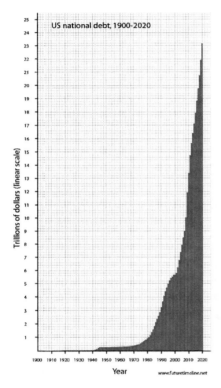

US national debt, 1900-2020

Everybody realizes that unless unsustainable federal spending is immediately addressed, our nation faces imminent demise, yet Congress does nothing about it.

Congress must rein in spending and cannot raise the debt limit again. No individual, family, organization, or nation can continually spend money it does not have and expect to survive.

America's national debt increased from $8.7 trillion in 2007 to $16.5 trillion by year end 2012. That's a doubling of our national debt in just six short years. Our own Department of the Treasury continues to project trillion dollar deficits and classifies this spending trend as "not sustainable."

Our nation is in deep financial trouble. Standard & Poor's lowered its outlook for the nation's long-term debt, there's serious speculation that the dollar will no longer be the world's global reserve currency, and the IMF predicts China will replace the United States as the dominant world economy in five years.

Reaching the debt ceiling should be a wake-up call for the government to get its financial house in order. The debt ceiling was raised in 2009 by $1.5 trillion to cover deficit spending and then raised another

$2 trillion in 2010 while Congress made no attempt to curb its spending. Instead, Congress arrogantly assumes the debt ceiling will be continually increased to allow more deficit spending on any program it desires.

Unbelievably, Congress again raised the debt ceiling another $2 trillion in 2011. The Republicans were in control of the House. Why did they raise this ceiling instead of cutting spending? This increase by itself saddled every man, woman, and child in the United States with an additional debt of over $6,500. And for what? To further fund spending outside of any constitutional authority on political pet projects designed to create dependency on government.

Our federal debt now exceeds the entire gross domestic product of the United States—with no end in sight. Unless addressed, we will implode from this crushing debt.

We cannot continue on this financial course. Congress has known since the start of its term that we were fast approaching this limit, yet no significant cuts were ever proposed. Why are we to believe that Congress will seriously address cutting spending after the ceiling is raised, when they shunned the process before? I say, "Do not raise the debt ceiling, and do not engage in deficit spending." Implement significant spending cuts now, whatever it takes, not only to alleviate the need to raise our debt ceiling, but to also start paying off our debt.

We can address our financial crisis without raising our borrowing limit—if the government desires to do so. Government receives about $200 billion dollars per month in tax revenue that can be used to pay our loan obligations. We are not in danger of defaulting on our debt. The government can then prioritize its obligations and use the balance of these receipts to pay for its constitutionally mandated programs—primarily defense and immigration, along with its Social Security and Medicare obligations.

Thereafter, we must eliminate our deficit spending practices or else, like the irresponsible family mentioned beforehand, our country will be forced into bankruptcy, resulting in an unimaginable world-wide financial calamity. The United States will not have any money for any obligation, and our country may very well cease to exist.

Reaching the debt ceiling provides Congress with the opportunity to examine all federal programs and cut waste, fraud, duplication, and anything else not allowed by the Constitution. I think it's morally wrong to shift the burden of payment for our unsustainable deficit spending to our children and grandchildren. They will not be able to satisfy it.

My solution is to enforce the existing constitutional provisions. Focus attention on limiting federal influence to its specific, enumerated powers and then enforcing the existing provision in Article 1 Section 9, which prohibits Congress from funding any program outside of its specific enumerated duties. It's already against the law for Congress to spend money on the majority of programs it funds today. Simply following the Constitution will solve every financial and domestic problem threatening the country today.

If Congress wants to solve this crisis they have the tools. It can encourage private-sector economic growth by lowering taxes and removing burdensome regulation. Cutting repressive taxes always results in the dual benefit of increasing revenue to the government and decreasing the need for government support. It's been proven effective when used by Kennedy, Reagan, and Bush. Why ignore it now?

Congress should also encourage procedures allowing the United States to become energy independent by immediately opening up federal lands to private-sector energy development. The United States has more domestic oil then all the OPEC nations combined, but government prohibits its development. Congress would rather see us spend $30 billion per month importing oil from abroad, than allow the private sector to invest that money into our own economy, creating jobs and generating federal revenue.

Congress' record of seriously cutting spending is dismal. We cannot allow them to pass more crushing debt to future generations by again raising the debt ceiling.

We must address our financial abyss by immediately balancing the budget, eliminating deficit spending, and enforcing existing constitutional provisions.

Balanced Budget

Congress has the moral responsibility to balance the federal budget. It is incomprehensible to me that we would saddle our children with debt that we are UNWILLING to pay.

According to the Constitution, federal spending MUST be limited to the enumerated powers specified in the Constitution. Spending on all non-enumerated programs is UNCONSTITUTIONAL, against the law, and should be completely phased out as quickly as possible. The federal budget must be balanced IMMEDIATELY.

Our current elected representatives in Washington are sacrificing the very survival of our nation through continued deficit spending. They are acting both irresponsibly and incompetently. Unless this stops, the United States, the greatest economic country on earth, will implode from this self-imposed, crushing debt.

I hear the term "shared sacrifice" bantered in Washington, meaning that the taxpayers should contribute more of their hard-earned money to Washington to fund additional, irresponsible federal spending.

I have a different definition. "Shared sacrifice" should mean that all the recipients of non-constitutional federal spending should understand that the country is broke, and that these federal handouts must stop.

The attitude in Washington must revert back to our founding principles with the understanding that government is the problem, and that economic prosperity can only be generated through the private sector.

Cutting repressive taxes generates economic prosperity and increases revenue to the federal treasury. Reagan actually doubled federal revenue during his term by cutting taxes.

We must encourage private-sector economic expansion by following the same path today by imposing across-the-board tax cuts for both businesses and individuals. Economic freedom requires that those generating income be able to retain it, so that these earnings can be used to hire additional employees, purchase capital equipment, or be otherwise invested. When government extracts this hard-earned capital from the private sector, it not only squanders the earnings of others, but also stifles economic expansion.

I am adamant that it's Congress's responsibility to balance the budget. It can be done.

First, we must reverse the asinine federal policies imposed by Washington onto the private sector that are stifling economic growth. We need to cut taxes; eliminate repressive, anti-free market regulation; and allow the private sector to use private investment to develop the United States' immense energy resources.

Simply allowing the U.S. to become energy independent will add over $30 billion per month to the U.S. economy, spurring unprecedented economic growth.

For the purposes of my analysis, I assume that Washington actually wants to allow the free market to solve our economic problems and has adopted programs to retract federal control from the private sector by reducing repressive regulations and taxes. Based on these actions, I assume that revenue will increase 8%, as it did under Reagan.

This balanced budget for Fiscal Year 2012 uses the projected revenue from the Office of Management and Budget for 2012[46] (adjusted upwards by 8% due to the removal of stifling federal policy), then subtracts the 2012 projected costs for constitutionally mandated programs and what I consider the legal obligations of Social Security and Medicare. All other costs are budgeted at 96% of the actual 2008 spending levels.

Check it out:

---

[46] All figures utilized within this analysis are from the "Office of Management and Budget Analysis from 2008-2019" on page 119. http://www.gpoaccess.gov/usbudget/fy10/pdf/fy10-newera.pdf

Balanced Budget for FY 2012 (in billions)

Revenue

2012 Revenue (Projected revenue of $3,081 * 1.08):	**$3,327**

Expenses

2012 projected Defense:	$ 604
2012 projected Social Security:	747
2012 projected Medicare:	500
2012 projected Interest:	378
Total 2012 Expenses:	**$2,229**

(96% of actual 2008 totals below)	
Other Appropriated Programs:	$ 506
Medicaid:	193
Other Mandatory Programs:	395
Total Expenses 2008 Actual @96%:	**$1,094**

Total Expenses:	**$3,323**

Projected Budget Surplus:	**$ 4**

This budget is a starting point only. Actual values could obviously be modified, as long as the overall goal is achieved—meaning immediately balancing the budget.

The figures included in this analysis are estimates from the OMB, and may not be accurate due to the dismal economic performance of recent years. Regardless, Congress has to understand that the budget must be balanced and then implement the required procedures to do so.

We must stop our out-of-control spending hemorrhaging now, or we never will. Our nation will no longer exist and our children and grandchildren will never know the blessings of liberty.

Peter Konetchy

Federal Investment

The Constitution grants the federal government authority to tax and spend whatever is necessary to perform its constitutionally mandated duties, but should the federal government "Invest" in America?

Many people, especially elected representatives, feel it proper that the government "invest in America" as the best means of allowing our country to remain competitive in the world.

I agree that investment is necessary, but disagree vehemently with federally directed "investment." There is a better way.

Who is better at investing money, those who earn it themselves, or those who forcibly confiscate it from those earning it?

A personal stake in the outcome of an investment, including putting your own money at risk, is critical to its success. Doing so forces the investor to evaluate if the required investment of time and money addresses a need of society, with a desired solution. If the investor is wrong he suffers severe personal consequences, but if right he reaps great reward.

There's great incentive on behalf of the investor to be efficient, frugal, and to sacrifice as needed, to ensure the success of his investment. A personal stake is a natural check against foolishness and adds sanity to the investment strategy.

Small businesses provide 75% of all new jobs in the United States. Entrepreneurs look at a problem facing society, and then place at risk their own money to address it with a solution of their choosing. If unable to self-fund their endeavor they must explain their plan to investors who then either invest, or decline, based on a critical analysis of the proposal. Faced with the very real probability of failure, personal hardship or ruin, entrepreneurs nevertheless risk all to achieve success.

Government investment is fundamentally different. Federal bureaucrats have no personal stake in the outcome of their investments and have no reason to care if they're successful. Unlike the private sector, this investment has not been earned by the bureaucrats, but extorted from the taxpayers. The government suffers no consequence if the investments fails, and more often than not, throws additional taxpayer funds at failed projects providing artificial life support long after private investment would have been withdrawn.

Government investment inflicts more harm to the economy than simply wasting money. It extracts scarce capital from the private sector which otherwise would be available for research and development, capital acquisition, promotion, and most importantly, expanding employment.

Federal "investment" is rarely based on need, but more often promotes a political agenda, or worse yet, rewards those providing partisan political support. Our government has been "investing" over one trillion dollars per year into political projects—of which most has been completely wasted.

Typical examples of wasted federal investment include battery maker A123 Systems whom the Washington Times reported received a federal investment of $250 million creating just 400 jobs [$625,000 per job]—prior to filing for bankruptcy.[47] The Obama Administration set aside $80 billion from the 2009 stimulus for green energy. Companies such as Solyndra, Evergreen Solar, Beacon Power, EnerDel, and scores more all took considerable taxpayer money prior to filing for bankruptcy.[48] Government policy, funded by taxpayer investment, encouraged the development of the Chevy Volt. According to Michigan's Mackinac Center for Public Policy, each Volt cost taxpayers $250,000.[49] It's doubtful any of these investments would have been made if federal policymakers were held personally responsible for the success of these schemes they imposed upon the people.

---

[47] The Washington Times, Oct 29, 2012, Jim McElhatton
Quarter-billion-dollar stimulus grant creates just 400 jobs

[48] World Net Daily, Oct 19,2012
OBAMA'S GREEN ENERGY HANDOUTS COSTING BILLIONS

[49] Tom Gantert, Dec. 21, 2011, Mackinac Center for Public Policy Chevy Volt Costing Taxpayers Up to $250K Per Vehicle

What about federal investment in social programs dealing with education, housing, food stamps, welfare, the environment, etc? I argue that unintended consequences from Washington's politically motivated one-size-fits-all policies have resulted in the direct disintegration of society. Who's better at addressing local problems, the state and local governments, or the federal government? Local control is always better. Those closest to the need are much more adept at implementing the appropriate solutions than politically motivated federal bureaucrats. A basic pillar of our constitutionally limited republic is that the individual states provide a proving ground for ideas to meet the needs of the people. What works well in one state will be emulated in other states, whereas inefficient programs fall by the wayside. Federal intervention eliminates innovation and hinders the ability of the states to best address the needs of their citizens.

The Constitution grants the federal government no authority to invest in the private sector for good reason. A small handful of politicians and government bureaucrats are not only incompetent, but incapable of adequately evaluating the needs of millions of individuals, and implementing the policies best suited to meet their needs. Only the people themselves are capable of doing so.

Our founding principles provide the obvious solution to misdirected federal investment—restrain government back to its enumerated responsibilities and once again allow the people to pursue their own happiness, to determine their own destiny. Allow the individuals who evaluated a problem, developed a solution, risked their personal fortune, and then succeeded; to reinvest their earnings derived from their success as they deem proper. Private investment is successful only if consumers decide the offered solution provides increased personal benefit at a reasonable cost, and then voluntarily choose to purchase the offered product or service.

Federal Investment evades this natural selection process, provides no positive benefit to the country, and should be terminated.

Liberty and Taxes

The amazing difference between our Founding Fathers and today's political leaders is that our founders fought to preserve and protect our liberties, while today's leaders willingly trample them in order to feed their insatiable lust for political power.

The Declaration of Independence affirms man's God-given, unalienable rights, and avers that governments are created to secure these rights. Our founders knew that direct federal control of the citizenry would suppress personal liberty. Therefore, the Constitution limits federal influence to specific powers outside the scope of the individual or states, such as for common defense, immigration, a national monetary system, national postal system, etc.; and excludes direct, federal influence over the lives, actions, and decisions of individuals. Our Constitution is a solemn covenant, which ensures that our representative government concern itself with the task of interacting with the world and protecting our liberties, while all else is the responsibility of the people themselves or the states in which they live.

In 1913, this covenant was broken with the ratification of the Sixteenth Amendment, which allowed a direct tax on income. In order to enforce this tax, the federal government demanded access to, and ultimately control over, the most detailed and private aspects of the lives of the citizens of the United States.

The income tax dealt two major blows against personal liberty. First, it provided the government with a virtually unlimited source of revenue, allowing it to feed and fuel its lust for power. Second, through the creation of the Internal Revenue Service, the full force of the federal government could be unleashed against individuals who dared to question or disagree with its policies. Fear of the federal government, and the power that's funneled through the IRS, encourages submission and quells dissent.

The tax system is no longer designed to simply fund the government. It's designed to control and to channel thought and action as the government deems proper.

Most people recognize that the current Income tax system is wrong. A few alternatives have been suggested including the Flat Tax and a National Sales Tax, but both would fail. The problem lies in the fundamental flaw of allowing the federal government to maintain control of the taxing system—and to directly tax the individuals themselves. Congress would still determine minimum income levels, grant tax-free status to individuals or groups they consider worthy, set the tax rates, determine allowable exemptions or deductions, and continue to intrude in all aspects of life under the guise of "Compliance Verification."

Alternative tax programs are designed to be revenue neutral, allowing the federal government to collect an equal amount of tax revenue, with the difference being only the source.

Individuals would continue to be obligated to submit or face harsh punishment, while the government would continue to have no incentive to become efficient or restrict its intrusive practices. If additional funding is desired, the tax burden is simply increased—or worse—government steals from our children through deficit spending.

The debt of the United States now exceeds the entire GDP of the country—and it's still growing. If not addressed, this crushing burden will quash prosperity for our progeny and our nation will become insolvent and cease to exist. Our priority must be to eliminate all non-enumerated spending, substantially lowering the funding requirements of the federal government and correspondingly reducing the required federal tax burden of the nation.

The framers of the Constitution realized that the federal government needed a revenue stream to perform its constitutionally mandated duties. Yet, they were also very concerned about placing an undue burden on the citizens of the country. They wisely chose to fund the government through **indirect taxes**, consisting of *"Duties, Imposts, and Excises."*[50]

As the goal was to fund the government, Hamilton explained how the appropriate indirect tax rates would be determined. If taxes were set too low, the federal government would lack its required funding. Excessive rates would discourage consumption, resulting in lower federal revenue. Through time and experience, a natural equilibrium would be attained providing the government its required revenue without discouraging commerce.

If additional funding was required, the Constitution provided the solution. Article 1 Section 2 states that *"Representatives and direct Taxes shall be apportioned among the several States . . . according to their respective Numbers."* Although the ability to directly tax the states has never been repealed, the 16th Amendment allows this provision to be ignored.

Under the original constitutional mandate, states, not the individual, are responsible for paying their share of the excess federal budget—not funded by the collection of Duties, Excises, and Imposts. It allows the states to experiment with various forms of taxation, such as a flat or sales tax, or to develop entirely new sources of revenue. In the best case scenario, states could generate revenue through economic development, such as the development of natural resources in Alaska, which could entirely shift the tax burden from individuals. In the worst case, the state's portion of the excess budget would be taxed directly to the citizens of that state resulting in an overall tax burden similar to that of today.

The purpose of the original, constitutionally mandated census was twofold—to provide the states with representation in the House, and to determine the percentage of the federal budget for which each state

---

[50] US Constitution; Article 1 section 8: The Congress shall have Power To lay and collect Taxes, Duties, Imposts and Excises, to pay the Debts and provide for the common Defence and general Welfare of the United States; but all Duties, Imposts and Excises shall be uniform throughout the United States;

is responsible. Without the direct taxation of the states, the census has been manipulated to provide political power and benefit to the ruling political class without any corresponding responsibility.

The major benefit of directly taxing the states lies in the re-implementation of Checks and Balances by the states against federal waste. The current income tax provides the federal government with virtually unlimited revenue and power with which to dispense any conceivable benefit through a massive, federal bureaucracy. Since these benefits are not drawn from state coffers, most states gladly accept and encourage these benefits. The fifty states supplement or duplicate many of the same services through their own state bureaucracy.

When the burden of federal taxation is shifted from the individual back to the state treasury, then the states will rightly complain when they are forced to pay for federal pork, waste, inefficiency, fraud, and duplicity, and will strive to eliminate this waste. Unlike the individual, states are less intimidated by the possibility of retaliation and able to confront the federal government on an equal basis.

States must be concerned with efficiency and value. Otherwise, high-tax, inefficient states, will lose population and tax revenue to states with a lower overall tax burden. Fifty individual states collecting tax by various means would naturally promote taxing efficiency. Replacing the income tax with a direct tax to the states will rein in governmental excess at all levels.

The only solution to solving our nation's problems is to revert back to the original constitutional tax provisions and indirectly provide the federal government with all revenue necessary to perform its constitutionally mandated responsibilities, but nothing more. All direct federal taxes against individuals and business enterprises must be eliminated, along with the IRS. Imagine the explosive economic expansion and prosperity for all that would result from the elimination of these federal burdens.

Reverting back to constitutional tax provisions will not be easy. The federal government will not willingly concede power and will instead implement an all-out attack against those insisting it do so—namely the states, and people of the United States. The states will also complain as they see their federal subsidies disappear. But in the United States, we are a government of the people, not a people of the government.

The government establishment will complain that it is heartless to curtail benefits to the needy, in spite of the fact that the people of the United States are among the most moral and charitable individuals in the world. It's a false assertion. The provision of charity would be simply shifted away from the federal bureaucracy. Elimination of the federal tax burden will allow people the means to voluntarily support charitable organizations with which they agree. Free men voluntarily provide charity to those in need.

The people of the United States provide the final check against government intrusion. It would be a great mistake to allow our current tax code to be replaced with another one that is directly imposed on the individual and controlled by the government. We have a proud and independent ancestry who pledged their lives and fortunes for our independence. Now is our time to renew this fight for liberty and roll back the tyranny of unrestricted government. Votes count. Insist that every elected government servant at the local, state, and federal level adhere to our founding principles, which are based on personal liberty and independence. Those who don't must be voted out and replaced.

Funding State Programs Without Federal Dollars

The population has been conditioned to believe that states need federal dollars to survive. They question "How can we pay for schools, welfare, health care or roads without federal help?"

As with every other problem the solution is staring us in the face. Enforce the existing provisions of the U.S. Constitution.

The framework of government in the United States, unique in the world, produced the most successful nation which ever graced the surface of this earth.

This is fact, not theory.

The reason being that the federal government is charged with addressing, and paying for, national duties—defense, immigration, and maintaining our nation's role in world affairs; while it's the responsibility of the states is to address, and pay for everything else, including the services required by the people living within their borders.

The division of power which worked amazingly well during the first two thirds of our nation's life has all but been eliminated today. Federal tentacles ensnare every aspect of society, and maintain their grip upon the states through the redistribution of revenue.

The problem is not that the people are not being taxed enough to address the social problems facing our nation, but how that money is being collected and utilized.

Government at all levels within the U.S. collected about $5 trillion dollars in 2012, distributed as follows:

Level of Government	Revenue Collected
Federal tax collections	$2.5 trillion
Total tax collected by States	$1.5 trillion
Total tax collected by Localities	$1.0 trillion
Total tax revenue collected	**$5.0 trillion**

The Constitution grants the federal government an extraordinary ability to tax and collect as much money as needed with the caveat that the raised revenue only be disbursed in the performance of its constitutionally enumerated powers.

Likewise, the states and localities were provided with the means of raising as much tax revenue as was required to perform the requirements of the state and localities.

This segregation of responsibilities provided the check against abuse on all sides.

The federal government collects as much money from the people as is collected by all the state and local governments combined, but it ignores the requirement to spend it on its specific constitutionally enumerated duties. Once collected, it uses a small percent to perform its constitutional requirements, and then dumps the remainder into a huge bureaucracy which supposedly analyzes the needs of society, and then doles it back to the states as it deems proper—with conditions attached, totally outside any conceivable constitutional authority. It's an extremely inefficient process, but greatly empowers the federal government. If the states want federal money they'll toe the line, if they refuse to accede to Washington's demands, they'll lose their federal allotment.

Visualize this alternative. Assume that all the tax revenue collected by the federal government, over and above what was required fund the constitutional duties of government, remained in the individual states from which it was collected allowing the states to use those funds as they determined proper—without federal conditions or restrictions. The savings would be phenomenal.

Peter Konetchy

First, we wouldn't need to fund the huge federal bureaucracy. No longer would this money flow through federal agency upon federal agency supposedly figuring out the problems to be addressed, the allowed solutions, and then the means and conditions upon which to redistribute these funds back to the states.

Second, we could drastically cut the size of the federal government. Since the states would directly address societies needs, there would be no need for non-constitutionally authorized departments such as the Department of Education or the Environmental Protection Agency. With no need for these services, gone would be the concept of base line budgeting which automatically doubles the size of government every 10 years. The states would be responsible for providing for the needs of their people without the need for federal oversight.

Third, we would reap substantial savings by eliminating the duplication and burdensome regulation of federal programs bundled on top of state programs. We currently have both federal and state unemployment, environmental, social, medical, agriculture, housing, and labor services—to name a few. Often these programs work against each other.

By allowing the tax revenue to remain where collected, all the needs of the state would be satisfied more efficiently than they are now. Rather than having one-sized-fits-all federal programs forced upon the states, the states could once again act as fifty individual proving grounds for innovative ideas—something woefully lost in the federal bureaucratic nightmare.

We can return to these founding principles by implementing State Nullification, combined with Negative Baseline Budgeting, to restrain the government back to its enumerated responsibilities.

As the influence of the federal government is eliminated from society, the states can assume responsibility for desired federal programs and adjust the state revenue collection as needed. As with every domestic situation, the states will be able to devise the means to deliver desired services to the people much more efficiently than the federal government.

Let's implement the proven procedures from our history, and discard the failed policies being forced upon us today.

A Case Against the Federal Fair Tax

Proponents of the Federal Fair Tax want to replace all federal taxes with a supposedly revenue neutral 23% national sales tax—theoretically eliminating the IRS in the process. The problem is that it addresses the wrong problem with the wrong solution. The problem is not revenue collection—its spending. The solution is not to "fairly" fund our bloated government, but shrink it.

Assume Fair Tax proponents work diligently for the next 5-7 years to replace all federal taxes with a revenue neutral consumption tax. What will be the state of the nation? Being revenue neutral, we would have continued to incur annual trillion dollar deficits meaning our national debt would have increased by at least 50%—an unsustainable amount well above 100% of GDP. In all likelihood, our nation could not survive this transition period and would have imploded from debt prior to implementation of the revised Fair Tax structure.

Is it possible retail sales could drop significantly with the imposition of a consumption tax? My neighbors have decided to take responsibility for their own destiny. They have a large garden, chickens, a cow, as well as a portable sawmill. They produce as much of their own food as possible, they have a wood burning furnace [using wood collected from their own property] so they don't buy taxable heating fuel; and with their own saw mill they produce their own lumber for their building needs. Working towards self sufficiency, their retail purchases along with the associated consumption tax paid has dropped significantly. What happens if a "significant" portion of Middle America does the same? Will the federal government start punishing people for becoming self sufficient?

Will I be committing a federal crime if I have my neighbor process some of my trees into lumber, allowing me to build a barn, if in exchange I help them install a fence around their pasture? This is barter, and neither of us would pay a consumption tax on product or labor. In the USSR battering increased from around 5% to over 50% once a similar consumption tax was implemented. Why do the fair tax proponents discount the very real possibility of retail sales dropping significantly with the imposition of a significant new consumption tax?

What about the argument that everyone will pay their fair share—prostitutes, drug dealers, or those on welfare? Most of these people don't pay income taxes now. Do we actually expect that a single mother on welfare will have her cost of living increased by 23% without an associated increase in federal benefit? Not in today's political environment. In the name of "fairness" her federal benefits will increase by at least 23% allowing her to buy the same amount of goods she could have bought before the consumption tax. Those not on the government's dole will continue to be forced to pay the tax burden of themselves as well as those receiving federal benefits.

The IRS may disappear, but some other agency has to take its place, otherwise who will send out the pre-bate checks? To whom will the retailers, or States, forward the collected consumption tax? Or, if tax revenue "unexpectedly" drops, who will scourer society searching for "tax evaders?"

Washington's destroying our economy by sucking as much money as possible away from the people. This money is no longer available within the private sector for job creation, capital improvement, research and development, promotion, etc. It doesn't matter if the money is taken through an income tax, consumption tax, death tax, etc., the bottom line is that it's not available for private sector job growth. Add to this the crushing regulation imposed by the EPA, Obama Care, OSHA, etc, and there is no reason to expect our businesses to prosper under a revenue neutral Fair Tax.

What's Washington going to do if, or when, tax revenue declines under the fair tax? Raise the consumption tax percent (encouraging even wider spread avoidance)? Re-implement the dreaded income tax? Or simply confiscate wealth in the name of national survival?

The only solution for the survival of our nation is to immediately balance the budget, cut spending, cut taxes to encourage economic growth, and decrease the federal government back to its constitutional authority. **There is no other solution**.

History has proven that when constitutionally restrained, Washington's burden averages 2-3% of GDP—about $1/8^{th}$ of the 25% we spend today. History has again proven that federal funding can be satisfied by duties, imposts, and excises, combined with apportionment of direct taxes against the states—not the people.

What's better, a bloated federal government funded by a new consumption tax, or a constitutionally restrained government void of any direct tax against the individual? You decide.

I suggest that we put all of our effort into scaling back federal power to its constitutional authority and once again fund the severely limited constitutional requirements of the federal government as our founders proposed, rather than focusing on a implementing a "fairer" way to fund federal bloat.

Free Enterprise—the Engine of a Free Society

Free Enterprise is the engine of a free society, driven by what Adam Smith calls an "invisible hand"[51].

Individuals choose products, services, and ideas that they consider most beneficial, and naturally pursue livelihoods generating their own greatest personal gain.

Prior to the Industrial Revolution, commerce was generally local and limited. The majority of people provided for their own needs and sold or traded their excess production to purchase what they could not produce. Farmers and their families often woke well before dawn and worked until after dark. They were at the mercy of factors beyond their control—rain, drought, fire, pests, cold, heat, etc. If all worked well, they would be successful; if not, they could become destitute.

The Industrial Revolution introduced a more efficient option of earning a livelihood. Individuals and companies began to focus their talents through specialization allowing them to satisfy the needs of society better and more efficiently. All manner of commerce developed, addressing specific needs such as food processing, textiles, shoes, transportation, etc. Instead of working in the fields from before dawn until after dusk—and still being subject to the whims of the weather—individuals had the option of being employed at organizations that provided products to the population at large. They earned hard currency that could be used to purchase products, no longer needing to personally produce them. Markets developed, adding stability to the economy.

The free market is the only economic system in the world truly devoted to satisfying the needs of society. If two stores offer the same product at the same price, they distinguish themselves through service and support. In a controlled economy, the consumer has no option and

---

[51] "An Inquiry into the Nature and Causes of the Wealth of Nations," by Adam Smith, published in 1776

is at the mercy of the state. In a free-market economy, the consumer has choice, and the entrepreneurs compete for his business. The merchants providing the highest quality product at a fair and reasonable price excel.

Opponents of the free-enterprise system depict capitalists as greedy parasites, but nothing could be farther from the truth. In addition to encouraging quality service and support, free market competition determines and sets a fair and reasonable long-term price. If it's too high, competitors will undercut, driving prices down. If the price is too low, costs cannot be met, and the companies will go out of business. If there is no market for the goods or service produced, the producing company will fade away.

In spite of all these benefits, free enterprise is under a coordinated attack by government and leftwing organizations. The reason is that free enterprise, unlike government, is successful and actually solves problems, whereas government simply addresses problems without providing solutions. (*If the problem was solved, there would be no need for the government program.*)

The success of bureaucratic government programs pale in comparison to the corresponding achievements produced by the free-enterprise system. If left unchecked, the free-enterprise economic system would render unconstitutional government programs useless. Rather than conceding power or success to the free market, government would rather control and direct this great force of freedom, rendering it impotent.

Large companies, such as "Big Oil," are constantly demonized as greedy and uncaring. Yet, Big Oil, for example, has been providing an abundance of low-cost energy to the world for decades. They have explored for and extracted new reserves, transported the crude to refineries, refined the crude to high-grade fuel, and then distributed the final product to distribution points throughout the world. This is very good. Without Big Oil, we wouldn't have oil, cars, plastics, synthetic fabrics, electricity, or most of the products we take for granted today.

In a free market, nobody is ever forced to buy a product or service against his will. If an individual doesn't like a product or service for whatever reason, he is free to forgo the purchase altogether, or to choose a competing product that better satisfies his needs at what he considers a fair price. These individual decisions, multiplied a million times over, enable the free market to satisfy the needs of the people.

The free-enterprise system is the engine of a free and prosperous society—as long as government allows it to function.

Health Care

I am disgusted by the federal government's usurpation of the United States' health-care system. It's not about health care, but about control of the people.

The United States is founded on the principle of limited government. **Read the Constitution**. Article 1 Section 8 enumerates the specific duties of Congress. As a protection against usurpation of power, the Tenth Amendment prohibits Congress from assuming any other power[52]. Complete government control of the health-care system is the most egregious, unconstitutional attack on the personal liberty of the people of the United States imaginable. If it's not reversed, we will not remain a free people.

The American health-care system is the best in the world. Anybody can receive immediate medical attention by simply showing up at a hospital. There is no discrimination based on income, age, race, or even citizenship. The great majority of Americans are satisfied with their health care.

The census bureau reports that approximately 85% of the U.S. population is covered by health insurance, leaving about 46 million uninsured. Of these, about 10 million are illegal aliens, and 28 million voluntarily op-out or are uninsured for 4 months or less. Only 2.7% of legal U.S. citizens, 8.2 million people, cannot pay for health services received.[53]

The health-care problem pertains to the cost rather than the quality of the care received by those who are unable to pay. The illegal alien problem, which is a tremendous cost factor, could easily be solved if the

---

[52] 10th Amendment to the US Constitution: The powers not delegated to the United States by the Constitution, nor prohibited by it to the States, are reserved to the States respectively, or to the people.

[53] The American Spectator, The Myth of the 46 Million—By Philip Klein on 3-20-2009

country had the will to deport illegal aliens after providing them with the required medical service. Those voluntarily opting out of insurance usually pay for the care they receive and are not a drain on the system. Our focus should be on the remaining 8.2 million people (2.7% of the U.S. population) who receive health care, but can't pay for it.

The government solution is a complete absorption of the entire U.S. health-care system by the government. Under this absorption:

1. Illegal aliens would continue to receive heath care on demand—without paying for services received;

2. Authorized services, fees, and compensation for medical personnel would be set by the government;

3. The quantity and quality of doctors would decrease;

4. Medical care would be rationed;

5. Senior citizens would be encouraged to receive end-of-life counseling, allowing medical attention to be focused on those considered worthy by the government;

6. Individual compliance would be achieved through penalties enforced by the IRS;

7. Individuals will be involuntarily forced out of their existing health-care policies and rolled into the government system;

8. Costs will increase—as proven by Social Security, Medicare, Medicaid, etc.;

9. *THE WORST OF THE WORST*—unelected government bureaucrats will be making health-care decisions on your behalf—not based on your needs, but on political considerations.

There is nothing positive for the American people in federalized health care. Let's analyze a few claims:

The quantity and quality of doctors would decrease. Federalized health care requires that doctors provide services that are prescribed by the government, such as abortion or euthanasia counseling, and limits unapproved treatments by eliminating payment for such services.

If a doctor provides a service they feel necessary, but not approved by a handful of federal bureaucrats, the doctor will be punished.

Most doctors adhere to the **Hippocratic Oath,** which states in principle, that they will do their patients no harm. This would include not performing abortions or practicing euthanasia.[54] If the government requires a doctor or hospital staff member to perform a procedure they may personally find abhorrent—such as abortion—the affected individuals would probably leave the profession rather than perform services that are against their moral character. The number of health-care professionals would decrease, and the collective pool of those remaining would have much less respect for the sanctity of life.

---

[54] Portion of the Hippocratic Oath: I will use those dietary regimens which will benefit my patients according to my greatest ability and judgment, and I will do no harm or injustice to them. I will not give a lethal drug to anyone if I am asked, nor will I advise such a plan; and similarly I will not give a woman a pessary to cause an abortion. In purity and according to divine law will I carry out my life and my art. I will not use the knife, even upon those suffering from stones, but I will leave this to those who are trained in this craft. Into whatever homes I go, I will enter them for the benefit of the sick, avoiding any voluntary act of impropriety or corruption, including the seduction of women or men, whether they are free men or slaves. Whatever I see or hear in the lives of my patients, whether in connection with my professional practice or not, which ought not to be spoken of outside, I will keep secret, as considering all such things to be private. Translated by Michael North, National Library of Medicine, 2002.

Medical care would be rationed.[55] FDA-approved Avastin is the world's best-selling cancer drug, but it is very expensive. The FDA is considering revoking approval of this drug—not because of its effectiveness, but because they believe that the benefits may not be worth the cost. This is the first step in rationing. What is next? Is it possible that the government will start to deny joint replacements to individuals over a certain age because the government doesn't think that the costs justify the benefits? These decisions should be made by the doctor and by the patient, and it is the patient's responsibility to pay for the service—not the government's.

History confirms that non-enumerated government programs are usually managed by incompetent government bureaucrats and are utilized to gain political advantage rather than to responsibly meet the needs of the recipients. Look at Social Security—which is bankrupt, Medicare—which is bankrupt, Department of Education—which has delivered the lowest test scores in U.S. history, and the Department of Energy—which has decreased the country's domestic energy supply and forced our dependence on foreign oil. Our government's competency record is dismal; yet they are usurping control of the entire U.S. health-care system and health-insurance infrastructure prior to addressing any of the failures associated with their other boondoggles.

What indication is there that government is even remotely competent to run health care?

None.

The Federalization of the nation's health care does nothing to address the 2.7% of the population who do not have the means to pay for the services they receive. It does nothing to address the 10 million illegal aliens accessing our health-care system with no intention of ever paying. What it does is completely destroy the health-care system that satisfies the needs of 97.5% of the U.S. population, lowers health-care quality, dramatically drives up costs, and empowers government to

---

[55]   FDA considers revoking approval of Avastin for advanced breast cancer By Rob Stein, Washington Post Staff Writer, Monday, August 16, 2010

confiscate additional money and distribute it as they consider politically advantageous.

If government is allowed to ignore constitutional restraint, "We the People" will have lost our liberty and sacrificed our children's liberty and the liberty of generations to come. Government must divest itself of all responsibility for the nation's health care and return responsibility to the people and the states through free-market principles.

Problem: Overreliance on Third-Party Payments

There is a problem with health care in the United States, but it has nothing to do with the quality of the care provided. The care provided by the United States health-care system is the best in the world, unsurpassed by any other system in any other country. What's broken is the manner by which it's delivered, which has been convoluted by governmental intervention. The result has been increased costs and limited choices.

Third parties, somebody other than the patients receiving the care, pay for the great majority of health care. The practice of employer-paid health insurance blossomed during WW II, when the government imposed strict wage controls. Employers were "allowed" by the government to offer health insurance to their employees as a means of bypassing these controls and attracting quality employees. Since then, the government has continued to encourage employer-provided insurance by providing the employer with a significant tax deduction, whereas a privately purchased policy receives none.[56]

Care for indigents and illegal immigrants are also paid for by a third party, the taxpayers. Extensive third-party payments disrupt the natural price and quality controls inherent in a free market economy, in that there's no incentive for consumers to monitor costs. When consumers purchase goods and services from of their own earnings, they're conscious of trying to get the greatest value for the lowest cost. It doesn't matter if it is a high or low ticket item.

Take milk for example, a small ticket item—not very expensive: In my community, milk normally costs about $3.79 per gallon. We drink a lot of milk. Since I'm paying for each gallon, I try to find the best deal. I'm aware that my local store occasionally sells milk for as

---

[56] Assume both the employer and employee pay a 30% federal tax rate. Also assume that a family health-care insurance policy costs $12,000/year. The out of pocket cost for the employer is $8,400 ($12,000–$3,600 tax deduction). The out of pocket cost for the private purchase of this policy the full $12,000.

low as $1.99 per gallon. I'm also aware of several non-local stores that regularly sell it for about $2.19 per gallon. Lastly, I'm aware of a local gas station that sells milk for $3.30 per gallon. When I buy milk, I try to maximize the power of my dollar by purchasing from the location that best balances price with convenience.

A car, as a second example, is considered a high-ticket item—expensive for most people. When purchasing for themselves, people again try to get the highest value for the lowest cost. To do so, they might look at different manufactures or dealers, evaluate the warranties provided, decide whether to buy new or used, check to see if they are eligible for employee pricing, inquire if a prior-model-year vehicle is available, or re-evaluate if they really need to replace their current vehicle. After completing this process, consumers purchase the product best meeting their needs.

These free-market shopping habits, multiplied millions of times, encourage the availability of quality products at reasonable prices. Suppliers of goods and services are also trying to determine the means of providing the highest possible quality at the lowest possible cost so that they may meet the needs of their consumers and remain successful. Yet, health-care payments by third parties completely eliminate any incentive for consumers to monitor the purchasing power of their health-care dollars.

Nobody is suggesting that emergency care be delayed until the cheapest physician is discovered, but if consumers had an incentive to control the cost of non-emergency, discretionary products and services, the associated cost would be dramatically reduced.

When a third party purchases goods or services, such as prescription drugs, mobility equipment, out-patient care, preventative care, counseling, etc., on behalf of others, there is no incentive for the patient to scrutinize costs. For example, a lower-price generic drug may have the exact same effect as the corresponding brand-name drug, but in a third-party-paid plan, the patient will never insist on the lower-cost drug. Likewise if somebody else, a third party, is paying for in home mobility equipment, the recipient doesn't really care what it costs. The consumer isn't directly paying for the product or service and takes whatever they're given without questioning costs. Third-party payment tends to eliminate free-market cost control from the health-care marketplace.

Third-party payments, *especially when paid by government,* **encourage fraud.** Although the great majority of health-care providers are honest, a significant number work at gaming the system. It is estimated that the government pays \$55 billion per year in fraudulent Medicare and Medicaid claims.[57]

For Example: The government receives invoices for goods and services. The invoice is hopefully reviewed for reasonability before it's paid. A fraudulent provider can easily add unperformed services to an invoice and be reimbursed for those services. When individuals are responsible for paying for their own care, invoices are better scrutinized making it harder to fraudulently bill for unperformed services.

Obama Care does nothing to address the third-party payment problem, but only makes it worse by greatly enlarging third-party payments by government. Anyone not enrolled in an authorized, private insurance program will be forced into the government-run insurance program. Remember, every social program the government has ever tried to implement has been a dismal failure—Social Security, Medicare, Medicaid, education, and now health care. All these programs are failing or bankrupt and have cost overruns grossly exceeding their original estimates.

The federal government is not the solution to the nation's healthcare woes. Any modification to the heath care system must remove government interference and reinstate free-market cost controls.

---

[57]   Reported by Alison Young, USA TODAY, 9-20-2010: Peter Budetti, director of the new anti-fraud office at the federal Centers for Medicare & Medicaid Services.

Problem: Health Insurers Providing Poor Service

During the health-care debate, the mainstream media and politicians tried to demonize the insurance companies as "greedy capitalists" whose sole purpose is to deny lawful claims to needful recipients.

Whenever government tries to assume unconstitutional power, it demonizes whomever it wants to regulate. Recent examples include energy providers, pharmaceutical companies, logging companies, bankers, and now health insurers. Organizations complicit with government, such as environmental groups, unions, trial lawyers, or homosexual groups, are left alone or given additional privilege.

All insurance companies have a duty to follow prudent claims procedures in an effort to discover fraudulent claims. If they think a claim is fraudulent, such as a claim filed after coverage has lapsed, they have a duty to deny. If they are incorrect, the rejection will be overturned through voluntary negotiations or in court.

Do health insurers make it a practice to unfairly deny claims and provide poor customer service? No. If they did so they would be forced out of business through their poor reputation, or by excessive court-ordered fines and penalties.

Every private enterprise in the United States provides better customer service than the United States government. Don't think so? Then try to get an answer from the INS (Immigration and Naturalization Service) via the phone!

A free-market system naturally encourages the highest quality of product and support. Satisfying the consumer's needs tends to increase the private enterprise's customer base, allowing them to generate a profit.

So, how is it possible that health insurers might provide consumers with poor service?

Most health insurance is purchased by either an employer or the government, on behalf of the patient. This being so, who is the insurance company's customer? It's either the employer or the government—not the patient.

In a free-market system, organizations survive when they offer a quality product to their customers at a fair price. Since the employer or government is the customer, the insurance company's purpose is to offer the employer or government a quality product at a fair price. The product not only includes a health insurance package, but also the necessary reporting, paperwork, and regulation compliance. Insurers are competing with other insurers for the employer's business and are under great pressure to contain costs.

Health insurers have great incentive to provide superior service to their customer, but much less incentive to provide the same quality of service to the patient. For example, if the customer (not the patient, but the head of the company's human-resource department) calls the insurer, a live person will most likely answer the call and address the question or concern immediately.

The patient is not the health-insurance provider's direct customer, the employer is. In order to maintain a relationship with the employer, the insurance company must provide the services contracted for in the health-insurance package, but they do not necessarily need to provide the same level of service for the patient as they do for the customer (employer).

For example, when a patient calls, they may be routed to an automated answering service, where they are required to navigate through innumerable options, never being able to talk with a person. Correspondence may need to be processed through standardized claim forms. It may not be a pleasant experience, but these procedures must be followed if the claim is to be paid. The reason for poor customer service is the fact that the patient is not the insurance provider's customer.

Let's change the scenario to deal with either homeowner's or auto insurance, which the consumer typically purchases directly. If you have a problem, you can immediately call your agent and file a claim. You receive superior service as the customer, since multiple insurers are directly competing for your business.

To further reinforce this point, consider the insurance commercials you see on TV—you're in good hands with Allstate, the gecko at Geico tries to secure your business, and the Aflac duck does the same. How many health insurance commercials do you see trying to secure your business? Very few to none. Their target market, the employer, does not buy health insurance packages from TV. But if you attend an industry trade show, many of the vendors will be health insurers trying to sell their packages to employers.

Health-care reform must reorient health insurers back to the patient, rather than the employer or government, as the customer. Otherwise, the patient will always tend to receive substandard care. Obama Care does nothing to address this problem, but only expands it.

Problem: State Mandates and Limitations

Each state has varying levels of mandated health-insurance benefits.

These are laws requiring insurers to cover services ranging from acupuncture to in vitro fertilization and providers ranging from chiropractors to naturopaths—and there are considerable differences among the states.[58]

State mandates have a direct effect on the cost of health-insurance policies available to residents. States mandating the most coverage force all their citizens to pay significantly higher premiums. Although the mandates are often described as "consumer protections," it's often the special-interest providers rather than patients who are pushing for these laws.

For example: in 2006, a healthy 25 year-old in New Jersey would need to pay $5,880 annually for an individual plan, yet pay less than $1,000 for the equivalent plan in Kentucky. [59] The reason is not due to the cost of providing health care, but is due to the difference in mandates between the states.

Free-market competition, unfettered by either state or federal mandates, will be the driving force to lowering health-insurance costs. It would be of great benefit to the New Jersey man in the example above to be able to save close to $5,000 by simply purchasing his policy in a different state.

More important than allowing purchase across state lines is the removal of all federal and state mandates from health-insurance policies. In a free society, people should be able to decide for themselves the coverage they require.

---

[58]   Should We Be Able To Buy Insurance Across State Lines? February 24th, 2010 by John Goodman

[59]   The Competition Cure, The Wall Street Journal Opinion Journal August 23, 2009 http://online.wsj.com/article/SB10001424052970203550604574360923109310680.html

For example: If a policy holder wants a high-deductible policy for catastrophic coverage only, WITHOUT coverage for office visits, prescription drugs, counseling, physicals, preventative care, pregnancies, dental, optometric, etc., let him buy a scaled-down policy at a greatly discounted price. He can choose to pay out-of-pocket for his routine needs and rely on his insurance for catastrophes only.

Conversely, if the same policyholder wants COMPLETE coverage with a low deductible, let him purchase an appropriate policy for that. It will be much more expensive, but will satisfy the desires of the purchaser. Currently, the state or federal governments determine the policy requirements, convoluting personal liberty and eliminating free-market controls.

Obama Care does nothing to remove governmental mandates, nor does it encourage greater choice and competition. It does exactly the opposite by dramatically increasing federal mandates, driving up costs, and limiting choice. It should be repealed.

Problem: Excessive Legal Costs Related to Health Care

Headline: *"CBO Underestimates Benefits of Malpractice Reform"*[60]

According to the Pacific Research Institute, medical-malpractice spending exceeds $240 BILLION per year—over 10% of total U.S. health-care spending.

Every year, close to 25% of all doctors are sued for medical malpractice. 90% of these doctors are found innocent, but they're still required to defend themselves in court, with the cost averaging $100,000 per defense—regardless of whether they are innocent or guilty.

Fear of lawsuits forces doctors to practice defensive medicine, meaning they order unnecessary tests, referrals, and procedures to protect themselves against allegations of medical negligence. Rather than analyzing each situation and prescribing the best care, doctors are aware that any patient may sue them at any time, and regularly order excessive, defensive procedures—not for the benefit of the patient—but solely to protect themselves in case of a lawsuit.

Medicine is not an exact science. People access the health-care system for help with a problem. The great majority of medical professionals try to analyze each patient's needs correctly and prescribe the best solution, but nothing is 100% certain. Recommended procedures are often assigned a certain success percentage, and prescription drugs more often than not have serious side effects. Listen to any drug commercial on TV. It seems as if half of the commercial addresses possible side effects from taking the advertised drug. As in any aspect of life, is it the duty of the individual to gather information and take personal responsibility for their care. If a patient is in doubt as to the diagnosis, benefits, or risks, it is that patient's (or the family's) responsibility to secure a second opinion until all the questions are answered.

---

[60] LAWRENCE J. MCQUILLAN; OCTOBER 23, 2009, CBO Underestimates Benefits of Malpractice Reform http://online.wsj.com/article/SB10001424052748703573604574491690229571588.html

---

Plaintiff lawyers have conditioned many in our society to transfer responsibility away from self to somebody—anybody—else. If a procedure doesn't produce the desired results, or if the individual happens to experience one of the possible side effects, too often, the societal solution is to sue the health provider rather than to accept personal responsibility. It now seems that health providers must guarantee success or risk being sued.

Plaintiff lawyers earn their fees by collecting a percentage of the settlement obtained on behalf of their clients. It's in the best interest of the plaintiff lawyers to file as many cases against as many individuals as possible. They will win their valid cases, but more importantly, they will receive possible settlements from innocent doctors whose malpractice-insurance companies find it more economical to pay a settlement than to expend the $100,000 average for defense costs.

What is the solution? Like all professionals, a small minority of doctors are negligent and deserve to be sued based on gross incompetence. I do not want to discourage these lawsuits, but the nuisance suits brought against the 90% of the innocent doctors must be discouraged.

In my opinion, a proper free-market solution would consist of requiring the loser of the lawsuit to pay the legal costs of the winner. As it now stands the defense overwhelmingly pays for the entire cost of litigation, but the plaintiff never reimburses the innocent defendants for legal costs they were forced to incur[61].

If the loser, plaintiff or defendant, were forced to pay all costs, the plaintiff lawyers would not find it economically feasible to use the shotgun approach of suing multiple defendants. For example, plaintiff lawyers would be greatly discouraged from suing the city, ambulance crew, fire department, hospital, doctor, drug providers, nurses, etc., hoping to extract a settlement from one or more of the targeted

---

[61] Plaintiff lawyers typically do not charge their clients legal fees when unsuccessful, but charge a significant percentage of the settlement when successful. Since the defense must pay their own legal costs, as well as the settlement, the defense in effect pay all legal costs incurred in litigation.

defendants. In this example, as it stands now, the seven defendants could be forced to spend close to $700,000 (using the $100,000 average defense cost), whereas the plaintiff attorney would invest only their time. If the loser is required to pay, a valid lawsuit will be directed against the responsible individual. A truly guilty individual will have incentive to settle out of court rather than pay all the legal costs of all of the parties. An innocent individual will have incentive to defend himself if he has confidence that his defense costs will be reimbursed.

Obama Care does nothing to address the problem of excessive medical malpractice costs. The problems resulting from the implementation of Obama Care—rationing, lack of effective drugs or equipment, delays, costs, etc. will be blamed on the health professional rather than on the underlying government policies. Under the current medical-malpractice system, doctors will likely continue to be sued—not only driving up the cost of health care, but also driving conscientious professionals out of the health-care business.

The health-care overhaul must encourage free-market principles within the legal system rather than continuing to encourage frivolous lawsuits against health-care professionals.

Solution: Free Market Principles

The United States is at a crossroads of its existence—fighting for its lifeblood. On one side are those who believe in personal liberty and a government held to constitutionally enumerated powers. On the other side are those who believe that individuals are incompetent to provide for themselves, and that it's government's role to provide for their needs. They see the Constitution as a "living" document whose meaning and powers change based on motives and desires of those in power.

The path we choose will determine whether the people of this great nation will remain proud and free, or subjected and dependent. I choose the former.

The health-care debate represents a *"line in the sand"* from which we cannot retreat. **The federal health care bill must be repealed!**

Proponents of government-run health care believe the free market is flawed, and that decisions by governmental bureaucrats and politicians are fairer. The truth is just the opposite.

A free market naturally provides needed goods and services to society at a fair price. Higher-quality products naturally force the obsolescence of lower-quality ones. Examples abound. Look at cell phones versus landlines or record players versus iPods. The same applies to health care. In a free market, producers and providers have incentive to develop cutting-edge products, technology, and procedures, offering the best solutions to our health-care problems.

Government intervention in the free market stifles the quality of goods and services by decreasing reward for risk and innovation. The greater the government intervention, the lower the quality of goods and services provided. Look at the quality of health care in countries with government-provided health care—Russia, Canada, and England, among others. These governments are concerned primarily with the accumulation of power, then with controlling costs, and lastly with providing basic health care to the masses.

Bureaucrats in government decide which procedures are allowed and how much they, the government, will pay for those procedures. Cutting-edge technology, which is normally expensive until it becomes main stream, is discouraged. In vain attempts to decrease costs, government imposes price controls and unfunded mandates on insurers and health-care providers. Rather than simply accepting these mandates, many professionals leave the market. The resulting shortage of personnel results in excessive wait times, a lower quality of service, and increased costs. The only solution available, after the government has caused these shortages, is the forced imposition of government-rationed health care.

This scenario is fact—not fiction. Consider that world leaders from controlled countries routinely travel to the U.S. for surgeries that aren't available in their countries.[62] Another more disgusting proof is the fact that that our Congress specifically exempted themselves and their staffs from the terms and conditions of the health-care bill being forced upon the rest of the nation.

Let's look at the current state of government-managed health care. Forty-five percent of health-care costs are paid through government programs, including Medicare and Medicaid.[63] Medicare is expected to be bankrupt by 2017,[64] possibly sooner if the government-induced economic downturn continues.

---

[62]   Newfoundland Premier Danny Williams set to have heart surgery in U.S. "Mr. Williams' decision to leave Canada for the surgery has raised eyebrows over his apparent shunning of Canada's health-care system." http://www.nationalpost.com/news/story.html?id=2510700#ixzz11gtV0pah

[63]   Senior Market Advisor, Published 5/13/2008; Medicare assets and expenditures
http://www.seniormarketadvisor.com/Exclusives/2008/5/Pages/-Medicare-assets-and-expenditures.aspx

[64]   Health Point pa, published May 14, 2009, Reports Kaiser Network News: http://www.healthpointpa.com/archives/medicare-trustees-say-the-fund-is-on-its-way-to-bankruptcy-by-2017/

Medicaid represents a huge drain on most state budgets. It's the largest single source of health-care coverage in the nation, covering low-income individuals. In order to limit costs, many states have lowered payments to health-care providers, resulting in the providers not being able to meet their costs. Many are opting out of the system, rather than losing money on each patient. The end result is that the quality of care provided to the Medicaid recipients is decreasing.

The only solution to the current health-care problem is the reintroduction of free-market principles. Any program adopted by government must address the following:

1. **Removal of the federal government as the provider and payee of health care.** Aside from the fact that there is no constitutional authority for the federal government to assume control of the system, the government has a history of implementing programs based on the accumulation of political power rather than on the realistic expectation of beneficial results. Social Security and Medicare are broke. Since the implementation of the Department of Education, U.S. students' test scores have plummeted compared to world standards. Since the creation of the Department of Energy, our domestic production of energy has dwindled. Do we want the same political blundering to destroy our health-care system? I don't.

2. **Illegal immigrants are an immense drain on the health-care system and the issue must be addressed.** I would suggest several procedures:

   a. If an illegal alien is admitted for care, their condition should be stabilized, and then the illegal should be taken into custody and deported.
   b. The interpretation of the 14th Amendment must be clarified, so that infants born to illegal immigrants in the United States are not automatically granted citizenship. The Amendment states specifically that you must be under the jurisdiction of the United States in order to be able

to grant citizenship to your offspring. [65] Illegal immigrants are not under the jurisdiction of the United States in that they have no visa, or permission to enter; they are criminals with no authority to grant citizenship to their progeny. They should be punished and discouraged rather than rewarded with citizenship.

c. If health care is provided to an illegal immigrant, that individual, or their family, should be held accountable for the charges—just like any U.S. citizen is held accountable. *(These fees will probably never be collected, but they will be on the record. If the responsible individual, or members of their families, ever try to immigrate to the U.S. legally, then the payment of this debt should be repaid prior to acceptance for immigration.)*

3. **Any reform must provide incentive for the patient to scrutinize costs—as is done in every other aspect of a free economy.** When a third party—such as the government, employer, or insurance company, purchases goods or services on behalf of others, there is no incentive for the patient to scrutinize costs. As far as the patient is concerned, it's free.

Remove the tax disincentives which discourage the purchase of health care by the individual. When selling directly to the consumer, numerous free market incentives could be offered to lower costs and ultimately decrease health care premiums.

4. **Health-care reform must control nuisance or frivolous lawsuits against health-care providers.** Fear of lawsuits forces doctors to practice defensive medicine, meaning they order unnecessary tests, referrals, and procedures to protect themselves against allegations of medical negligence. Plaintiff lawyers earn their fee by collecting a percentage of the settlement obtained on behalf of their clients. It's in the best interest of the plaintiff lawyers to file as many cases against as

---

[65] 14th Amendment to the US Constitution: "All persons born or naturalized in the United States, and subject to the jurisdiction thereof, are citizens of the United States and of the State wherein they reside."

many individuals as possible. They will win their valid cases, but more importantly, they will receive possible settlements from innocent doctors whose malpractice-insurance companies find it more economical to pay a settlement rather than expending the $100,000 average for defense costs. A simple solution to this problem lies in requiring the loser of a lawsuit to pay the attorney fees of the winner.

5. **Eliminate governmental mandates.** Government mandates have morphed health insurance into pre-paid health care. Government mandates often require insurers to cover costs for procedures such as office visits, prescription drugs, counseling, prenatal care, etc. How has government been granted this authority? It never was. Any health-care reform must allow the consumer to purchase the health insurance provisions they desire, not the provisions the government mandates.

6. **Allow the free market to address the health-care needs of society.** The free market will provide vastly superior care to those able to pay for it. Those in need must rely on charity from others—just as they do now; but the care should be provided as voluntary, free-market charity, rather than through government-imposed programs. The people of the United States are the most charitable in the world and will take care of the indigent voluntarily. Absent government involvement, voluntary charitable organizations would abound to care for the indigent. The Shriner's Hospitals are an example of this type of generosity.

Without government interference in all matters related to health care, options would blossom, from the unfettered ingenuity of a free people, to meet all the needs of society. For example, medical schools may find it in their best interest to offer free or low-cost, clinics to serve the routine needs of the local community. The clinic could be staffed by senior-level medical students and supervised by professors. Not only would it provide routine care to those in need, but it would also provide the students with invaluable experience in providing health care.

To adequately address the health care requirements of the nation we must work to repeal Obama Care, remove federal influence, and allow the people, in conjunction with the doctors of their choice, to implement the best solutions to their health care needs.

It's worked throughout history.

The last option we should implement is a government imposed solution to a government created problem.

Social Safety Net

Prosperity breeds compassion. The Unites States is a very prosperous and compassionate nation.

The people of the United States have willingly accepted the responsibility to support those in need. The question facing us today is, *"what is the best means of providing support for those in need—voluntary charity by individuals or community, or the forced federal redistribution of funds by the government?"*

Ever since Lyndon Johnson's introduction of the "War on Poverty," the rough percentage of U.S. citizens considered poor has remained relatively constant. We, as a nation, have transferred many trillions of dollars in the fight against poverty without making a significant difference.

The government establishes "means testing," meaning they look at the individual's income and social status (married, supporting children, etc.) to determine qualifications for benefits. Generally speaking, single individuals with little or no income receive the greatest benefit. Those responsible for children receive even more. The more kids, the more benefit.

The obvious consequences of this policy are the discouragement of marriage and the encouragement of out-of-wedlock births. Neither one of these consequences is beneficial for society. Married couples are generally more responsible for themselves and their families than single parents. In addition, an intact, two-parent household is generally much more beneficial for children than a single-parent household. Yet, it's much easier to qualify for benefits as a single person, so those desiring assistance from the government programs are economically discouraged from marriage. Greater benefits are also provided with more children. Therefore, single women with many children are rewarded with the most benefit.

Many recipients of governmental aid find it easier to remain on aid than to take the initiative to become self-sufficient. There is little incentive to work, since aid is cut as soon as income is earned. Children raised outside of a strong family structure are not exposed to family values and tend to lack personal responsibility and a solid work ethic. Many children follow their parent's example and become dependent on government aid.

Without the goal of self-sufficiency, the perceived need for education decreases. Many children receiving aid drop out of school. Without a job or education, they often find trouble and have a higher-than-average tendency toward crime and incarceration. An uneducated, unmotivated, self-perpetuating, angry dependent class evolves.

Government imposed safety net programs are a backward solution, the opposite of what responsible individuals would do, possibly implemented with noble motives, but resulting in great destruction to society—especially those they were supposed to help.

If government aid isn't the solution, what is?

As in every aspect of a free society, the solution lies with the people themselves.

Without government aid, people in need would naturally turn to family or friends. Nobody enjoys asking for help, yet the discomfort isn't necessarily bad. It's a motivating factor to solve problems and get back on your feet as quickly as possible. Family and friends will offer help as needed, but will likely expect the recipient of their charity to make a good-faith effort to better himself.

Family and friends will not encourage the dissolution of marriage. On the contrary, they'll probably offer encouragement to keep the union together through tough times. They will not encourage out-of-wedlock births or support promiscuity. Family and friends will encourage recipients of charity to act responsibly and better themselves. If the appropriate effort is not exerted, then the voluntary charity will most likely be terminated.

What happens without family and friends? Then you look to the community. Virtually every church in the United States will offer support and assistance to those in need. Like family and friends, churches will encourage the family to remain intact through tough times. They will not encourage out-of-wedlock birth, and will offer the needed support and encouragement to overcome the difficulties as quickly as possible.

Other community-based support comes from organizations such as the Salvation Army, YMCA, charitable food kitchens, and charitable food banks.

The differences between government and community support are stark.

Government support encourages the breakdown of families and the establishment of a long-term dependent class. It's not theory; it's demonstrable. Look at the social destruction found in virtually any city supporting a population dependent on government. Detroit is a prime example of a once-great city decimated by governmental social programs. Inner cities are not the only problem, the same thing is happening in the suburbs and rural communities being inundated with government support.

Community support, consisting of family, friends, churches, and local charitable organizations, encourage success for those in need. It's based on morality, personal-responsibility, and self-respect. Voluntary support from family, friends, or local charitable organizations tends to develop and maintain strong communities.

Providing a safety net for those in need is important for any society. The question is how best to provide for those in need. The provision of voluntary charity by caring individuals is far superior to the government's forced redistribution of wealth.

Federal Unemployment Benefits

I realize it's a difficult situation when a person loses a job. That being said, what is the proper response and role of the federal government in dealing with unemployment, and how does that contrast with the role and responsibility of the individual?

Sporadic, unexpected, unemployment is a natural byproduct of any economic system, and most people, at some point in their lives, already have, or will, involuntarily lose a job.

What would be the response by the individual to a job loss if there were no government-sponsored unemployment compensation?

The individual would become aware that they are responsible for themselves. They would observe how others in the community prepared for and reacted to unexpected unemployment and they would act accordingly.

Employees would probably have a greater appreciation of the job that provides a livelihood for themselves and their families. They would probably, either consciously or unconsciously, strive to provide the best possible service for their employer in order to keep their company successful and retain their jobs.

Realizing that they are responsible for themselves and their families, people would have a tendency to save money for the proverbial rainy day rather than spending excess funds on appealing, but unnecessary, consumer goods.

If a job is lost, the unemployed would immediately start looking for alternative employment to provide for themselves and their families—even if it is outside their area of expertise or at what they consider a lower level of status than they desire. If necessary, they could work multiple jobs to provide for the needs of themselves and their families until their optimal employment is secured.

Personal expenses would be cut as much as possible, allowing the unemployed to survive on as little money as possible.

If a job could not be found, the unemployed could rely on voluntary charity from family, friends, and the community until employment and self-sufficiency is attained.

Providers of voluntary charity would likely hold the recipient responsible. If the recipient were acting in a way the providers considered irresponsible, the voluntary charity would most likely be terminated.

How would the free market respond if no government-sponsored unemployment compensation existed?

The genius of the free market is its ability to provide solutions that satisfy society's needs in an efficient and cost-effective manner.

If the need existed, insurance companies would provide consumers the option to purchase private unemployment insurance as a stopgap measure between jobs. Free market competition would provide different options and terms based on the desires of the policy holder. A barebones policy would probably be relatively inexpensive, with the cost of the policy increasing relative to the benefits provided. Regardless, the cost would be much less expensive than state sponsored insurance since there would be much less of a tendency of the recipient to take advantage of the system. Those desiring to provide for themselves could forgo this expenditure and rely on their accumulated savings to meet their needs while looking for another job.

Trade unions or employers could voluntarily design and offer unemployment or termination packages as an incentive to attract new members or quality employees.

For those desiring to provide voluntary aid to the unemployed:

- Money could be raised for a private unemployment foundation—similar to that being done by the Shriners hospitals for children.
- There are many private, charitable organizations advertising for voluntary donations to causes such as "Save the Children" throughout the world. For those desiring to help the unemployed, the same type of fundraising and distribution programs could be established.
- Most churches already have community-outreach and support programs that help the unemployed. These programs are often ignored due to the ease of receiving a government benefit. Elimination of the government benefit would encourage the utilization of church-based programs, which would tend to uplift the moral character of society.

What is the responsibility of the state in dealing with unemployment?

According to the 10th Amendment, the responsibility for unemployment falls to the states or to the people themselves.

If the citizens of a state desire, the individual states could implement unemployment compensation programs to address the needs of the citizenry. State programs could span from zero involvement—relying totally on personal responsibility and voluntary charity, a workfare-type program where benefits are paid in exchange for state-mandated labor, or to programs that provide a direct cash benefit without work or responsibility requirements.

States with efficient programs would attract industry and develop a strong economic and tax base, whereas states with inefficient programs would discourage economic development and lose tax revenue. States with inefficient programs would have great incentive to improve and emulate successful, proven solutions.

What happens when the federal government provides unemployment benefits?

The federal government has no money of its own. Any benefit provided by the government has been forcibly extorted from yourself, your neighbors, and your friends, under penalty of incarceration for non-compliance.

The federal government is a huge bureaucracy that has no real incentive to help the unemployed. As unemployment decreases, the bureaucrats charged with dispensing benefits lose power. They establish requirements, and if you meet these criteria you receive benefits. Often the criterion are broadened to allow for additional recipients, such as those voluntarily becoming unemployed, or to extend the length of time benefits may be received.

Most people receiving unemployment are good, responsible people appreciative of the benefits they receive, yet a significant percentage of recipients are freeloaders, manipulating the system for their personal advantage.

Responsible people, through the receiving of benefits, are gradually conditioned to expect the government to take care of them in time of need. They lose a sense of personal responsibility for themselves and their families and tend to become dependent on government. They're conditioned to accept as normal that government will provide for their needs, and tend to lose the understanding of personal responsibility.

Unsavory politicians understand this dependency and try to cultivate it. The more dependent a society becomes on government, the more power and control the government has over its citizenry.

Many unemployed become accustomed to unearned benefits and postpone searching for employment until their benefits expire. Once the benefits expire, they tend either to manipulate the system to gain additional benefits, or to take the initiative to look for employment.

There is no constitutionally enumerated power granting the federal government authority to pay unemployment benefits—to forcibly transfer wealth from those who earn it to those who do not.

A free country must ask what is best for society—to naturally encourage a sense of personal responsibility along with the reinforcement of family and community ties, or to subtly and persistently discourage personal responsibility, break down family and community ties, and promote a dependence on government.

The answer is obvious. The development and expectation of personal responsibility is far better for the individual, community, state, and country than is dependence on government. Our founders, along with the people and states that ratified the Constitution, knew this to be the case when they omitted government charity from the enumerated powers. There has been, and always will be, some level of unemployment. If left alone, the transitory period is short, and the individual is again gainfully employed.

The federal government should have nothing to do with unemployment compensation and these federal programs should be phased out. In a free society, charity is provided voluntarily by the community, free market, and lastly the state, if the people want government oversight, but never by a centralized federal government.

Social Security: Fixing a Broken Program

Social Security is a program, possibly founded upon good intentions, that is grossly and continually mismanaged by Washington politicians. With good reason, there is no enumerated power in the Constitution granting the federal government authority to impose and manage a centralized retirement system, but the government did it anyway. Regardless of the intentions, the end result is a vast expansion of federal authority through the forced dependence of the elderly on government for their retirement security.

Social Security pays benefits from Social Security taxes collected. It was able to sustain itself when 16 taxpayers supported each retiree, but today, only three taxpayers support each recipient. In a few years, this ratio will drop further, and the remaining taxpayers will not be able to support the burden—driving Social Security to financial ruin.

To its credit, the government foresaw this problem in the 1980's and significantly raised Social Security taxes to stockpile money for future benefits. Yet, due to political greed and incompetence, government regulations forbade the creation of an actual trust account into which the stockpiled cash could be deposited. Instead, it was mingled with other government revenue, and immediately squandered on pet political projects. The government provided IOU's acknowledging receipt of the money, but had no reserve from which to pay it back.

A similar situation occurred in the movie "Dumb and Dumber." Two broke individuals, with good intentions, acquire a suitcase full of money. Needless to say, they waste it all through binge spending, but acting "responsibly," provide IOUs for each withdrawal. When it comes time to account, there's no money—only a handful of worthless IOU's. Our government has done the exact same thing. Congress has already spent the accumulated excess. The pending, catastrophic shortfall is postponed only by unfunded IOU's. If a private corporation accounted for retirement funds as our government has, the principals would be in prison.

If the overall goal is to allow individuals to fund their retirement, then private enterprise offers the solution.

In 1981, the Social Security Administration allowed municipalities to opt-out of the Social Security system. Galveston, Texas took advantage of this opportunity and implemented a private plan—totally outside the scope of the federal government.

They designed a program with three goals:

1. To provide better retirement benefits then Social Security,
2. To require no increase in withholding tax, and
3. To be risk free.

Furthermore, they wanted benefits to be like a bank account, which could be passed on to family members upon the account holder's death.

The goals were met. An equivalent retirement deduction was withheld from each employee's check and deposited into their own retirement account. This money was invested in secure, risk-free, annuities protecting the program from the fluctuations of the stock market. After 30 years the program exceeded all expectations, providing benefits up to 300% greater than Social Security.[66]

A similar private-sector solution was implemented in the country of Chile, transforming their destitute, pay-as-you-go, government-run Social Security system into a successful, secure, fully funded, privatized system.[67] We can implement the same type of program with equal or better results in this country.

---

[66] National Center for Policy Analysis: Galveston County: A Model for Social Security Reform http://www.ncpa.org/pub/ba514

[67] CATO Policy Report: The Success of Chile's Privatized Social Security; http://www.cato.org/pubs/policy_report/pr-ja-jp.html

We're faced with the choice of either trying to fix our failed government system or implementing the types of proven, free-market solutions demonstrated to work in Galveston and Chile.

I believe that Social Security must be transitioned away from government control to the private sector—with the understanding that government is obligated to honor its commitment to those who are currently retired and receiving benefits, and to those currently working and paying into the system.

My proposal for addressing Social Security reform is as follows:

1. The federal government has an obligation to provide benefits to all who have paid into the system. All currently retired individuals must continue to receive their full benefits from the federal government. Payroll taxes were forcibly extracted from their earnings, and government has a moral obligation to honor its commitment by providing the promised retirement benefit.

2. Those not yet entering the job market should have the opportunity to be responsible for their own retirement. As was demonstrated successful in both Galveston and Chile, they could invest in proven, successful, fully funded, private-sector retirement programs yielding a much higher return than Social Security. A competitive, private-sector retirement market will develop to satisfy this need just as it is now doing with the 401(k) programs.

3. Those currently working, but not yet having reached retirement age should have the choice to stay in the Social Security system, continue paying their payroll taxes to the government, and receive their promised benefit or to opt-out and invest their payroll taxes in a private-sector solution. Those who opt out of the Social Security system would forfeit any future Social Security benefits, but would have them replaced with higher-yield, private-sector benefits. Younger workers would probably find it to their advantage to opt out, while older workers would probably remain in the system.

4. Due to political incompetence, there is no Social Security Trust Fund, and the federal obligation must be funded from current revenue. Possible options for funding include:

   - Increase federal collections by cutting government regulation, allowing robust economic growth. Federal revenue doubled during Reagan's presidency once he cut repressive regulation and taxation. If the same policy is followed, the increased revenue should be used to pay the Social Security deficit.
   - Greatly increase energy royalties by allowing private energy companies to develop our domestic energy reserves and allow the United States to become energy independent.
   - Implement my One-Eight, One-Nine program and reshuffle spending away from non-constitutional programs—such as the Departments of Education, Energy, Health and Human Services, or Housing and Urban Development—to satisfy the Social Security obligation.

5. Once Social Security is transitioned to the private sector, the federal government must be prohibited from paying retirement benefits or supporting, in any fashion, individuals who have been negligent in providing for their own retirement. Individuals must be responsible for their own retirement or rely on voluntary charity from family or community.

Following these suggestions, the federal government's Social Security obligation would be completely phased-out over time, all obligations would be honored, and future generations would benefit with higher returns and greater flexibility.

Unfunded government obligations, consisting primarily of mandated Social Security and Medicare expenditures, are currently estimated at 100 trillion dollars, equating to over $300,000 for every man, woman, and child in the United States. Our generation accumulated this debt, and it is the responsibility of our generation to address it. This spending MUST be stopped, or else our nation will cease to exist. The United

States will fold under this crushing debt exactly as did the Soviet Union and Greece.

Aside from being a financial disaster, Social Security encourages the continued dependence of individuals on the federal government. When acting outside of its enumerated powers, the federal government largely consists of incompetent bureaucrats motivated by political power—with seemingly infinite access to *other people's money*. They do not act in our best interest and do not deserve our trust. Return retirement responsibility to the individual, who actually has a vested interest in ensuring it is handled competently.

Please read the following articles describing the success of privatized Social Security Systems.

The first article is written by Ray Holbrook and describes the Galveston system. The second article is written by José Piñera and describes the Chilean model.

Galveston County: A Model for Social Security Reform[68]

Tuesday, April 26, 2005 by Ray Holbrook and Alcestis "Cooky" Oberg

The current debate over Social Security reform is reminiscent of the discussions that occurred in Galveston County, Texas, in 1980, when county workers were offered a retirement alternative to Social Security: At the time they reacted with keen interest and some knee-jerk fear of the unknown. But after 24 years, folks here can say unequivocally that when Galveston County pulled out of the Social Security system in 1981, we were on the road to providing our workers with a better deal than Franklin Roosevelt's New Deal.

The Problem with Social Security. Social Security is a pay-as-you-go system under which taxes collected from today's workers are used to pay today's retirees. That was sustainable in the past; for example, in 1950 there were 16 workers providing benefits for each retiree. However, today the ratio has dropped to 3 workers for each retiree, and by the year 2030 the ratio will be 2 to 1.

America's demographic changes and the program's expansion have driven the initial Social Security tax rate from 2 percent (1 percent each from employer and employee) to 12.4 percent today, and threaten to drive it even higher. This unsustainable trend is why policy makers are looking for ways to reform the system.

One of the most prominent proposed reforms would allow younger workers to divert some of the payroll taxes they already pay to create personal retirement accounts. The burden on future taxpayers would decline as retirees draw retirement benefits from their personal accounts, reducing the demand for taxpayer-funded benefits. Current and near-retirees would be unaffected and would continue to receive currently scheduled benefits. But how should the new accounts be structured? Some point to Chile, Britain, Australia or one of almost 30

---

[68] National Center for Policy Analysis: Galveston County: A Model for Social Security Reform
http://www.ncpa.org/pub/ba514

Peter Konetchy

countries that have incorporated personal investments into their public pension programs. But there are examples much closer to home.

The initial Social Security Act permitted municipal governments to opt out of the system—a loophole that Congress closed in 1983. In 1981, employees of Galveston County, Texas, chose by a vote of 78 percent to 22 percent to leave Social Security for a private alternative. Brazoria and Matagorda counties soon followed, swelling the private plan to more than 5,000 participants today. In the private plan, contributions are similar to those for Social Security but returns are quite different.

The Galveston Plan. In 1979, many county workers were concerned about the soundness of Social Security, as many people are today. We could either stay with it—and its inevitable tax increases and higher retirement ages—or find a better way. We sought an "alternative plan" that provided the same or better benefits, required no tax increases and was risk-free. Furthermore, we wanted the benefits to be like a savings account that could be passed on to family members upon death.

Our plan, put together by financial experts, was a "banking model" rather than an "investment model." To eliminate the risks of the up-and-down stock market, workers' contributions were put into conservative fixed-rate guaranteed annuities, rather than fluctuating stocks, bonds or mutual funds. Our results have been impressive: We've averaged an annual rate of return of about 6.5 percent over 24 years. And we've provided substantially better benefits in all three Social Security categories: retirement, survivorship and disability.

Galveston officials held meetings that included debates with Social Security officials and put it to a vote: Galveston County employees passed it by a 3-to-1 margin in 1981—just in time.

The Galveston Plan was implemented just before the U.S. Congress passed a reform bill in 1983 that closed the door for local governments to opt out of Social Security.

To be sure, our plan wasn't perfect, and we have made some adjustments. For instance, a few of our retired county workers are critical of the plan today because they say they are making less money than they would have on Social Security. This is because our plan allowed workers to make "hardship" withdrawals from the retirement plan during their working years. Some workers withdrew funds for current financial problems and consequently robbed their own future benefits. We closed that option in January 2005.

Galveston vs. Social Security. Upon retirement after 30 years, and assuming a 5 percent rate of return—more conservative than Galveston workers have earned—all workers would do better for the same contribution as Social Security:

1. Workers making $17,000 a year are expected to receive about 50 percent more per month on our alternative plan than on Social Security—$1,036 instead of $683. [See the Figure.]
2. Workers making $26,000 a year will make almost double Social Security's return—$1,500 instead of $853.
3. Workers making $51,000 a year will get $3,103 instead of $1,368.
4. Workers making $75,000 or more will nearly triple Social Security—$4,540 instead of $1,645.
5. Galveston County's survivorship benefits pay four times a worker's annual salary—a minimum of $75,000 to a maximum $215,000—versus Social Security, which forces widows to wait until age 60 to qualify for benefits, or provides 75 percent of a worker's salary for school-age children.

In Galveston, if the worker dies before retirement, the survivors receive not only the full survivorship but get generous accidental death benefits, too. Galveston County's disability benefit also pays more: 60 percent of an individual's salary, better than Social Security's.

Two government studies of the Galveston Plan—by the Government Accountability Office and the Social Security Administration—claim that low-wage workers do better under Social Security. However, these studies assumed a low 4 percent return, which is the minimum rate of return on annuities guaranteed by the insurance companies. The actual returns have been substantially higher.

Guidance for Today's Reformers. Congress could consider making participation in any privatization plan voluntary at first. We made our plan voluntary in the beginning and 70 percent joined. It later became mandatory, and now there is full participation. Also, if some workers remain uncertain about investing a portion of their contributions, the plan could include a guarantee that low-income earners receive the same funds they would get with total participation in Social Security.

Our experience has shown that even though low-income workers would do better, a guarantee would ease their worries. Moderate—and higher-income workers would do much better, as ours do, because they have invested more in the plan and are not prejudicially punished or "topped out" on retirement benefits, as they are in Social Security.

In today's debate about whether to partially privatize Social Security, the Galveston County plan is sometimes demagogued. But our experience should be judged factually and fairly, not emotionally, politically or on the basis of hearsay. We sought a secure, risk-free alternative to the Social Security system, and it has worked very well for nearly a quarter-century. Our retirees have prospered, and our working people have had the security of generous disability and accidental death benefits.

Most important, we didn't force our children and grandchildren to be unduly taxed and burdened for our retirement while these fine young people are struggling to raise and provide for their own families.

What has been good for Galveston County may, indeed, be good for this country.

> *Judge Ray Holbrook was Galveston County judge from 1967 to 1995, and oversaw the creation and administration of the Galveston County alternative plan. Alcestis "Cooky" Oberg is on USA Today's board of contributors.*

The Success of Chile's Privatized Social Security [69]

by José Piñera

> *José Piñera, who as Chile's minister of labor privatized the state pension system, is president of the International Center for Pension Reform and co-chairman of the Cato Institute's Project on Social Security Privatization.*

It's an honor for me to share with you some of the experiences we have had in Chile with our new private pension system. I would like to comment on how the new system works, how we were able to make the transition from the old system to the new one, and what have been the main economic, social, and political consequences of the new system. I will not explain the shortcomings of the old pay-as-you-go system in Chile. Those shortcomings are very well known because that is the system that is failing all over the world.

In Chile we accomplished a revolutionary reform. We knew that cosmetic changes—increasing the retirement age, increasing taxes—would not be enough. We understood that the pay-as-you-go system had a fundamental flaw, one rooted in a false conception of how human beings behave. That flaw was lack of a link between what people put into their pension program and what they take out. In a government system, contributions and benefits are unrelated because they are defined politically, by the power of pressure groups.

So we decided to go in the other direction, to link benefits to contributions. The money that a worker pays into the system goes into an account that is owned by the worker. We called the idea a "capitalization scheme."

We decided that the minimum contribution should be 10 percent of wages. But workers may contribute up to 20 percent. The money contributed is deducted from the worker's taxable income. The money

---

[69] The Success of Chile's Privatized Social Security http://www.cato.org/pubs/policy_report/pr-ja-jp.html; 11/4/2011

is invested by a private institution, and the returns are untaxed. By the time a worker reaches retirement age—65 for men, 60 for women—a sizable sum of capital has accumulated in the account. At retirement the worker transforms that lump sum into an annuity with an insurance company. He can shop among different insurance companies to find the plan that best suits his personal and family situation. (He pays taxes when the money is withdrawn but usually at a lower rate than he would have paid when he was working.)

As I said, a worker can contribute more than 10 percent if he wants a higher pension or if he wants to retire early. Individuals have different preferences: some want to work until they are 85; others want to go fishing at 55, or 50, or 45, if they can. The uniform pay-as-you-go social security system does not recognize differences in individual preferences. In my country, those differences had led to pressure on the congress to legislate different retirement ages for different groups. As a result, we had a discriminatory retirement-age system. Blue-collar workers could retire at 65; white-collar workers could retire more or less at 55; bank employees could retire after 25 years of work; and the most powerful group of all, those who make the laws, the congressmen, were able to retire after 15 years of work.

Under our new system, you don't have to pressure anyone. If you want to retire at 55, you go to one of the pension-fund companies and sit in front of a user-friendly computer. It asks you at what age you want to retire. You answer 55. The computer then does some calculations and says that you must contribute 12.1 percent of your income to carry out your plan. You then go back to your employer and instruct him to deduct the appropriate amount. Workers thus translate their personal preferences into tailored pension plans. If a worker's pension savings are not enough at the legal retirement age, the government makes up the difference from general tax revenue.

The system is managed by competitive private companies called AFPs (from the Spanish for pension fund administrators). Each AFP operates the equivalent of a mutual fund that invests in stocks, bonds, and government debt. The AFP is separate from the mutual fund; so if the AFP goes bankrupt, the assets of the mutual fund—that is, workers' investments—are not affected. The regulatory board takes over the fund and asks the workers to change to another AFP. Not a dime of the workers' money is touched in the process. Workers are free to change from one AFP to another. That creates competition among the companies to provide a higher return on investment and better customer service, or to charge lower commissions.

The AFP market opened on May 1, 1981, which is Labor Day in Chile and most of the world. It was supposed to open May 4, but I made a last-minute change to May 1. When my colleagues asked why, I explained that May 1 had always been celebrated all over the world as a day of class confrontation, when workers fight employers as if their interests were completely divergent. But in a free-market economy, their interests are convergent. "Let's begin this system on May 1," I said, "so that in the future, Labor Day can be celebrated as a day when workers freed themselves from the state and moved to a privately managed capitalization system." That's what we did.

Today we have 20 AFPs. In 14 years no AFP has gone bankrupt. Workers have not lost a dime. Of course, we created a regulatory body that, along with the central bank, set some investment diversification rules. Funds cannot invest more than x percent in government bonds, y percent in private companies' debentures, or z percent in common stocks. Nor can more than a specified amount be in the stock of any given company, and all companies in which funds are invested must have credit ratings above a given level.

We set up such transitional rules with a bias for safety because our plan was to be radical (even revolutionary) in approach but conservative and prudent in execution. We trust the private sector, but we are not naive. We knew that there were companies that might invest in derivatives and lose a lot of money. We didn't want the pension funds investing workers' money in derivatives in Singapore. If the system had failed in the first years, we would never have been able to try it again. So we set strict rules 14 years ago, but we are relaxing those rules. For example, only three years ago we began to allow the funds to invest abroad, which they weren't allowed to do initially, because Chilean institutions had no experience in investing abroad. The day will come when the rules will be much more flexible.

Let me say something about the transition to the new system. We began by assuring every retired worker that the state would guarantee his pension; he had absolutely nothing to fear from the change. Pension reform should not damage those who have contributed all their lives. If that takes a constitutional amendment, so be it.

Second, the workers already in the workforce, who had contributed to the state system, were given the option of staying in the system even though we thought its future was problematic. Those who moved to the new system received what we call a "recognition bond," which acknowledges their contributions to the old system. When those workers retire, the government will cash the bonds.

New workers have to go into the new private system because the old system is bankrupt. Thus, the old system will inevitably die on the day that the last person who entered that system passes away. On that day the government will have no pension system whatsoever. The private system is not a complementary system; it is a replacement that we believe is more efficient.

The real transition cost of the system is the money the government ceases to obtain from the workers who moved to the new system, because the government is committed to pay the pensions of the people already retired and of those who will retire in the future. That transition cost can be calculated. In Chile it was around 3 percent of gross national product. How we financed it is another story. It will be done differently in each country. Suffice it to say that even though governments have enormous pension liabilities, they also have enormous assets. In Chile we had state-owned enterprises. In America I understand that the federal government owns a third of the land. I don't know why the government owns land, and I don't know the value. Nor am I saying that you should sell the land tomorrow. What I am saying is that when you consider privatizing Social Security, you must look at assets as well as liabilities. I am sure that the U.S. government has gigantic assets. Are they more or less than the liabilities of the Social

Security system? I don't know, but the Cato project on privatizing Social Security will study that. In Chile we calculated the real balance sheet and, knowing there were enough assets, financed the transition without raising tax rates, generating inflation, or pressuring interest rates upward. In the last several years we have had a fiscal surplus of 1 to 2 percent of GNP.

The main goal and consequence of the pension reform is to improve the lot of workers during their old age. As I will explain, the reform has a lot of side effects: savings, growth, capital markets. But we should never forget that the reform was enacted to assure workers decent pensions so that they can enjoy their old age in tranquility. That goal has been met already. After 14 years and because of compound interest, the system is paying old-age pensions that are 40 to 50 percent higher than those paid under the old system. (In the case of disability and survivor pensions, another privatized insurance, pensions are 70 to 100 percent higher than under the old system.) We are extremely happy.

But there have been other enormous effects. A second—and, to me, extremely important—one is that the new system reduces what can be called the payroll tax on labor. The social security contribution was seen by workers and employers as basically a tax on the use of labor; and a tax on the use of labor reduces employment. But a contribution to an individual's pension account is not seen as a tax on the use of labor. Unemployment in Chile is less than 5 percent. And that is without disguised unemployment in the federal government. We are approaching what could be called full employment in Chile. That's very different from a country like Spain, with a socialist government for the last 12 years, that has an unemployment rate of 24 percent and a youth unemployment rate of 40 percent.

Chile's private pension system has been the main factor in increasing the savings rate to the level of an Asian tiger. Our rate is 26 percent of GNP, compared to about 15 percent in Latin America. The Asian tigers are at 30 percent. The dramatic increase in the savings rate is the main reason that Chile is not suffering from the so-called tequila effect that plagues Mexico. We do not depend on short-run capital flows because we have an enormous pool of internal savings to finance our investment strategies. Chile will grow by about 6 percent of GNP this year, the year of the "tequila effect." The stock exchange has gone down by only 1 or 2 percent and will be higher at the end of the year. Chile has been isolated from short-run capital movement because its development is basically rooted in a high savings rate.

Pension reform has contributed strongly to an increase in the rate of economic growth. Before the 1970s Chile had a real growth rate of 3.5 percent. For the last 10 years we have been growing at the rate of 7 percent, double our historic rate. That is the most powerful means of eliminating poverty because growth increases employment and wages. Several experts have attributed the doubling of the growth rate to the private pension system.

Finally, the private pension system has had a very important political and cultural consequence. Ninety percent of Chile's workers chose to move into the new system. They moved faster than Germans going from East to West after the fall of the Berlin Wall. Those workers freely decided to abandon the state system, even though some of the trade-union leaders and the old political class advised against it. But workers are able to make wise decisions on matters close to their lives, such as pensions, education, and health. That's why I believe so much in their freedom to choose.

Every Chilean worker knows that he is the owner of an individual pension account. We have calculated that the typical Chilean worker's main asset is not his small house or his used car but the capital in his pension account. The Chilean worker is an owner, a capitalist. There is no more powerful way to stabilize a free-market economy and to get the support of the workers than to link them directly to the benefits of the market economy. When Chile grows at 7 percent or when the stock market doubles—as it has done in the last three years—Chilean workers benefit directly, not only through higher wages, not only through more employment, but through additional capital in their individual pension accounts.

Private pensions are undoubtedly creating cultural change. When workers feel that they own a fraction of a country, not through the party bosses, not through a politburo (like the Russians thought), but through ownership of part of the financial assets of the country, they are much more attached to the free market, a free society, and democracy.

By taking politicians out of the social security business we have done them a great favor because they can now focus on what they should do: stop crime, run a good justice system, manage foreign affairs—the real duties of a government. By removing the government from social security, we have accomplished the biggest privatization in Chilean history—someone even called it, paraphrasing Saddam Hussein, the mother of all privatizations, because it has allowed us to go on to privatize the energy and telecommunications companies.

That has been our experience. Of course, there have been some mistakes. There are some things that should be improved. There is no perfect reform. With time and experience, I know I would do some things differently. But on the whole, I can tell you that it has been a success beyond all our dreams.

The Success of Chile's Privatized Social Security http://www.cato.org/pubs/policy_report/pr-ja-jp.html; 11/4/2011

Immigration

Can the United States survive as a nation with an open-borders policy?

Think of the nation as your own home. Would you allow an intruder to enter your home without your permission, eat your food, sleep in your bed, use your possessions, and possibly do your family harm? Of course not. People secure their homes and arm themselves to protect their families from harm and their possessions from being stolen.

It's a completely different situation when you invite guests into your home, voluntarily provide them with room, board, and supply all their needs until they're able to do so themselves.

These same concepts apply to our nation. Legal immigrants enter our country as our guests, have a sponsor to provide for their needs, and seek to assimilate into our culture. On the other hand, illegal immigrants sneak into our country without permission, often without any means of support, forcing law abiding taxpayers to spend untold billions on their care and sustenance. Being illegal, they tend to shy away from interacting into our society, learning English, or actively striving to assimilate into our culture.

Illegal immigrants are not harmless individuals simply trying to improve their lives any more than bank robbers are harmless individuals simply short on cash. Both are criminals, and both are destructive to society.

Illegal immigrants impose a significant burden on society. The emergency rooms of many hospitals are overflowing with illegal immigrants demanding health care without paying for the services they receive; social-service programs are burdened by providing housing and support; public schools are forced to accommodate the children of illegals; and law enforcement agencies must often allocate an inordinate amount of their resources to address illegal immigrant crime.

The current open-borders policy has turned the lower third of Arizona into a virtual no-man's land often populated by roving bands of armed drug dealers and human traffickers. Rather than controlling the borders, the federal solution is to erect billboards warning U.S. citizens that this portion of our sovereign nation is unsafe due to these roving thugs.

We must stop the flow of illegal immigrants into our country while encouraging quality individuals desiring to immigrate legally.

Legal Immigration is a win-win situation for both the immigrant and the United States. All immigrants desiring to enter our country should be prescreened to make sure they satisfy the following criteria:

1. Have an overwhelming desire to assimilate into our culture and become productive citizens of the United States; to embrace the uniquely American values of liberty, personal responsibility, and self-determination; and be willing to learn, read, and speak English when interacting in society.

2. Possess a talent or ability beneficial to our society.

3. Have a sponsor, a current US citizen in good standing, able to provide housing and support for the immigrant until he becomes self-sufficient. It is highly improper for the United States taxpayers to be required to support immigrants to this country.

4. Be in good health and of high moral character.

Why do we have such an extensive illegal immigrant problem?

The simple answer is that our elected representatives lack the fortitude and leadership to confront the illegal immigration problem and instead, encourage it.

Our borders are porous; law enforcement is prohibited from addressing or confronting the illegal immigrant problem; more than a few locally elected officials provide sanctuary cities, encouraging illegal immigration; and illegal immigrants are able to secure taxpayer-funded social services and financial benefits.

To top it all off, unscrupulous politicians view an uneducated, dependent, illegal-immigrant population as a potential voting bloc, providing them with the additional votes required to maintain power.

As a country, how can we stop illegal immigration?

We must to decide if we want to control our borders or not. The politicians in Washington are either fearful of taking a stand, or view illegals as a source of political power, and have no desire to stop illegal immigration. Conversely, the great majority of the people understand the threat and want illegal immigration stopped.

What policies can be enacted to reverse Illegal Immigration?

- Elections count. Elect representatives who understand the destructive nature of illegal immigration, and who possess the character and fortitude required to address the problem.
- Discontinue taxpayer-funded benefits to illegal immigrants. Do not provide them with housing, education, health care, or welfare.
- Allow law enforcement officers to address illegal immigration as they do any other infraction. Whenever an officer stops anybody for any infraction, it is common practice to check for proper identification, outstanding warrants, adequate insurance, and even whether the driver has been issued a concealed weapons permit. It's only common sense to allow officers to also check the individual's citizenship status to verify if they're in the country legally or not—just as they check to verify if the driver's license is valid or invalid.
- Illegal immigrants are criminals, and when they are discovered, they should be jailed and deported. Repeat offenders should be imprisoned.
- We should fully support our border patrol and allow a border fence to be constructed where it's deemed necessary.
- We must reverse our current policy of allowing babies of illegal immigrants to become automatic citizens of this country. The 14th Amendment grants citizenship to babies born in the United States, "under the jurisdiction of the United

States."[70] Babies of illegals are not under our "jurisdiction," and accordingly, illegal immigrants cannot confer legal citizenship upon themselves.

Immigration policy is an enumerated power of the federal government granted by the Constitution[71]. Congress should establish and enforce rules for immigration consistent with the general welfare of the United States.

Currently, they are not doing so. Federal policy actually encourages illegal immigration and is the primary roadblock to effective enforcement. (Note the federal government's extreme criticism of the mild Arizona law supporting established, but ignored, federal law.)

If the federal government refuses to enforce immigration policy I believe the states have constitutional recourse. Article 1 Section 10 grants the states the ability to defend themselves from invasion.[72] I classify the uninhibited flow of illegals across undefended borders as an "invasion." The Constitution allows the states to act in their self-interest when invaded. I would strongly suggest that the governors of the borders states, faced with the invasion of illegal immigrants, use whatever means they determine are necessary to stop this invasion and provide for the well-being of their citizens—including patrolling their borders with their own National Guard or border agents combined with incarceration and deportation.

---

[70] US Constitution, 14th Amendment: All persons born or naturalized in the United States, and subject to the jurisdiction thereof, are citizens of the United States and of the State wherein they reside.

[71] US Constitution, Article 1 Section 8: To establish an uniform Rule of Naturalization.

[72] No State shall, without the Consent of Congress, lay any Duty of Tonnage, keep Troops, or Ships of War in time of Peace, enter into any Agreement or Compact with another State, or with a foreign Power, or engage in War, **unless actually invaded, or in such imminent Danger as will not admit of delay**.(emphisis added)

How should we address the millions of illegal immigrants currently residing in the United States?

People skirting our immigration laws are criminals just as are people breaking other laws. The situation is no different from a bank robber who had eluded capture for many years, lived a quality life, and was subsequently caught. The criminal must be punished for their deeds and make amends to those they harmed.

We are a nation of laws, and when we selectively enforce some laws, and ignore others, our society is weakened. The remedy to illegal immigration must be based on existing law and must be in the best interest of the United States.

Regardless of the length of time an illegal has been in this country, we cannot allow him to grant himself legal citizenship. It's completely against logic and the rule of law. Immigrants must apply for and obtain United States Citizenship legally.

I propose a plan that is simple and fair.

1. Specify an enforcement date. All illegals residing in this country, including the children of illegals, must voluntarily return to their legal country of origin prior to the enforcement date. If possible, they should document their productive lifestyle by securing the following type of information:

    a. Proof of gainful employment
    b. Proof of self-sufficiency
    c. Documentation of rent or mortgage payments
    d. List of acquired assets
    e. Net worth statement
    f. References from U.S. citizens in good favor

2. All illegal aliens who voluntarily return to their country of origin prior to the enforcement date would be allowed to apply for U.S. citizenship. When applying for a visa, they should be able to prove that they did reside in the United States in

good standing, had no criminal record, did not rely on public support, provided a needed skill or benefit to society, and voluntarily left the United States when asked prior to the enforcement date.

3. Those proving they were a benefit to the United States would be granted a visa, and then be allowed to navigate through the Legal Immigration maze. As with all immigrants, they would need a sponsor and would not be eligible for federal benefits.

4. Those considered a drain on society, as demonstrated by a criminal record or by prior acceptance of taxpayer support, would be rejected.

5. Illegal immigrants who choose not to obey the law and do not apply for legal citizenship would be considered criminals. When discovered during the normal course of business they should be deported and not be allowed to legally immigrate to this country thereafter.

It's important that everybody know the rules and the timetable. Those choosing to remain illegally in the United States, after the enforcement date, will have disregarded the option to become legal immigrants, and must face the consequences of their decision.

Long-term illegals currently residing in this country—who follow the law, can demonstrate they will be a benefit to this country, and who wish to assimilate into our society, will be welcomed as our guests.

For a free society to survive, we must enforce known, fair, and consistent laws. Our existing immigration laws are known, fair, and consistent, and must be enforced; otherwise we do a great disservice to those who came before us, and even a greater disservice to those following.

Legal immigration, correctly screened, has the potential to greatly benefit our society and should be encouraged. Illegal immigration is destructive to the United States and the American culture and must be controlled.

Abortion

You never have the moral right or authority to kill an individual you consider inconvenient to your life.

Let me explain my view on abortion this way. Some senior citizens require extended care. Assume 50% of the U.S. population, *about the same percent that supports abortion,* believes that caregivers should be able to decide if the seniors under their care should be involuntarily killed if they become a burden or an inconvenience.

Should there be a law allowing these caregivers the "choice" of whether or not to terminate another's life?

OF COURSE NOT! Even if 99.9% believed it proper, killing others for your own convenience is wrong. *You never have the moral right or authority to kill an individual you consider inconvenient to your lifestyle.*

The same reasoning applies to unborn babies in the womb. The most innocent among us should be nurtured and protected, rather than slaughtered on demand.

Our country is founded upon the principle that all men are *"endowed by their creator with unalienable rights, that among these are Life, Liberty, and the Pursuit of Happiness."*

Life is an unalienable right from God. Governments are instituted to secure these rights for everyone—especially the most innocent and defenseless amongst us, the unborn.

Our society has been conditioned to view a baby in the womb as a "fetus," or mass of flesh, not as a human baby. It's a misconception. At eight weeks after conception, the baby has a human form with a regular heartbeat. Its arms, fingers, toes, and all major organs are clearly forming. It's a baby—defenseless, and protected within its mother's womb. By the end of the second trimester, the baby moves, sleeps and wakes, and has hair, fingernails, taste buds, and skin; it's a fully formed, yet still developing, human being.

It's not the baby's "choice" to be aborted. Quite the contrary; life strives to survive.

A baby in the womb is an innocent and defenseless being totally dependent upon its mother for protection and sustenance. They do not want to die any more than any other living creature desires death. Once born, the baby cries when it is hungry, cold, or uncomfortable and is at peace when it's cared for.

Abortion is wrong—it devalues life and contradicts our Judeo-Christian morality and the principles upon which our country was founded. Life is a miracle, a precious gift from God. The devaluation of life does not stop with abortion but reflects itself in the devaluation of all human relationships. People are seen as objects rather than human beings. Selfishness, coupled with self-indulgent perversions become commonplace throughout society.

The devaluation of life opens the door for other crimes against humanity such as euthanasia. Abortion has already introduced the practice of killing innocent babies considered inconvenient. Once accepted, this concept can be expanded to include others in society considered inconvenient, such as the disabled or elderly. Obama Care already replaces treatment with end-of-life counseling for the elderly—the first step towards euthanasia.

Rather than being aborted, unwanted babies should be brought to term and then given up for adoption to desiring parents. The long-term solution to unwanted pregnancies is a rededication to the time-honored values of dignity, self-respect, and fidelity.

In the tragic event that the physical health of the mother is in question, the decision must be left to the parents, counseled by those they trust, with a firm reliance on the grace of God.

Partial-Birth Abortion

Partial-Birth Abortions are never justified. It's a gruesome procedure consisting of the cruel and painful murder of a viable, healthy baby. The baby is rotated out of the safe and normal head-first delivery to a dangerous feet-first birth. The baby is then delivered alive (except for the head). Scissors are jammed into the live baby's scull, and the baby's brains are sucked out, killing the baby. The dead baby is then removed from the mother.

This is nothing less than infanticide—the murder of an inconvenient baby.

The baby has a fully functional nervous system, allowing it to experience the unbearable pain associated with the procedure.

This gruesome procedure is employed for the sole purpose of eliminating an inconvenient and unwanted pregnancy, and is *NEVER* employed to save life of the mother[73].

It sickens me to address this issue, but it sickens me more that it is allowed to continue.

---

[73] In 1992, Dr. Martin Haskell presented his paper on this procedure at a Risk Management Seminar of the National Abortion Federation. He personally claims to have done over 700 himself (Interview with Dr. Martin Haskell, AMA News, 1993), and points out that some 80% are "purely elective." In a personal conversation with Fr. Frank Pavone, Dr. Haskell explained that "elective" does not mean that the woman chooses the procedure because of a medical necessity, but rather chooses it because she wants an abortion. He admitted to Fr. Frank that there does not seem to be any medical reason for this procedure. *There are in fact absolutely no obstetrical situations encountered in this country which require a partially delivered human fetus to be destroyed to preserve the life or health of the mother* (Dr. Pamela Smith, Senate Hearing Record, p.82: Partial Birth Abortion Ban Medical Testimony).

What is the solution? Unwanted babies should be delivered and placed for adoption with desiring families. There is a great demand for adoptable babies in the United States. So great in fact, that many families are forced to adopt from overseas.

Let's once again work towards securing the unalienable, God-granted right of Life for the most defenseless amongst us, unborn babies.

Education

Before federal intervention, the U.S. boasted one of the best educational systems in the world.

I started school in the 1960's. The main focus was on core curriculum consisting of English, math, history, science, social studies, and geography. We were expected to do our homework, and were penalized otherwise. If we hadn't mastered the minimum requirements of the grade, we were held back.

Fast forward to today. The school's main goal is to provide a safe and wholesome environment with education following as a secondary goal.

The school my children attended not only started to provide breakfast, but to actively promote it. We received flyers encouraging us to participate in the school breakfast program, informing us that discounts were available to eligible families. Although possibly conceived with good intentions, the breakfast—and now dinner—programs shift child-rearing responsibility away from the parent to the government. It also takes time out of the school day that could be used to teach core subjects.

Homework fell by the wayside. It was very unusual for my children to ever bring homework home. I talked to the teachers, who explained that many children simply didn't do homework. Rather than have these kids fall behind, all subject matter was addressed in class. The only homework assigned was the completion of unfinished class work.

The teachers explained to us that their entire curriculum was geared to the poorest performers. A math teacher told me that one child lacked parental supervision, didn't do homework, stayed up till the early morning hours, and then consistently fell asleep in class. This teacher decided to gear his curriculum towards this specific under-performer—doing a disservice the others in the class.

At dinner my wife and I would talk to our kids about what they learned in school. More times than I care to remember, my kids would tell me that they watched Disney movies in class, such as Toy Story, because they had finished their work and were waiting for the others in their class.

We could no longer accept what we considered a substandard education, so we decided to home school our children until they reached high school, then sent them to a private Christian school that better agreed with our principles.

What has happened to our public schools to make them fail?

1. Lyndon Johnson's war on poverty ended up creating a dependent class of people who have been conditioned to expect others to care for them. Governmental assistance programs have replaced a sense of personal responsibility with sense of dependency. This general lack of personal responsibility and dependence is passed from generation to generation. Many children from dependent families are attending school with no reason or desire to learn. They don't need a job—government provides for them. Many schools have geared their curriculum towards these non-achievers, in effect becoming babysitters rather than educators.

2. The curriculum has been consistently dumbed down. Social courses, such as sex education, health, marriage, nutrition, diversity, etc., along with the serving of breakfast and dinner, have displaced the core classes of history, English, science, math, social studies, government, etc. To further dumb down the kids, the school introduced technological aids when inappropriate. In second grade, my son was given a calculator with which to solve math problems. Learning the principles behind the subject was rendered unnecessary by a couple of keystrokes. The kids no longer learned the principles, just how to compute a result.

3. We need to teach a sense of pride in our country. We live in the United States of America, a country based on limited government and personal liberty which has unleashed the greatest prosperity man has ever experienced. It's a fact that must be reinforced, cherished, and nurtured, or else it will be lost. Our schools often downplay the greatness of the United States in that:

- The Pledge of Allegiance is often ignored;
- Free markets, prosperity, and achievement are equated with greediness;
- It's explained that industry and production generate pollution;
- Students are taught that a free society is naturally unfair;
- We cannot recognize our rights as God given;
- Personal liberty and responsibility are de-emphasized, while public programs are extolled.

What do I think are the solutions?

1. We need to remove the federal government from education and return authority to local communities and states. There is no constitutional authority for federal interference in education. Rather than concentrating on providing the best education, federal programs impose a one-program-fits-all solution, which is based on the accumulation of power, political payback, and political correctness. If we allow thousands of local communities to offer what they consider to be the best education for the lowest cost, then the best solutions will tend to be emulated throughout the country.

2. We must re-introduce free-market solutions to education. Free-market principles naturally promote reasonably priced exceptionalism. As it stands today, education is an extremely expensive, inefficient, government-protected monopoly. The free market solutions should be implemented by the states or local communities, but never by the federal government.

One option is to have the states provide parents with educational vouchers that could be used to fund education rather than funding the schools directly. Parents could use these vouchers at any accredited school, whether public, private, or religious, and would naturally choose schools that best met their expectations. Competing schools would have an incentive to develop the required curriculum and practices to provide the best overall education. Successful models would be copied by unsuccessful schools, which would tend to improve the entire education system. The poorest performing schools would naturally fall by the wayside, since nobody would choose to attend.

3. We must allow local school boards to fire under-performing teachers and reward exceptional performance through pay-based incentives. The great majority of teachers are caring and diligent. The current tenure practices tend to protect under-achieving teachers. If teachers were treated like private employees, rewarded for exceptional performance and penalized for poor performance, the quality of teachers and teaching would naturally improve.

4. We must encourage educational right-to-work and allow non-union teachers in schools. Today's teachers unions insist upon policies that tend to drive up the cost of education while lowering quality. Allow local communities to hire the best qualified teachers regardless of union affiliation.

5. Allow free-market choice to encourage a variety of charter or private schools offering different areas of focus and interest. Allow the parents and students to choose. Some schools will focus on college preparation, others towards the arts, while others may be geared towards vocational training. All would need to satisfy the minimum requirements of the state or community, but parents and students could choose the venue that best fit their needs.

The education of our children is extremely important for meeting the needs of our nation and should be geared towards teaching the unbiased core curriculum of English, history, math, science, social studies, geography, literature, and language. The federal government, with its politicized mandates, must be removed from the educational system. States and local communities, bolstered by free-market choice, are the only means of restoring quality education to our children.

Energy Independence

The United States is blessed with an abundance of domestic energy resources, vastly more than most of the countries from which we import.

OIL: The U.S. is sitting on the world's largest, untapped oil reserves, estimated at about 2.3 trillion barrels—nearly three times more than the reserves held by Organization of Petroleum Exporting Countries (OPEC) nations and sufficient to meet 300 years of demand, at today's levels, for auto, truck, aircraft, heating, and industrial fuel, without importing a single barrel of oil.[74]

COAL: The United States' estimated recoverable reserves of coal stand at 275 billion tons, an amount that is greater than any other nation in the world and which is capable of meeting domestic demand for more than 250 years at current rates of consumption.[75]

NUCLEAR: The United States has developed the technological expertise to safely construct and maintain nuclear plants and has 104 nuclear power reactors in 31 states, operated by 30 different power companies. Nuclear power accounted for almost 20% of the total domestic electricity generated in 2008.[76]

NATURAL GAS: The American Gas Association estimates the national inventory of natural gas reserves is approximately 300 trillion cubic feet. This 'on-the-shelf' inventory is the foundation

---

[74] The U.S.' Untapped Oil Bounty By Jim Ostroff, Associate Editor, The Kiplinger Letter, June 30, 2008
http://www.kiplinger.com/businessresource/forecast/archive/The_U.S._s_Untapped_Bounty_080630.html#ixzz14PAmgpuq

[75] About Coal, Fred H. Hutchison, Edited on: March 27, 2009, http://www.clean-energy.us/facts/coal.htm

[76] Nuclear Power in the USA, Updated 29 October 2010, http://www.world-nuclear.org/info/inf41.html

along with growing national resource estimates that may point to as much as a 100 year natural gas supply in America. [77]

With all of our energy wealth, why isn't the United States energy independent?

According to Kiplinger, the U.S. Government is the major obstruction to energy independence. In spite of our huge domestic oil reserves, the United States government has assumed control over the great majority of these reserves and has disallowed their development.

Oil Shale: Roughly two-thirds of the U.S.'s oil shale fields in Colorado, Wyoming and Utah are in federally protected areas and are closed to development. (1.5 trillion barrels—or 200 years worth of supply at current usage levels.)

Tar Sands: The sands are located predominantly in Utah, Alaska, Texas, California, Alabama, and Kentucky on federal and state lands that, by laws and administrative orders, are closed to mineral and petroleum development. (Around 75 billion barrels)

Outer Continental Shelf (OCS): Something in the neighborhood of 90 billion barrels of oil sit beneath the ocean bed 50 to 100 miles off the Atlantic, Pacific and Gulf coasts. Presidential bans and congressional prohibitions have made the tracts off limits to oil company exploration, at least until 2012.

ANWR: About 10 billion barrels of oil are locked away here, with little possibility that federal lawmakers will open the door.

In order to meet our energy requirements, the U.S. is forced to import more than 60% of our oil. Our federal government would rather allow our domestic oil reserves to remain untouched in the ground,

---

[77]   American Gas Association 4-4-2012: US Natural Gas Reserves at Record Levels

and transfer close to $400 billion per year out of the U.S. economy to purchase our needed supply.[78]

Imagine the economic boom that would take place if this $400 billion remained in the U.S. economy rather than being sent overseas—much of it to countries wishing us harm. Economic growth and prosperity would be phenomenal. Unemployment would drop to virtually nothing. Federal, state, and local government welfare spending would be slashed. The increased supply would naturally drop the price of oil from its current, artificially inflated price to its true cost, based on free-market competition. The cost of every product and service used by consumers would decrease, due to the ripple effect of lower fuel costs (cheaper transportation—driving, flying, freight, etc.), cheaper plastic products, and cheaper manufacturing costs. Every effect is beneficial.

Eliminating oil importation will drastically increase national security. Whether we admit it or not, we are now held hostage by the countries from which we import oil. Take, for example, the possibility that hostilities escalated between the West and the Middle East. One weapon the Middle East could use against the West would be the curtailment of oil exports, which would immediately drive up the cost of fuel, create shortages, and be very detrimental to the economy of the West. Chances are that our political "leaders" would rather suffer insult and humiliation, than stand up for our national interest. A prime example is the civilized Western nations allowing Iran to continue with its development of nuclear weapons, which can be used not only against our ally, Israel, but also to destabilize the entire region.

The invisible hand of the free market delivers an abundance of goods and services at fair prices to meet all of society's needs. Government decisions are predominantly based on political posturing, accumulation of political power, and succumbing to the demands of special-interest funding groups. Government intervention is always destructive to the free market and is primarily responsible for shortages of goods and

---

[78]   S. Imported 382 Million Barrels of Oil in August, Spending $29.3 Billion http://www.pickensplan.com/news/2010/09/14/us-imported-382-million-barrels-of-oil-in-august-spending-293-billion/

artificially increased costs. Federal interference in domestic energy production is no different and has been especially detrimental to the general welfare of the nation.

Why would government impose these restrictions to energy independence?

Government accumulates power by addressing problems. Not solving, but addressing. A huge governmental bureaucracy has been created to address energy problems. If the government allowed the free market to solve these problems, there would be no need for further government attention, and this bureaucracy could be disbanded. Government would then lose control, influence, and power over the population. Rather than allowing the problem to be solved, our "leaders" in government would rather maintain their influence and control over the people by perpetuating this problem.

What are my solutions for achieving Energy Independence?

1. Remove government from energy development and oversight. The enumerated powers of Congress, detailed in Article 1 Section 8 of the Constitution, provide the government with no authority to micromanage the energy industry. (The Commerce Clause provides government with the ability to regulate the flow of goods and services between the states and internationally, but it never provided Congress with the ability to micromanage the industry.)

2. Eliminate the Department of Energy. Any valid, constitutional oversight can be handled by the Department of Commerce or the Department of Defense (for nuclear concerns). The Department of Energy's purpose has morphed into perpetuating the energy problems to seemingly justify its existence. Rather than allowing the free market to address and solve energy problems, they are stifling the free market and imposing politically motivated solutions.

    a. They disallow development of our proven energy reserves;

b. They're encouraging the imposition of Cap and Trade legislation to limit carbon emissions, which is based on faulty science and which has the potential to drastically drive up the cost of energy.

c. They are spending billions of dollars of taxpayer funds on the development of unnecessary alternative fuels. *If we compared water to oil, our government would disallow the use of our abundantly available water, and then spend billions of dollars on alternative water sources, trying to replace what they have prohibited. It's a ridiculous situation, yet our government's doing it.*

3. Allow the states to negotiate private sector contracts to extract energy from federal land within their borders—with clear performance standards. Grant long-term leases to the energy developers, providing them with the confidence that they will be able to achieve their expected return on the capital investment required to develop and extract the energy resources properly. Royalties can be negotiated to provide benefit to both the state and federal treasuries.

4. Eliminate all taxpayer-funded energy development. Developers of conventional energy—oil, coal, nuclear, hydro—have the responsibility to provide the needed capital to develop and deliver energy. Providers of alternative green energy—solar, wind, tidal, etc.—should have the same responsibility. Instead, they finance their projects with public funds and have no financial incentive to succeed. Many have wasted their entire federal investment before filing for bankruptcy. We must restore the financial incentive to succeed along with the financial loss resulting from inefficiencies or for developing a useless product.

5. Pass legislation that would protect energy developers from frivolous lawsuits designed to delay or halt energy development.

6. Eliminate the proposed implementation of Cap and Trade. This legislation is based on the faulty science of manmade

global warming. It creates an artificial market to trade carbon credits (which will greatly benefit a small group of connected investors), increases costs for all energy users (which will be passed onto consumers through increased costs), creates a huge federal enforcement agency, and inserts its tentacles into all aspects of society (such as requiring all homes to have a federal government inspection verifying they meet governmental environmental standards before being sold).

7. Allow oil producers the ability to build new refineries, as they deem necessary, to adequately refine our domestic oil reserves.

8. Eliminate bureaucratic, governmental regulations that drive up the cost of energy. For example, eliminate the requirement that various grades of gasoline be refined and distributed to various parts of the nation based on seasonal temperature fluctuations.

9. Encourage the development of nuclear energy. It's clean, safe, and reliable. Require the developers of nuclear power to propose the means of safely disposing of nuclear waste during the bidding process.

10. Allow energy providers to charge the appropriate fees, not only to develop and deliver energy, but also to maintain the delivery infrastructure. Government-imposed price limitations generally backfire by limiting the capital available to maintain the energy infrastructure. Let the developers charge what they consider necessary to maintain the system. The free market encourages fair and appropriate pricing.

The private sector could easily develop the domestic energy reserves of the United States allowing us not only to become energy independent, but to become exporters of energy throughout the world—if the federal government got out of the way. Let the free market function to satisfy the energy requirements of the United States.

Legal Reform

I'm watching TV and see ads soliciting plaintiffs for lawsuits! It's not just a single ad, but multiple, different ads during a single TV show such as:

> *"If you or your loved ones have worked in shipbuilding, construction, or whatever, and may have possibly been exposed to asbestos, call this number. You may be eligible for a financial settlement."*

The same thing happens with medicine:

> *"If you have taken this drug and have experienced any of these side effects, then call us and we may be able to recover a significant financial settlement."*

This message can be replaced with virtually any product or service, and then used by lawyers hoping to file a lawsuit on your behalf allowing them to receive a significant percentage of any settlement.

Lawsuit abuse is not limited to solicitation by shady lawyers. There are hosts of frivolous lawsuits filed by individuals hoping to shift responsibility from themselves to what they consider deep-pocketed organizations.[79] The plaintiffs, more often than not, have nothing to lose. It costs just a few dollars and a little time to file the suit. The lawyers, hoping to recover a percentage of the settlement, do not charge for their time.

---

[79] A sample of frivolous lawsuits from http://www.sickoflawsuits.org/threats/JunkLawsuits.cfm

A New York securities trader sued a Manhattan strip joint for "serious injuries" he sustained during a lap dance. The man, who is married, alleged that a stripper employed by the Hot Lap Dance Club near Madison Square Garden swiveled and smacked him in the eye with the heel of her shoe during an early morning performance last November. (The Associated Press, March 17, 2008)

Yet the defendant is required to hire the needed legal representation to defend themselves. Each lawsuit can easily cost many tens of thousands of dollars in defense costs. Some corporations have adopted a policy of settling suits, even though they are completely innocent, since it's cheaper than providing a defense in court.

Many lawsuits are valid and address true grievances. The quandary lies in how to limit frivolous lawsuits without impacting valid grievances.

I have great confidence in the jury system. The circumstances pertaining to each lawsuit are different, and a jury should be able to hear the facts of the case and determine the outcome. I do not want to limit in any way the judgment of the jury or the ability of aggrieved parties to bring suit against those who do them harm.

In my opinion, a reasonable solution lies in requiring the loser of the suit to not only pay their own legal costs, but also the legal costs of the winner. As it stands now, the defense pays all costs. They pay for their own defense, and then pay the plaintiff's lawyer via a percentage of the settlement. The plaintiff lawyer does not typically get paid when they lose, but the defense still pays their legal team dearly.

The Loser-Pays solution has several beneficial effects:

- **First:** The real risk of losing a suit will eliminate frivolous lawsuits filed by individuals who are simply trying to extort a settlement from deep-pocketed organizations.
- **Second:** Innocent defendants would be willing to defend themselves if they realize that they are likely to be able to recover their defense costs.
- **Third:** Guilty defendants will be much more likely to admit responsibility and offer a reasonable settlement to atone for their damage. If the settlement does not meet societal standards for reasonability, then the case can be tried in front of a jury.
- **Fourth:** There are no limits on truly damaged individuals who wish to bring suit and recover damages that are considered reasonable and proper by a jury of their peers.

- **Fifth:** The legal caseload will decrease, with people settling their suits outside the court system.

Lawsuit abuse is very detrimental.

The cost of virtually every consumer product is increased to cover actual or potential legal costs. Every time you purchase a lawn mower, food product, toaster, medicine, or any other conceivable product, you're paying for the legal costs and associated bureaucratic workload forced upon the producer. For example, sleeping pills often have a ridiculous warning label such as "Caution: May cause drowsiness." [80] The cost of the product includes all the actual and potential legal costs incurred by the manufacturer and retailers, plus the costs of their legal departments trying to figure out how to best limit future suits.

New product development is curtailed. Manufacturers spend many millions of dollars to conceive, develop, test, and market new products they believe will be beneficial to society and that will allow them to make a profit. Regardless of the potential benefit of a new product or drug, the product may never be developed if the manufacturer's legal department foresees the possibility of excessive, potential lawsuits.

Products and services beneficial to society are eliminated. Ignorant and/or malicious parties are able to use the court system to postpone indefinitely projects they consider undesirable. Take, for example, the United State's energy development. A small, but

---

[80] Why do sleeping pills have warning labels that state: "Caution: May cause drowsiness?" Because most sleeping pills contain benadryl (diphenhydramine) which the chief *side effect* is drowsiness. The reason most likely that they have to say that, is because someone took one, it made them drowsy and then they did something stupid (like ran his car over a cliff) and his *attorney* sued the medication manufacturer saying "the box did not say that the *sleeping pill* could make you drowsy" . . . thus getting his client a million dollars for which the attorney made $333,333.33 (33%).

(http://www.anyqa.com/Other/468-1-general-2.html)

---

vocal group of environmentalists are able to stop nuclear power development, coal processing, and oil extraction in the United States. A very effective mode-of-operation for these special interest groups is to continually challenge energy producers through the court system, delaying development and driving up costs. For example, hundreds of nuclear power plants were ordered, and subsequently canceled in the United States during the late 1960's and early 1970's—primarily due to cost overruns and delays caused by legal challenges.[81] Domestic oil development on federal lands and in shallow, offshore water has virtually been stopped. Safe nuclear power generation and oil exploration still occurs throughout the world, but it's been stopped in the United States through the court system.

Lack of personal responsibility. Perhaps the most damaging aspect of lawsuit abuse is the changed attitude Americans now have regarding personal responsibility. No longer are accidents accepted as accidents; they're considered, by far too great a percentage of the population, a potential lottery winning. If someone has a car accident, they try suing the manufacturer; if someone is hurt in gang violence, they sue the city; if a price scanner is set incorrectly, the store is sued. People need to become responsible for their own lives.

Lawsuit abuse is a huge problem in the United States, and it must be addressed. In my opinion, a great first step would be to introduce a loser-pay system for all legal costs.

---

[81] The chairman of the Consumers Power Company has opened negotiations with natural gas suppliers for possible conversion of the defunct Midland nuclear power plant to natural gas, the utility said today. The nuclear power plant was 85 percent finished when work was stopped in July 1984 because of lack of money and opposition to its completion. The initial cost estimate of the power plant was 267 million. Consumers says it spent $4.1 billion on the project when it was abandoned as a nuclear plant.

Global Warming

I believe in "Climate Change."

From my review of available information, it seems that Earth's temperature has been fluctuating since its creation, and will probably continue to do so in the future. I disagree with the idea that Climate Change, or Global Warming, is caused by humans and represents one of the greatest threats facing mankind.

I don't know what causes the Earth's climate cycles. One theory relates it to solar activity combined with variations in the Earth's orbit. A recent National Geographic article informed that Mars is experiencing a warming cycle similar to Earth's[82]. Unless man's activity is billowing over to Mars, man seems to have nothing to do with the warming of the inner planets. Whatever it is, I believe it's natural and outside of man's control, and that man couldn't change Earth's temperature if he tried.

I recently read in an article, *"Melting glaciers in Western Canada are revealing tree stumps up to 7,000 years old where the region's rivers of ice have retreated to a historic minimum, a geologist said today."*[83] It infers strongly that the landmass in Western Canada, currently covered by glaciers, was once much warmer and able to support forests.

Another article stated, *"One thousand years ago Vikings thrived in the green coastal meadows of Greenland during what we now call the Medieval Warming. It was warmer than today, the summers were longer, and there was ample grass and hay for the Vikings' dairy cows. Then Greenland's climate*

---

[82] National Geographic News, Kate Ravilious;February 28, 2007; "Mars Melt Hints at Solar, Not Human, Cause for Warming, Scientist Says"; http://news.nationalgeographic.com/news/2007/02/070228-mars-warming.html

[83] Melting Glacier Reveals Ancient Tree Stumps; By LiveScience Staff; posted: 30 October 2007; http://i.livescience.com/4702-melting-glacier-reveals-ancient-tree-stumps.html

suddenly got colder. The Little Ice Age had begun. Sea ice moved south, and the Vikings' sailing ships could no longer get through to trade wood for seal furs. Shorter summers produced less hay to feed the Viking cows through longer, colder winters. The last written record found in the abandoned Viking colonies was dated 1408."[84]

Reports like these support the theory that climate change on Earth is natural, cyclical, and regular—totally outside of man's influence.

Proponents of man-induced Global Warming infer that man-made pollution is the primary cause of Earth's warming. Yet volcanic activity alone is estimated to be responsible for the release of 130 million tons of carbon dioxide into the atmosphere annually. Volcanic activity is not pleasant, and spews many toxins into the air, as does man, but natural atmospheric operation cleanses the skies of this debris and returns it as nutrients to the soil. Everything on Earth works in harmony.

Water vapor is classified as the greatest greenhouse gas by far.[85] Its primary source is evaporation from the ocean. Man cannot, and

---

[84] Melting the Facts about Greenland's Ice Sheet; CFact News; April 28, 2006; http://www.cfact.org/a/886/Melting-the-facts-about-Greenlands-ice-sheet

[85] Water vapor constitutes Earth's most significant greenhouse gas, accounting for about 95% of Earth's greenhouse effect. Interestingly, many "facts and figures' regarding global warming completely ignore the powerful effects of water vapor in the greenhouse system, carelessly (perhaps, deliberately) overstating human impacts as much as 20-fold.
Water vapor is 99.999% of natural origin. Other atmospheric greenhouse gases, carbon dioxide (CO_2), methane (CH_4), nitrous oxide (N_2O), and miscellaneous other gases (CFC's, etc.), are also mostly of natural origin (except for the latter, which is mostly anthropogenic).
Human activities contribute slightly to greenhouse gas concentrations through farming, manufacturing, power generation, and transportation. However, these emissions are so dwarfed in comparison to emissions from natural sources we can do nothing about, that even the most costly efforts to limit human emissions would have a very small—perhaps undetectable—effect on global climate.

---

should not try to, control it. To me, it's a miracle of God that water vapor envelopes our earth. It helps to shield us from the sun's radiation and provides protective insulation, keeping us from freezing to death. Without the greenhouse gas of water vapor, life as we know it could not continue to exist on earth.

Obviously, we should be good stewards of the earth on which we live. A prosperous, free-market economy, with private property ownership, encourages high environmental standards. What is cleaner, a typical home in the United States, with a 90%+ efficiency furnace and flush toilets, or a dirt-floored hut in a third-world economy, relying on an open fire pit and open latrines? Obviously, it's the United States.

The free market addresses the needs of man and naturally provides for a clean environment.

Steam-engine locomotives and horses were filthy and inefficient, yet they provided the best transportation solutions at the time. The free market has naturally replaced them with cleaner and more efficient electric-locomotives, automobiles, and planes. In a free market, products continually evolve to meet all the needs of man.

Conversely, state-controlled markets discourage a clean environment. My wife grew up in Russia and told horror stories of how young girls, washing their hair in rivers, became diseased and lost their hair, because unbeknownst to them, pollutants such as raw nuclear waste was routinely disposed of into the river upstream from where these girls bathed. It wasn't an isolated experience. The land and air in state-controlled societies is filthy compared to the United States.

If environmentalists are so concerned about cleaning up the planet, have them go to countries like Africa, China, India, or Russia, and encourage a market-based economic system to generate prosperity, which will naturally improve the standard of living and clean up their environment.

Monte Hieb: Global Warming: a Closer look at the Numbers (http://www.geocraft.com/WVFossils/greenhouse_data.html)

The concept of man-made global warming is a hoax perpetuated by government and environmental groups to accumulate power, wealth, and control over the population. It has no basis in science and should not be used to impose government regulation and control upon the country.

Committee of 12

Congress completely and consistently ignores any constitutional boundaries and is literally destroying this country. Our elected representatives do not understand the greatness of limited government or their role in securing the liberty of the people.

Government is the problem, but this same government is arrogant enough to think it's the solution. And what is their solution? To create a committee of 12 established politicians to address the most pressing problems the country is faced with.

Adhering to the Constitution apparently never even crossed their minds.

I recent read an article discussing the rationale for the new "Super Committee" or the "Committee of 12."

"WASHINGTON—After weeks, months, of bitter feuding, Congress has finally agreed on who cannot be trusted to solve the country's complicated fiscal problems: The U.S. Congress, all 535 members. And Congress has a solution: a special committee.

Both Republicans and Democrats have proposed drumming up a committee of 12 legislators, handpicked by both parties, to deal with the most complicated issues involved in a likely debt-ceiling compromise. It will be up to this "super committee" to complete the epic task of cutting $2.8 trillion in spending from the federal budget." [86]

I consider this new Committee of 12 unconstitutional, since it fundamentally alters the structure of Congress.

Article 1 Section 1 of the U.S. Constitution specifically states:

---

[86] Congress will hand the sticky details to a bipartisan committee of 12; August 01, 2011|By David A. Fahrenthold, Washington Post; http://articles.boston.com/2011-08-01/news/29839317_1_committee-members-debt-limit-deficit-cuts

Peter Konetchy

"All legislative Powers herein granted shall be vested in a Congress of the United States, which shall consist of a Senate and House of Representatives."[87]

I've read this section many times and cannot find any reference to a constitutional entity called the "Committee of 12" or "Super Committee." All I see is a House and Senate.

What am I missing? Nothing.

The purpose of the House is to directly represent the interests of the people. The purpose of the Senate, though lost with the passage of the 17th Amendment, is to represent the interests of the state.

Who is represented by this new "Committee of 12"?

This third entity within Congress, the Committee of 12, represents neither the people nor the states, but an entrenched, Congressional establishment desiring to fast track bills that elite politicians in Congress want passed. It provides Congress with its own representation, which supersedes the representation of the People (House) or the States (Senate). The "Committee of 12" was established totally outside of any conceivable constitutional authority.

The Constitution states that bills originate in the House or Senate, and once passed, they are forwarded to the other body for approval. After passage by both bodies of Congress, they are forwarded to the President for approval. [88]

The Committee of 12 changes the constitutional procedures established in Article 1 Section 7 of the Constitution. Bills Congress considers "truly important" or "significant" now originate in this new Committee of 12. After receiving a simple Committee of 12 majority vote (seven or more), the bill is then presented to the House for an up or down vote—without the ability to amend, and then submitted to the Senate for a similar up or down vote—again without the ability to amend.

---

[87] US Constitution, Article 1 Section 1
[88] US Constitution, Article 1 Section 7

Does anyone else, beside me, fear that the people or the states are losing representation? There are six Senators and six House members on this "Committee of 12." What is the purpose of the remaining 429 House members or 94 Senators? They have no input into the bills and no ability to amend them. They simply rubber stamp or reject the bills presented to them.

Imagine the pressure to accept the decision of this "Committee of 12" on the non-committee members. If they reject a desired bill, are they blackballed? Are they threatened with lack of funding or support in their upcoming re-election? Are they threatened with a primary challenger? Are they threatened?

We face extremely serious challenges in this country that must be addressed. Every single domestic problem facing our nation today is a direct result of Congress overstepping its constitutional authority and imposing its will upon the people.

Let me clarify. Our nation is on the brink of collapse because Congress ignores every aspect of the Constitution and does anything it damn well pleases.

This "Committee of 12" is another example of the complete disdain for the constitutional process. Our elected representatives have abdicated their responsibility and handed it off to a select few. It's another encroachment of our constitutional safeguards by those in power and is very dangerous and unconstitutional.

We don't need an unconstitutional Committee of 12.

The solution to all our problems is staring us in the face—the U.S. Constitution. Limit congressional influence and power to specific, enumerated powers in Article 1 Section 8. Then limit spending to these same enumerated functions, as required by Article 1 Section 9.

Problem solved.

Dump the "Committee of 12."

Fairness Doctrine

The Fairness Doctrine is based on the premises that the people of the United States are not receiving fair and balanced information and that its government's role to monitor the dissemination of information and punish those who do not report what the government considers fair and balanced.

Free people choose the ideas and viewpoints to which they wish to be exposed.

People in the United States have access to an unlimited amount of information through equally unlimited mediums—radio, television, newspapers, magazines, books, Internet, lectures, and conversations—and freely choose to access what they consider desirable and ignore what they consider offensive.

If you scan through the radio dial, you're exposed to just about anything people have an interest in listening to: rock and roll, light rock, rap, jazz, classical, religious, and talk radio. Within talk radio, samplings of topics available include home improvement, computer technology, photography, gardening, finance, investments, farming, and politics.

In a free society, the market, rather than a government authority, dictates the available programming.

For example: A radio program addressing soil preparation, fertilization, and farming techniques will probably not find a market in New York City; yet the same program could be popular in the Midwestern breadbasket states.

If a significant percentage of people in a listening area are interested in a subject, the radio program will be likely to support itself through advertising, and the topic will probably be broadcast; otherwise, the program will be dropped.

Another example: I do not believe, nor think it proper, that the federal government would force a rap music station to include a "reasonable" balance of classical music in its programming.

I think it safe to assume that the Fairness Doctrine would apply only to monitoring and controlling free political speech found offensive by government.

The political ruling class in Washington finds in incomprehensible that the general population may disagree with their policies and actions. Rather than evaluating their own actions and their effects on the country, politicians would rather control the discourse and have their actions skewed positively.

Consider this farfetched? I don't think so. According to the Heritage Foundation, both Presidents Kennedy and Nixon used the power of the government, through the Fairness Doctrine, to quell dissenting information.[89] Barak Obama has repeatedly chastised both Rush Limbaugh and Sean Hannity and counseled the nation not to listen to these individuals. Senate Majority Leader Harry Reid has done the same thing.[90] If the Fairness Doctrine were reinstated, the political

---

[89] Telecommunications scholar Thomas W. Hazlett notes that under the Nixon Administration, "License harassment of stations considered unfriendly to the Administration became a regular item on the agenda at White House policy meetings." (Thomas W. Hazlett, "The Fairness Doctrine and the First Amendment," The Public interest, Summer 1989, p. 105.) As one former Kennedy Administration official, Bill Ruder, has said, "We had a massive strategy to use the fairness doctrine to challenge and harass the right-wing broadcasters, and hope the challenge would be so costly to them that they would be inhibited and decide it was too expensive to continue." (Tony Snow, "Return of the Fairness Demon," The Washington Times, September 5, 1993, p. B3.)... "Why The Fairness Doctrine Is Anything But Fair" Published on October 29, 1993 by Adam Thierer

[90] Harry Reid's letter to Mark Mays, October 2, 2007, mischaracterizing Rushes "Phony Solider" comments.

ruling class could use the full force of the federal government to stifle dissent.

Rush Limbaugh, Sean Hannity, Mark Levin, and other conservative talk show hosts address current events from a constitutional basis and in light of our founding principles of limited government and personal responsibility. The ruling class in Washington does not want these values discussed or reinforced and tries to silence the hosts. There are plenty of "news" outlets promoting the expanding scope of government—including most major news networks such as ABC, CBS, NBC, CNN, MSNBC, public broadcasting, and virtually all major newspapers and print magazines, but the population chooses not to turn to them. Since the Fairness Doctrine was eliminated under Ronald Reagan, established media outlets have lost significant market share and influence and are now being replaced by the "alternative" media—including conservative talk radio and Fox News.

People choose not to listen to liberal philosophy, as demonstrated through the bankruptcy of Air America, and the few liberal talk show hosts have a hard time retaining an audience.

The First Amendment to the U.S. Constitution[91] specifically states, "Congress shall make no law . . . abridging the freedom of speech, or of the press . . ." The Fairness Doctrine directly contradicts this amendment and should never be reinstated.

A free society must have freedom of thought. Government should never be allowed to control, dictate, or manipulate the content of information disseminated to the people.

The mindset of the controlling Washington elite can be epitomized by the statement of Michigan's Senator Debbie Stabenow. In a radio interview on February 5, 2009, Stabenow told radio host and WND

---

[91] Congress shall make no law respecting an establishment of religion, or prohibiting the free exercise thereof; or abridging the freedom of speech, or of the press; or the right of the people peaceably to assemble, and to petition the Government for a redress of grievances.

columnist Bill Press that it was time to bring back the so-called "Fairness Doctrine."

"I think it's absolutely time to pass a standard. Now, whether it's called the Fairness Standard, whether it's called something else—I absolutely think it's time to be bringing accountability to the airwaves. I mean, our new president has talked rightly about accountability and transparency. You know, that we all have to step up and be responsible. And, I think in this case, there needs to be some accountability and standards put in place."

(February 05, 2009 © 2010 WorldNetDaily)

Term Limits—Good or Bad?

We have a problem in Washington. It's called *"Politicians."*

The people of the United States simply want government to leave them alone. It's their desire to elect federal representatives who perform their constitutionally enumerated duties, while leaving all else to the people or the states.

Through reliance upon our founding principles, our country amassed great prosperity and attained the highest standard of living in the history of mankind.

What's happened in the United States?

While we were busy living our lives and "pursuing our Happiness," our elected representatives were equally busy expanding the scope of government. They've chosen to ignore any constitutional restraint, effectively implementing the state of tyranny our forefathers fought to defeat.

Rather than appreciating the success of our country, meddling politicians—the scourge of a free society—decided to justify their existence by searching for problems. They concluded that the free-market system, the natural result of Adam Smith's Invisible Hand, was unfair, and that it was government's duty to address these shortcomings. They decided to forcibly redistribute income from the productive to the unproductive, improve the education system, secure reliable energy, clean the environment, save endangered species, feed the hungry, manage our retirement, and save the world from human destruction. All these initiatives were, and continue to be, dismal failures. They've created a "nanny" state where people are no longer responsible for their own lives, but are dependent on, and totally regulated by, government.

What's the solution?

Many people feel that term limits are the solution. They reason that once elected, politicians lose their sense of purpose and their appreciation of personal liberty and morph into rulers rather than representatives. They feel that the solution lies in limiting the length of their stay, disallowing them the time to have their principles corrupted.

I disagree with the conclusion.

I believe that term limits, in effect, throw the proverbial baby out with the bathwater. In a free nation, people must be able to elect the representatives they believe will best represent their interests. Term limits would throw the good and stable representatives out with the bad. We'd lose any long-term sense of consistency in government.

I believe that there are two courses of action, which must be pursued to address incompetence in government.

1. People need to wake up and elect morally responsible individuals who are willing to fight for our founding principles of limited government and personal liberty. These principles have kept our country safe, free, and prosperous—with the sad side effect of allowing the population to become complacent. We've allowed our politicians to function autonomously, without citizen supervision. Instead of working on our behalf, they were instead growing government, increasing their personal power and influence, and diminishing our personal liberty.

    Since the election of 2008 and the ensuing implementation of disastrous federal policies, the people have awakened. Politicians of both parties who have trampled our liberties have been thrown from office and replaced with representatives pledging to restore constitutional restraint. We must hold these newly elected representatives accountable and supplement their numbers in forthcoming elections. We must remain ever vigilant.

2. We must repeat the 17th Amendment to the Constitution, which allowed the selection of Senators by popular vote.

Our Constitution severely limits the power of the federal government and assigns to it the responsibility of defending the nation and the authority to act on the country's behalf in the world community. All other power falls to the people or states. The purpose of the House of Representatives is to directly represent the people in matters pertaining to the federal government. If the federal government tries to trample the people's rights, it's the representative's responsibility to fight on behalf of the people.

Every member of the House is elected every two years and their district is quite small allowing the people to stay familiar with their actions. If people are dissatisfied with their representatives they can vote them out of office. It happened in 2010 with a "historic" shift from democratic to republican control of the House. The system worked.

The original intent of the Senate was to represent the interests of the individual states. The Senators were appointed by the state legislatures for the purpose of ensuring that the federal government was held to its enumerated powers and did not infringe on the responsibilities of the states. The Senators were held accountable to the state legislatures. If they reneged on their duties, they would be replaced. Back in 1913, the 17th Amendment changed all that.

Since the Senators are now elected directly by the people, they've lost their allegiance to the state. Their role has changed from checking the federal government's growth and influence to securing federal benefits. The more benefit secured, the more successful the Senator is deemed to be. This focus naturally encourages the expansion of federal power.

It costs a lot of money to mount a statewide Senate campaign—tens of millions of dollars in many instances. In order to raise this money, Senators accept contributions from special-interest groups including unions, environmental groups, and other organizations with specific agendas. Once the Senator is elected, their allegiance is often pledged to their contributors, rather than to the state or its citizens. The resulting legislation is often harmful to the country, but beneficial to the donors.

Repeal of the 17th Amendment will refocus the role of Senator on checking the growth of the federal government and protecting the rights of the state. Some may insist that appointment of Senators is unfair, but in light of the Senate's purpose, it is proper.

Consider how ambassadors are appointed to represent the United States at the UN and abroad. Their allegiance is to the United States, and they are charged to protect the United State's interest. The same applies to the Senate. The Senators should be concerned with protecting the interests of the states.

How ludicrous that the federal government is suing states over implementation of immigration policy or that the states are suing the federal government over the terms and conditions of the Health Care bill. If the Senators were fighting for the state's interest, immigration would be addressed, and the Health Care bill would not have been passed.

Term limits is a gimmick that masks the underlying lack of responsibility and morality. The first line of defense against federal corruption and incompetence is a vigilant electorate. The second is repealing the 17th Amendment.

National Popular Vote

I do not support the National Popular Vote (NPV) movement, which seeks to assign state electors based on the nationwide popular vote, rather than the statewide popular vote.

The Electoral College was established to protect the rights of the smaller states. Every state is assigned electors based on their representation in Congress, one for each senator and one for each representative. Michigan has 16 electors, two for our senators and 14 for our Congressional representatives.

There was no popular vote for president when the Constitution was ratified. The states selected their electors who then chose the President. The system made sense. The duties of the federal government were limited to only those functions performed on behalf of the "General Welfare" of the states. Washington performed services which the states could not effectively perform themselves—defense, immigration, etc. The federal government was granted no power or authority over the people's lives and was specifically prohibited from interfering in such by the 9th and 10th amendments. There was no need for the people to select the President.

There are only two systems currently in use by the states to select their electors, Winner-Take-All and District. Both represent the will of the people in the individual states.

Winner-Take-All: Specifies that the presidential candidate winning the popular vote of the state receives all of that state's electoral votes.

District: Specifies that the state's two electoral votes, applicable to the senators, be assigned to the presidential candidate wining the popular vote of the state. The Electoral votes associated with the Congressional districts are allocated based on the popular vote in each state Congressional district.

Michigan is a winner-take-all state. Whichever presidential candidate wins the popular vote in Michigan receives all 16 electoral votes.

The NPV movement wishes to add a third system for the allocation of electoral votes.

National Popular Vote: This system proposes that the state assign its electoral votes to the presidential candidate receiving the most votes cast nationwide, rather than the candidate receiving the most statewide votes.

If Michigan decided to utilize the Nation Popular Vote system, all of Michigan's electors would be assigned to the presidential candidate receiving the most votes nationwide, regardless of the will of the people of Michigan.

Assume, for example, that two candidates are running for office, Candidate A and Candidate B. When the Michigan's votes are counted, Candidate A received 63% of the vote, while B received the remainder of 37%. Assume further that the nationwide vote split for Candidate A at 49.97% and Candidate B at 50.03%.

How would Michigan's 16 Electoral votes be cast?

System	Candidate A	Candidate B
Winner-Take-All	16	0
District	11	5
National Popular Vote	0	16

In this example, the Winner-Take-All and District systems represent the will of the voters of Michigan. The National Popular Vote does not.

What are the potential problems with the NPV?

- It would allow candidates to campaign in high-population areas and ignore the rest of the country.

Candidates would rank the nation and actively campaign by population centers, rather than by state. Low population centers throughout the Midwest would be ignored.

If you look at electoral maps, the great majority of the countries landmass typically votes red, conservative, whereas the high population centers typically vote blue, liberal. The NPV would encourage campaigning based on population distribution rather than state.

- It would encourage the party in power to dole massive federal benefits to high-population areas to purchase this voting bloc with taxpayer money.

We already have an extensive percentage of the domestic population dependent on government. Millions more illegals are streaming across our borders receiving additional federal benefit. The natural inclination is for the party in power to try to capture these votes. The tendency is to provide as much benefit to these people as possible, effectively buying their vote with taxpayer dollars.

- Voter fraud is a massive problem, but it's currently limited to individual states. If the NPV were enacted, thousands of activists could be dispatched to high-population areas throughout the country to cultivate fraudulent votes.

Imagine, in the above example, if "unsavory" Candidate "A" needed 250,000 additional votes to win the nationwide popular vote. Activists working on his behalf could be dispatched to New York, Boston, Detroit, Chicago, Philadelphia, Los Angeles, Denver, etc. to "find" the necessary votes to push him over the top to win. It happened in Minnesota when Al Franken was elected, and it could happen again. Politics is a nasty business.

- A recount in a national election is virtually impossible. How could you possibly recount the popular vote of the entire nation? How could you control the honesty and integrity of the recount if activists were deliberately trying to manipulate the election? You couldn't.

The Electoral College is not broken and does not need to be fixed. Neither is the Constitution broken. What's broken is the elite political establishment, which seeks to ignore the Constitution and manipulate the system in any way possible to perpetuate their personal political power.

The popular vote of the President helped to usher in the era of big government. The positions of presidential candidates are no longer limited to the constitutionally enumerated responsibilities, but address how best to provide for the needs of the electorate—well outside the president's authority and job description. More often than not the people vote for the candidate providing the most direct benefit rather than the candidate best able to perform their constitutional duties.

The NPV is not the answer. It's designed to further perpetuate big government, massive spending, and a permanent dependency on the federal government. If passed, the only result will be the further destruction of our country.

The answer is to get back to our constitutional roots, limit the federal government to its enumerated authority, and once again allow the people and the states to address the needs of society. This will refocus federal elections towards providing for the security of our nation and discourage the election of candidates intent on implementing politically based social policy well outside of constitutional authority.

Federal Right-to-Work

I support the right-to-work movement in Michigan 100%.

States that have enacted right-to-work legislation have drastically improved their economic standing, and have actually increased union membership. It's truly a win-win situation and would be very good for Michigan.

An underlying principle of personal liberty is the ability to negotiate employment with an employer, free of third-party restrictions—union or government.

Right-to-work is a personal or state issue, but definitely not a federal one. The federal government should never address it.

The genius of the Constitution is that the authority of the federal government is limited to national duties such as defense, immigration, etc., which are incapable of being performed by the people or the states. Labor relations are definitely not an enumerated federal duty and the federal government has been granted no authority over this aspect of the people's lives. It's prohibited from imposing bureaucratic, one-size-fits-all, centrally controlled, highly regulated, federal labor-related programs on the people.

Centralized federal control always restricts personal liberty and should be shunned. Congress has already detrimentally interfered in employee-employer relations by passing many laws encouraging unionization and interfering with the free market—well outside any constitutional authority.

I am adamant about the repeal of these laws—the Wagner Act, the Davis Bacon Act, the Minimum Wage Law, various child labor restrictions, and all other federal labor regulations which do more harm to the economy than good. The people, free market, or states are more that able to address the situation.

The reason state sponsored Right-to-Work initiatives are even an issue is to counteract federal involvement in free market labor relations. The true solution is the repeal of all federal labor relation laws and allow the states to impose whatever laws, or lack of law, they feel best represents the interest of their states.

Peter Konetchy

Seven:

THE PLAN

Consider General Washington's plight at Valley Forge in the winter of 1777-78. He had suffered a string of defeats at the hands of the British who flaunted their superiority through the occupation of Philadelphia, the seat of our fledging government. While our troops were hungry, cold, and demoralized, the British occupiers lived in relative opulence in our heated homes growing fat on our food. Some leaders of the Revolution began to question General Washington's competence and thought the possibility of winning the war was hopeless.

In defiance of all odds we persevered and won our independence, spawning the greatest nation on earth.

Those of us cherishing the sacrifices of our forefathers face a similar situation today. We also have suffered a long string of defeats. For decades we've seen the gross expansion of federal power manifest through the creation of dependency on government; the redistribution of wealth; the effective nationalization of education, banking, housing, health care, and energy to name but a few; and the complete and utter disregard of constitutional compliance.

Many established leaders claim that our cherished principles, including a constitutionally limited government, are forever dead; and they have been willing for decades to compromise, if not flat out capitulate, with those trying to subdue us. They can no longer comprehend the fact that the federal government was created, and solely exists, to serve the needs of the states as enumerated in the Constitution; and instead promote the fabrication that the federal government is supreme, its representatives are our rulers, the people are their subjects, and the states exist to serve.

I vehemently disagree.

I cannot allow our most cherished principles to be compromised away by worthless leaders not beginning to understand the value of what they ignorantly discard.

Those in Washington have proven through their actions that they are incapable of imposing the required self-restraint to curb their insatiable lust for power.

Our founders understood and cherished liberty. Their counsel to us, through word and action, is to assert our birthright as free and independent men, never accepting attacks on our liberties from anybody, foreign or domestic.

Independence is an attitude manifest by action. Free and independent people do not submit to false authority. No aggressor can defend against the unbridled passion for Liberty and Truth.

How can we counter the assault on our liberties by our own government, by those charged with securing our liberty but doing the exact opposite?

We must first understand our goal as restoring the balance of government as originally prescribed by our founders. Jefferson addressed this balance when he confirmed the states created the federal government to perform special purposes on their behalf and delegated to it certain definite powers, reserving to each state the residuary mass of right to their own self-government.[92] We've lost this balance resulting in the federal suppression of self-government by the people and states.

---

[92] Kentucky Resolutions: "[The States] *constituted a general government for special purposes—delegated to that government certain definite powers, reserving, each State to itself, the residuary mass of right to their own self-government; and*

All is not lost. The proven solution has been bestowed upon us by our founders as prescribed through the Constitution. The problem lies not in the Constitution but in the fact that those currently charged with executing its responsibilities have convoluted its pure principles from securing our liberties into demanding our submission.

We must stand strong as a people, as states, and lastly as the federal government to fight the infringement of our liberties.

---

that whensoever the general government assumes undelegated powers, its acts are unauthoritative, void, and of no force:"

The Role of the People

The majority of the people in this country hunger for the return of our traditional American values of morality, self reliance, voluntary charity, patriotism, and freedom from government. We the people are the force of last resort.

We can't allow ourselves be cowered into submission through political correctness but must speak our minds, not rudely, but with confident truth. Those seeking to dominate us have no problem spewing forth the filth of their ideas, and if we allow the dissemination of lies without refute, the lies will be accepted as truth.

We can't accept the indoctrination of our children to philosophies antagonistic to our self preservation. Those seeking our demise twist our history into the unrecognizable, and present falsehoods as truth, in order to deceive the uninformed in their charge. We must educate ourselves, and those we love, and counter with truth the deceptions presented. Ask, and then listen to, what your children are being taught in school. If the teaching goes against your morality and values, confront those doing so and have them justify their actions. Evil unopposed flourishes, but when confronted it wilts.

We need to have the principled discipline to personally reject acceptance of federal benefit and instead take responsibility for ourselves and those we love. If we need help, rely on family, friends, or community to get through the tough times. The federal government has no money of its own, but provides benefit by extorting from one group to seduce another. It plays a role similar to a drug pusher providing "free" product to entice new users. Once people accept this benefit they have a tendency to become dependent on it, expect it, and lose the will to be responsible for themselves. The fostered result is the loss of self responsibility and self respect, bitterness towards those who succeed, and submission to the dominance of federal control.

We live in a representative republic and are able to elect, from our peers, the individuals to represent us at all levels of government. Thoroughly vet those running for office. Elect moral representatives to the state and local governments who understand the limited authority of the federal government, and refuse be intimidated, bribed, or threatened to accede to usurped authority. Once elected hold them accountable. The scourge of the earth is a politician elected on their promise to secure liberty, who then abuses this trust and turns their attention to the selfish accumulation of wealth and power.

The Role of the States

The states have a critical role in restraining abuse.

They created the federal government through mutual compact, and this government exists for the sole purpose of serving the needs of the states through the performance of its granted authority. Yet, the federal government has unilaterally elevated itself to a position of superiority over the states. This is a false and dangerous assertion. I ask the question, who signed the Constitution on behalf of the federal government? The answer is clearly "Nobody." The federal government was created by the states to serve the states. The only parties who can judge the propriety of action by the federal government are those responsible for its creation—the states.

Jefferson correctly stated within the Kentucky Resolutions of 1798:

> *"that to this compact each State acceded as a State, and is an integral part, its co-States forming, as to itself, the other party: that the government created by this compact was not made the exclusive or final judge of the extent of the powers delegated to itself; since that would have made its discretion, and not the Constitution, the measure of its powers; but that, as in all other cases of compact among powers having no common judge, each party has an equal right to judge for itself, as well of infractions as of the mode and measure of redress"*[93]

Regardless of their position of strength, the states docilely accept as valid unconstitutional dictates forced upon them by the federal government. It's critical that state legislators understand the proper division of powers and refuse to accept unauthorized dictates when thrust upon them. The states bind themselves to tyranny by fear or greed, but not by authority.

---

[93]   Ibid

The proper balance of government obligates the states to restrain federal authority to its granted powers. The states never authorized the government the ability to continually tax in excess of that needed to perform its duties, and more dangerously, to use this ill-gotten gain to purchase the dependency of both the states and people. The obvious solution to government overreach is for the states to nullify, [refuse to acknowledge, implement, or enforce], all federal action exceeding its specific delegated authority.

The Kentucky Resolutions of 1798 provided precedent for states to nullify unauthorized federal dictates. The federal government can bellyache as loudly as it desires, but the only constitutional course of action is for the states to nullify unconstitutional acts which are unauthoritative, void, and of no force.

Nullification is a potent force. As the individual states pass their State Nullification Resolutions[94] the federal government loses its power to interfere with, or control through funding, state mandated responsibilities. When enough states honor their Nullification Resolutions the only province left to the federal government will be to exercise its constitutionally authorized powers.

The states must understand that the federal government is irrelevant when acting outside of its authority and act accordingly.

---

[94] For a complete explanation of state nullification please review *State Nullification* within the Solutions chapter of this book.

The Role of the Federal Government

As the people and states express their independence, the federal government will naturally become populated with constitutionally minded individuals. As quickly as is possible, when Congress is again dedicated to performing their responsibility of securing the Liberty of the people, the following policies should be adopted.

Immediately balance the budget and eliminate unsustainable deficit spending. Crushing debt is destroying our economy, devaluing our money, holding us hostage to creditors, and enslaving our children. Unless we regain control, this debt will destroy our nation.

Thereafter, phase out non-authorized programs from federal control through the concept of Negative Baseline Budgeting.[95] Bureaucratic boondoggles, financed through repressive taxation, and implemented by mountains of regulation, are stifling not only economic activity but our cherished Liberty.

Implementation of these two policies will go far towards solving every domestic problem facing our nation today. It will realign the balance of government so that federal responsibility will be focused towards the security of our nation, and everything else will be addressed by the people through their own personal endeavor, an unrestricted free market, voluntary charity, or lastly programs provided by the state.

This plan is common sense. It's based on personal responsibility and Constitutional enforcement. The tools for our survival have been freely given to us and have proven overwhelmingly effective. Let's use them.

We are Americans. Celebrate and defend our greatness, don't let it be compromised away by those who are unappreciative.

---

[95] For a complete explanation please review the Negative Baseline Budget section within the Solutions chapter of this book.

Samuel Adams correctly addressed the independent spirit of free Americans when he said:

"If ye love wealth greater than liberty, the tranquility of servitude greater than the animating contest for freedom, go home from us in peace. We seek not your counsel, nor your arms. Crouch down and lick the hand that feeds you; and may posterity forget that ye were our countrymen."

EIGHT:

ZHANNA'S FIRST-HAND ACCOUNT OF LIFE IN THE SOVIET UNION

Written by: Zhanna Konetchy

Introduction

I immigrated to the United States from Russia at the age of 34. When people learned that I grew up in the Soviet Union, I noticed a curious and sincere interest about my life there. Many people asked me to write about it. I'll try to describe the life of the average family in the Soviet Union as I remember it during the years that were called, by the socialist media and communist apparatus, "the era of the prosperous developed socialism."

This period, when Brezhnev was a General Secretary of the Communist Party for eighteen years, was often overlooked because of the more "exciting" period of Soviet History, Stalin's oppressions, appeared to be more fascinating to people. The Brezhnev period did not grab too much attention because it was "mild tyranny"—no mass murders, no massive GULAGs, or mass starvation—therefore it was quite boring. The life during "the era of the prosperous developed socialism" reveals the rather dull existence of people, who were completely owned by state, who tried to adopt to their miserable reality the best they could, and most of whom were completely conditioned through years of fear and generational brainwashing, to become complacent and disillusioned that they lived in the most thriving country in the World. In the face of any shortcomings, the rhetoric of the Party was, "Only the state, represented by the central government, can cope with this difficult task."

The Soviet citizens maybe realized that their lives were not as prosperous as in some other countries, however, they believed that their lives were better protected then those who lived in the capitalist countries. They were satisfied to be safe from the worry of being unemployed and pleased to be shielded from fears about their retirement, health problems, and education.

When you'll read the following chapters, I want you to keep in mind that these people were lead to believe that they were not poor people. In the socialistic system it could not be so! It would be in disagreement with the socialistic principals of equality, so we were instructed that poverty was a phenomenon found only in the capitalist countries.

And how could the soviet people know any different? The media was completely owned by the state and had to carry the Party line. Most of the people could not travel abroad to see the truth for themselves.

The State ordered restrictions on travel abroad: once in three years people were allowed to visit other socialist countries such as Cuba, Bulgaria, East Germany etc., and once every five years capitalist countries such as Britain, France, Canada, etc. Also, before they would get permission to go, they would be carefully checked by Party representatives to verify if their ideological views were strong enough not to fall for the capitalist propaganda. It was made known to the traveling group that one of them was an undercover KGB agent, to make everyone in the group suspicious of the others. Traveling abroad parents could not take their children with them to discourage them from defecting.

The few who were allowed travel to the USA (mostly on a business trips) were very carefully checked and warned not to spread "rumors" about the "illusions of prosperity" they would see.

In my opinion it is too bad that this period was overlooked because it could help us to understand better what the USA is facing now, how much freedom we have already lost, and how far we have already gone into socialism, autocracy, and statism. You name it. It has all and the same face—the face of despotism.

In the following chapters I also shared my memories about "perestroika" to shatter some "illusions" Americans have about the "turning of the Soviet Union away from socialism to capitalism."

Another trivial thing, many are curious, was it hard to learn English?

As my English teacher used to say, anybody can learn foreign language with the grade "B."

I could compare the studying of English with little children learning their own language—through visual actions and by guessing the words, which sometimes would result in ridiculously funny confusion. The biggest fear for me was to not appear stupid in the eyes of others because I would not know what some word meant. As soon as I passed through this fear I did not hesitate to ask questions or explain what I intended to say. Learning English became easier.

The funniest phenomenon was when I mixed the use of the languages in a group of people consisting of both Russians and Americans during our last visit to Russia about 15 years ago. I found myself speaking to Russian people in English, assured in my mind that I was speaking to them in Russian, and vice versa speaking to Americans in Russian. I would understand my mistake only when I saw the confused expressions on their faces. I would then think to myself, "Oops, I used the wrong language," and we all would laugh.

For the Start

I grew up in a small coal-mining town in West Siberia.

In the Soviet Union "small town" usually meant that distributions of food, clothing, and other products were poorer than those of the larger cities.

There was a strict nomenclature for distribution of commodity fixed by the Center according to the "importance" and "productive capacity" of their citizens. Moscow and Leningrad (St. Petersburg) were the cities of the residency of the central government and had the best distribution of goods at their stores. Next step down were province capitals, then region capitals, etc. Therefore, the people who lived in the small towns or villages had poorer choices of consumer goods and services. Sometimes in the village stores you would not be able to buy anything but bread and vodka. The villagers had to raise all their necessities themselves by having a little kitchen garden, a few chickens, a pig, a cow, etc.

I loved mathematics at school and attended Tomsk University, from which I graduated in 1982 with a degree in ballistic engineering.

My choice for the college was not just due to a love for mathematics. I equally loved art and literature. However, during school years I noticed that any subject could be skewed and distorted by political correctness except for the mathematics which was ruled only by facts and logic. That fact made my preference.

I was married in Russia and had a daughter.

After the death of my first husband, Providence crossed my path with Pete's. Ours was a classical romantic story of writing letters to each other across the globe, meeting for the first time face to face in Moscow, and then coming to the U.S. where we got married and spent 20 happy years together.

In my younger years I always had a dream to visit the United States, probably because it was a sacred dream of my father. My father always praised the United States in his conversations.

He told me about the full satisfaction of work derived from the freedom to keep the fruits of your own labor. In the contrary, the Soviet regime always used some punishment for underperformance rather than reward for success. Ideologically, reward would create inequality, somebody would be richer than others, while punishment brings everyone to an equal state.

My father told me that anyone using their talent and hard work would succeed in the United States, unlike in the USSR. This was something foreign for the average Soviet person—to be able to reach prosperity without a need to betray their high morals and principles by seeking special corrupting connections to achieve a more comfortable life. As the saying goes, "One hand warms other hand."

My father told me about freedom of expressing your own opinion without fear of being disciplined by the centralized "apparatus." He brought me a borrowed book, Business in America by Smelyakov that was not widely available for reading in the USSR. Surprisingly, this book had a quite accurate description of living in the United States and the advantages of capitalism.

My Parents

My mother was a teacher and my father worked at the coal mine as a "propaganda" artist. Practically every plant or factory in the USSR had artists who would decorate the Soviet parades or paint billboards glorifying Lenin, the Communist Party, the Soviet style of life, etc. My father always liked to do artistic work; however, the political side of it was very unsatisfactory for him. He had no choice and couldn't do anything about it.

I could sense my father's constant discontent about how he was denied by the regime the ability to support his family as well as he could, if hypothetically, he worked for the free market and earned what he was worth. In the Soviet reality, he knew that he could be better rewarded only by overstepping his ethics, i.e. start cheating the system, stealing, or even joining the Party. My father despised doing that.

Once he told me that he wished that government would pay him what he earned in full and he would pay for his own needs, including his own children's education. With that concept all people would be in much better affluence. I brought up this story in one of the arguments I had with a liberal woman here in the U.S., pointing out that it was said by a man who lived in the socialist society under the Soviet regime. She cut me off right away and spewed out that my father was greedy. She clearly understood that my father lived in the Soviet

---

[96]   http://www.hist.msu.ru/ER/Etext/cnst1977.htm#7

Union; however, I don't think she even realized that my father was paid by the government only about $14 a month as a salary from which he also paid income tax. Greedy for wanting to have what he rightfully earned (not to take it from the neighbors through redistribution) and pay for his own expenses?

My mother quit her job for three years after my birth to take care of me. Most women would go back to work right after maternity leave. They would place their infants in an "infant nursery school" at the age of three months old, right after their maternity leave expired. My mother's wage was not that large an addition to their poor budget anyway; however, the main reason she stayed home was that my parents did not want to have me under the supervision of the state at such a young age. So many children were under the supervision of one nurse in the nursery school that they were not often cared for properly.

Later the Soviet government changed some laws for young mothers. In the USSR, the stillbirth and infant death rates were so high in comparison to other "civilized countries" and also the birthrate was so low that the government tried to resolve these problems by giving pregnant women two fully paid months of maternity leave both before and after delivery. Thereafter, young mothers would have partially paid maternity leave for up to 18 months, and non-paid leave for up to three years with the guarantee of keeping their job. After that law passed all women stayed home taking care of their children through the age of three.

After I reached the age of three, my mother returned to work, and I was placed in the "nursery school." Basically, all children in the USSR went to nursery schools, epitomizing "raising children by the village."

Since all parents worked, children were left at home without supervision after their school day. Neighbors or strangers seemed to enjoy disciplining, scolding, and nagging children who weren't their own. I remember seeing on TV a show where a British lady, who was living in the USSR with her child for some time, was very annoyed with that fact. In the interview she told it was getting on her nerves that every stranger seemed to think it was his or her duty to discipline her child.

At the nursery school, all kids would be separated into same age groups. Each group would have about 25-30 kids under the supervision of one teacher with the required college pedagogue degree, and an assistant. Children would have three meals there [my favorite was 4 p.m. tea with cookies] and an afternoon nap.

Funny, I do remember from my nursery school years how we had celebrations to honor "Grandpa Lenin," particularly on his birthday, April 22nd, sang songs and read poetry about "Grandpa Lenin," and learned how "Grandpa Lenin" loved all the children around the world.

School and College

The USSR Constitution, adopted October 7, 1977.

*"**Article 25.** The USSR has a unified and constantly improving public education system, which provides general education and vocational training for citizens, provides youth with communist instruction and intellectual and physical development, preparing them for work and social activities.*

__Article 45.__ Citizens of the USSR have the right to education.

This right is ensured by free provision of all types of education, the institution of universal secondary education of young people, the extensive development vocational, college and university education based on learning communication activity and production; by provision of state grants and privileges for students, free issue of school textbooks, educational opportunities in the school in their native language, to create the conditions for self-education."

We started school at the age of seven and had ten grades. For the first four years, we had the same teacher who followed us from grade to grade. That was different from the United States where every grade in the elementary school had a different teacher. We had elementary grades from 1st to 4th, junior grades from 5th to 8th, and senior grades from 9th to 10th.

The first day of school was always September 1st everywhere in the country (including the colleges), and school lasted through the end of May. Our school week consisted of 6 days with Sunday off. Each lesson lasted 45 minutes and there were 10-15 minute breaks in between. There was neither recess for the student as you know in the U.S., nor a lunch break. Whoever wanted to have lunch had it at their own discretion in the school cafeteria when they could fit it in, such as during the longest break between classes or after the school hours.

Like in the U.S. we had four vacations, however, based on different grounds: winter vacation was around New Year, fall vacation was during the celebration of the October Revolution (November 7th), and spring break would be a week before March, 31st (no particular holidays). It was always fun to return back from vacation on April Fools' Day and play tricks on fellow friends! And, of course, we all enjoyed our long summer vacation.

While students would be on their vacation, teachers still had to attend their work and go to school every day without any real reason to be there and would just fritter their working hours gossiping. However, teachers did have a two-month vacation during summer, the longest of all employees in the country.

Housing was very cramped, and most students lived within one or two blocks from their schools. We didn't have school busses and most of us simply walked to school. Those students who lived far from school had to use public transportation and pay for it themselves. We did not have "snow days," but sometimes little children wouldn't have school during very cold days.

Most of the schools were overcrowded and for the proper functionality all students were divided into two scheduling groups: morning and evening. Every other semester, half of the students would go to school from 8 a.m. to 2 p.m. and the other half would go from 2 p.m. to 8 p.m. The next semester these students would switch turns.

When I started school in 1966, ballpoint pens were unknown, and all our work was done with dip pens. Pencils were allowed to be used only for drawing and graphing. We would carry special spill-safe ink containers to school in the little fabric sacks. To insure proper calligraphy habits, fountain pens were not allowed until the middle grades. I remember the first ballpoint pens appeared when I started the fifth grade, about 1970. The Soviets made a rocket and sent men into space before they made a ballpoint pen!

The Center had the publishing monopoly and all student textbooks were the same throughout the Russian Federation. Textbooks were not free of charge when I went to school. The student's parents had to buy school books at the book stores as well as all other school supplies: notebooks, pens and pencils, etc. Students started to use the first free-of-charge text books in 1978, shortly after I finished school. According to the Act #1029 of 11.24.1977, in 1978 the free textbooks were supplied only to the elementary schools and by the year 1983, free textbook supposed to be in use through high school also. In colleges we used free textbooks borrowed from the college library.

Home schools were something unheard of. Homeschooling would be interpreted as a neglect of the child's education and parents would lose the child. My guess, the true reason was about the difficulty of controlling the homeschooling and children's proper communist instructions.

Of course, the learning had political propaganda and was secularized, both in the schools and in the colleges.

"The church in the USSR is separated from the state and the school from the church." [97] Whereas before the revolution "God's Word" was a essential subject in every Russian school.

Regularly, the local government inspectors, the school elite bureaucrats, would come to classes to check how well teaches would follow the centralized curriculum. Being a teacher, my mother was always nervous about these visits. She used to say that it was done with one purpose only, "to criticize the teacher." This criticism was supposed to improve the quality of education.

Besides the curriculum, the Education Ministry of the USSR dictated the soviet teacher's doctrine:

Teachers had to be a mentor to raise the students *"as a useful member of the communist society"*, to raise them in the *"attitude toward labor as a vital necessity and a true pleasure; taking care and having a prudent attitude towards communistic property—the material basis of the new system, approved by the*

---

[97] from the Article 52 of the USSR Constitution, adopted in 1977

truly humane Communist morality, which determines the everyday behavior of people." [98]

They had to ideologically convince the students, and make it second nature for them, that *"the ideal Communist man is opposed to the bourgeois (that is capitalistic) selfish ideals: of being eager for success, wealth and power, and petty-bourgeois ideals of the spiritually ascetic beggar, who is trusting in 'God' or the 'helmsman.'"* [99]

Duteous to this doctrine my mother had to instruct her students on the local history about how badly the coal mine owners, the bourgeois, treated their workers before the Revolution, and how much it was improved with the Soviets in charge.

One of her students got up and told my mom that her statement was simply not true. The fourth grader argued that his grandfather, who worked at the coal mine before the Revolution, told many good things about his boss. He told that the owner of the mine would send birthday presents to the workers and their children, knew everyone by name, and regularly checked their living conditions, etc. My mom was just speechless. She did not know how to respond to the boy, because deep down she knew that he was right, but by Soviet instruction she could not openly support the student's statement.

When teachers have a "sword hanging over their heads" there always will be some kid who would make a teacher watchful of their answers. Once I rattled my history teacher with the simple question, "Where did Lenin work?"

Well, after Lenin finished his studies at the Law School in Kazan University, he really did not practice law. Therefore, he did not earn his living by providing some service and by his own definition was a "parasite on society." Lenin lived off sponsors, "the intelligencia," [100]

---

[98] Translated   by   Zhanna   Konetchy   from   the   article
КОММУНИСТИЧЕСКОЕ ВОСПИТАНИЕ [Communist Education]
[99] ibid
[100] Meaning Intellectuals

whom he despised greatly, but who helped him to finance the Socialist Revolution. Of course, my history teacher could not say something like that to me, and because she had such a long pause before she gave me her answer, I sensed that she could not tell me what she was really thinking.

After finishing the 8th grade and 10th grade, we had final exams followed by a prom. Most boys would be drafted to the Army right after graduation. Every male had to serve in the Army after they reached 18, but were given a deferment while going to college. All college boys had to go through the ROTC program, and all Medical school graduates (including women) were automatically enlisted in the reserve.

To enter college in the Soviet Union was quite competitive. After making a choice of the college and a faculty, we had to pass four entrance exams on its campus. Exams included the major subjects of the chosen facility. For example, with my choice of a technical physics major, I had to pass two Math exams, a physics exam, and write a Russian literature essay. Another example, to enter the economic faculty the students had to pass Math, history, social studies, and write a Russian-Literature essay. Students with the highest scores were accepted.

Every faculty had a designated course scheduled for us for every semester and students were not able to change these subjects or their schedule.

It was the understanding among the Russian students of my generation (1970's) that American college education was of much higher quality than Soviet college education.

As the old saying goes, "nothing is for free", the "pay off" for the free college education came as a compulsory work assignment after graduation. Actually, college graduates were able to choose a place of work, but only from a list authorized by the Labor Department and sent to the Dean of the faculty. Frankly, it was not exactly a free choice, but every graduate had worry-free "guaranteed employment."

The procedure was following:

The Dean of the faculty received a list of the organizations, factories, or plants that made requests through the Department of Labor. All graduates were listed according to their grades. The students with the best grades would have the wider choice. The leftovers were for the slackers.

There was a law that college graduates had to work at the place of their appointment for three years and could not resign. That was a "payback duty" to the State in "gratitude for the free education."

After three years of the obligation these people were free to quit their job and seek a different place to work eventually. Fact is that the tangle of the Soviet residential system and internal passports system discouraged the work or residency changes (read about it in the chapter "Internal Passport: Serfdom, Soviet Style"). Therefore that "payback duty" would last until retirement.

Pictures

A coal mine in my native town with pile of slag in background

The railway station in the city of Novosibirsk around 1968

**My father during his service in the Air Force
with a picture of Lenin he painted**

My Parents on their honeymoon in 1958

**Family gathering with a new Radio—my father's parents on the left
and mother's parents on the right**

My grandfather holding me at his home

My nursery school in 1963—I'm in the middle row, 2nd from the right

New Year carnival at nursery school—I'm 2nd from the right

My parents holding me outside my Grandparent's house

I'm carrying bread outside my apartment building

Ready for the first day of 2nd grade in my holiday school
uniform—1967 (my every day uniform had a black apron,
holiday's had a white one)

My mother, Tamara, and her newly-wed husband, Victor.
Victor relates a heart-wrenching story about the murder of his
family, and growing up as an orphan, within the section titled
"My Family History and Accounts of Repression"

Freedom of Speech

Article 50 of the USSR Constitution adopted on October 7, 1977.

"In accordance with the interests of the people and in order to strengthen and develop the socialist system, the citizens of the USSR are guaranteed freedom of speech, press, assembly, meetings, street processions and demonstrations."

My father told that Khrushchev eased "freedom of speech." After Stalin passed away, people were able to criticize the government timidly, and only in the privacy of their homes. Usually Russian guys liked to gather in the kitchen and discuss politics being sarcastic about government while drinking vodka or beer. The people were allowed to "bark, but not bite." That was quite different from the Stalin years when people were afraid to say anything even to their spouses.

For the first time after the decades, Khrushchev opened the borders. Foreigners could visit only a few cities that had the best standards of living and the best general appearance.

Soviets had to improve the world opinion about of freedom of speech in the USSR. Some elements of so called "freedom of speech" appeared in the media; however, it was heavily censored by the Center. Of course, censorship was disguised as only applying against profanity, harmful insults, and betrayal of the country.

There were no GULAGs any more for "enemy elements," but there were mental institutions for "the unwilling to cooperate elements." Like during the Stalin regime, these facts were covered up and were revealed only after the "OK" was given by the Gorbachev administration in late 1980's.

Starting with the earlier 1960's, a few satirists made an entertaining career as "royal jesters." They were allowed to publically criticize their "masters" with scripted jokes approved by the Center.

Some journalists were a little bit cleverer trying to show us signs of the truth that they could not report but we could figure out ourselves. For instance, one journalist was reporting about the problem of a power shortage in Europe with conflicting video showing the full blast of electric lights and flashing electric advertising behind his back.

The Marx and Lenin's words "rotten capitalism" were used so often at schools and in the media that people turned it to sarcasms saying, "for so many years the damn capitalism is rotting, and rotting, but never seems to be able to deteriorate." However again, you could say it in the privacy of your home, but not from the public podium, especially if this podium is to be found on the University grounds.

My philosophy teacher at the University was "mildly punished" for his right of "free speech." He was not sent anywhere but only fired for telling the truth to the students about problems in the Soviet society. One of our students, who was infused with socialist propaganda, found the criticism of the socialism as irreconcilable with the principles of socialist society and issued a complaint to the dean. Our dean knew that the teacher was right. In the deep down agreement with this philosopher, the dean did not proceed with any charges against him. This student would not stop, and after his complaint was ignored, he went directly to the KGB, who sent a warning to the history and philosophy faculty to fire this philosopher. On his last day of teaching, this professor told us whole story. Our students had their own punishment for a whistleblower. They beat him up!

My Favorite Holidays

My favorite holiday was New Year's Day. We did not celebrate Christmas. Christmas was erased from the people's memories by Lenin's "Red Terror" against Christianity right after the Revolution. The Christmas tree was turned into the New Year Tree, and the Star of Bethlehem on the top of the tree turned into the Star of the Soviet Union. There were no angels on the tree. Lenin generously left "Father Frost" (the Russian Santa Claus) for the children's amusement, but there was no religious connection of any kind.

The New Year celebration was a carnival. Parents would make costumes for their children. No costumes were commercially made and sold. Children were visited by Father Frost and the Snow Maiden and participated in a lot of games, dancing, and other fun. Father Frost would pass children presents—a small sack of assorted candy and chocolates. And the biggest kick was that in each sack was one pretty apple and one orange. In Siberia we did not have oranges or quality apples sold at the stores, which is why these rarities were so special for children! These presents were distributed by the trade unions, meaning given by the government. Not exactly distributed!

Our parents paid for these presents. Government would supply the trade unions with the deficit candy, apples, and oranges, and the trade unions would divide them between the children of their members.

During the early 1990's, Christmas was officially returned as a national Russian holiday. I have never forgotten a ridiculously humorous comment from a lady in her seventies, "Now they (referring to the government) gave us this holiday, but they never instructed us how to celebrate it!"

I remember my parents and grandparents would always celebrate Easter. My Father was fascinated that the Soviets could never "kill" Easter from the hearts of the people.

My grandma would dye eggs by boiling them with onion skins, which gave them a dark brick-red color, kind of golden rustic and very pretty. She would always put one egg in front of the icon of Jesus that she had in the corner of her living room. She would cook a big feast with my favorite food, a big tub of rolls. I always enjoyed coming to her house for Easter.

I have another pleasant memory of my grandmother. Every time I would visit her, she would give me a glass of milk fresh from the cow. It was warm, very fluffy and airy. Not too many people in the U.S. (except farmers perhaps) have experienced that taste. It is much better than a milkshake.

Another fun traditional Russian holiday was July 7th, the Day of St. John the Baptist. It was not a national, but a combined folk and religious holiday. People would dump buckets of water on each other on the streets. It did not matter whether they knew each other or not. It was fun for kids, though! I tried to avoid going anywhere that day, or if I had to, I would bring my dog with me. She was a very kind dog, but looked quite ferocious to those who didn't know her. People stayed away from us, and I stayed dry. A pagan legend said that if you found the "flower of the fern" on the eve of John the Baptist Day, then that flower would open the treasures of the earth.

This would be fun, lol!

Free Health Care

Article 42 of the USSR Constitution adopted on October 7, 1977.

"Citizens of the USSR have the right to health care. This right is ensured by free, qualified medical care provided by state health agencies; by extension of the network of therapeutic and health-building; by development and improvement of safety and health regulation; by conducting of broad prophylactic measures, measures to improve an environment; by special care for the health of the younger generation, including the prohibition of child labor, with exception of school and labor training; by the scientific research aimed at preventing and reducing morbidity, to ensure a long and active life of the citizens."

In Russia, in general, services of any kind were limited, and polite people performing these services were a rare exception.

Healthcare services were not immune from rude employees also. Of course, I would never claim that everyone who worked in the healthcare was rude and many doctors and nurses were very considerate. The doctors and especially the nurses were among those government employees who had the lowest monthly wages. And how else it could be with free healthcare?

Even a healthy person has to encounter the necessity to visit a doctor sometimes. So did I on very rare occasions. Once, I twisted my ankle outside of my University dorm. Visual signs gave me idea that it was broken, however I was not quite sure. I decided to wait until morning to go to the hospital and was surprised by the appearance of an emergency ambulance crew in my dorm room. I didn't call the ambulance—one of my roommates did without my knowledge. The head of the crew yelled at me for supposedly calling them without good reason. He examined my leg, said that there was nothing wrong with it, and I could walk downstairs to the ambulance.

Our dorm room was on the eighth floor and our elevator was always out of order. I was not in the position to disagree and hobbled downstairs to the ambulance which took me and my roommate to the nearest outpatient hospital. The X-ray confirmed that I indeed had a break in my ankle. After casting my leg, the doctor gave me crutches to move to the hallway of the hospital. The crutches belonged to the hospital and could not be taken off the property. They did not sell crutches in the hospital either.

In the hallway, I found out that my roommate was no longer there and the receptionist did not know if she was coming back. Here I was—no crutches, no assistance, in the middle of January (icy roads and very cold), quite far away from the dorm, with a cast on my leg. It was a traditional old type plaster cast which can't be used for walking.

I asked the receptionist if I could use their phone. To my surprise, she let me—she probably had to get rid of me before the closing hours. I called my dorm. Surprise again—somebody answered! I asked some guys to help me to return to the dorm. Three guys came to get me. Once at the hospital, they caught a cab to drive me back to the dorm. When the taxi driver found out that we wanted to go only 2-3 miles, he laughed that I could easily hop back to the dorm.

Dental care in the Soviet Union is the most picturesque illustration of all the problems associated with "free" socialist healthcare.

It reminds me of the dentist "torture" scene in the movie "Marathon Man." That is exactly how dental treatment was performed in the Soviet Union—no kidding! The same as it happened in the movie, drilling was performed without anesthesia of any kind. In the movie the "dentist services" given to Dustin Hoffman were also for free—just as it was in the Soviet Union.

It was common that Government would not supply dentists with the cement for fillings. Without cement, these fillings would not last more than a couple of weeks and would fall out (not the doctor's fault). Because of this rationing, people had to go a few times a year to have the same tooth fixed again, and again, and again. In a few months, the tooth would be gone and need to be pulled out.

All other healthcare departments also had similar poor supplies, unless it was for government elites. For example, in the hospitals there were no disposable syringes. The same syringe was used for all patients standing in line, only the needles were changed. That caused a high incidence of hepatitis.

> *"Between 1980 and 1987 the incidence of hepatitis B doubled, and 52-68% of new infections were linked to medical procedures in hospitals and clinics. Between 12% and 15% of all hepatitis B infections in Moscow were linked to blood transfusions."*[101]

The Soviet pharmaceutical research was very poor. The elderly would literally use aspirin as a universal painkiller because nothing better was available—just like Obama's well known prescription, telling the older lady to take aspirin rather than surgery.[102]

Drugs, eyeglasses, dentures, or crowns were not free of charge.

In the delivery hospitals there were not enough pads for women. Babies were wrapped in reused linen. Most of these rags were so old that they had holes.

I believe if an American woman would have experienced giving birth in a Soviet hospital, she would not describe it is as anything but a nightmare.

My own memory of the Soviet delivery hospital in 1986.

First, the woman in labor was placed in a special pre-delivery room with a few beds in it, in my case it was eight beds, with a few other women in labor. The beds had mattresses without sheets, but wrapped in vinyl for easier cleaning. All these women were supervised by one or two doctors.

---

[101]   Zhores A Medvedev, Evolution of AIDS policy in the Soviet Union.
[102]   Video of Obama: https://www.youtube.com/watch?v=U-dQfb8WQvo

I personally had a nice doctor, but many women told stories that they were yelled at by staff to "shut up" if the woman in labor would cry from unbearable pain.

When a woman was ready to deliver, the doctor told her to walk into the delivery room. This room had a few quite tall stainless steel tables with a smaller drop table, also stainless steel, at the end for the convenience of the nurse to work with the baby after delivery.

I walked to delivery room, was helped to climb on the table and then left alone without supervision—the nurses had a lunch break. I was horrified that, if something would happen, the baby would drop down about couple feet to the end "drop" table. I started calling hoping somebody would come. One of the nurses came grouchily.

A few deliveries could be performed at the same time at the same room. After delivery, the baby was washed, brought to the mother to take a first look, and then baby was taken to a babies' room and mother had to walk to the recovery room, or she would be brought there on the roller bed, depending on her conditions.

Finally, that room had regular beds with the sheets. I had a room for two. In many other hospitals more than six women were in the same room.

Because of the very high percentage of baby fatalities in the Soviet Union, all women, together with babies were kept in the hospital until baby's umbilical cord would dry out and fall off—about a week.

As I already mentioned, women had to beg the staff for pads. It was not actually pads, but some old rags that were washed regularly and then sanitized in the special ovens. Relatives and husbands were not allowed to bring pads from outside because of sanitary restrictions. Wearing underwear was also disallowed. I have no idea why, probably for the same sanitary reasons.

I don't remember if there were showers. I think there was one in the room I stayed in but it was out of order. Anyway, there were no bath towels otherwise women would tear them up for their pads. We did have a toilet in our room. My mother remembered they did not have showers at all in her delivery hospital, it was in a smaller town, and the one bathroom on a floor, down the hall, was extremely dirty and cold.

During this week, the babies were always separated from their mothers and brought to them only during scheduled feeding hours. Mothers were strongly recommended to release their milk after the feeding into metal cups which were collected by nurses. This milk was used to feed the babies in between their scheduled feeding hours—literally—"feeding by the village."

The visitors, including husbands and parents, were prohibited either to come inside the rooms or have direct contact with the new mother and the baby. Sanitary restriction!

The week when the women were hospitalized with their babies, their husbands usually would come to visit them and stand under the hospital windows. There was always a bunch of men under the hospital windows, sometimes climbing on trees, trying to see their wives through the windows. During summer, if the windows were opened, husbands and wives would be yelling to each other the latest news. The winter created a little problem for a verbal communication.

Upon the mother and baby's release from the hospital, the husband would bring all the necessary new cloths and blankets. The baby would be dressed up by the staff and brought to the happy parents in the waiting room. That would be a first time when husband and relatives could see the baby.

Free healthcare lasted until the USSR was bankrupt.

During all years of the socialist regime the Soviet government **made a concrete promise** of the free healthcare for everyone. It was the best justification for socialism for everybody—the elderly and young. It was explained to the people that there were no other countries in the entire world that had better health security then those under the socialism. It was explained that people of the capitalist countries had to worry about how they would be able to pay for their healthcare, not in the USSR. People were forced to support the socialist healthcare system by their "slavery" work all their lives, completely unaware about it, because there were no health care taxes or any other fees taken from their payroll for them to see. The same thing occurred with retirement, education, etc.—no taxes were itemized for people to see that they were in fact paying for these services. Soviet citizens knew only about their progressive income tax that averaged 13% taken monthly from their salaries.

Nobody had the slightest doubt that free healthcare would always be available for them. During the 1990's, when hyperinflation occurred, the government discontinued "free healthcare" with the only explanation that they did not have any more money to sustain it. And just like that, free healthcare was gone! And just like that, all elderly were dropped off the promised free healthcare and left without any idea how to pay for their health needs.

On top of that, they lost all their savings due to hyperinflation, which I'll address in my next chapters about "perestroika."

The Internal Passport: Serfdom, Soviet Style

From Wikipedia: *"Serfs were laborers who were bound to the land."*

From the dictionary: *"A member of the lowest feudal class, attached to the land owned by a lord and required to perform labor in return for certain legal or customary rights."*

To attach "laborers" of the Soviet Union to a place, the Soviet government used the Internal Passport system. The Internal Passport, unfamiliar in meaning for any US citizen, **but very similar to the concept of e-verify**, was not just an ID document. This kind of "Super ID document" often defined and controlled the person to which it was presented. *Kinda like a "vaccine passport?!"*

Without the Passport, one could not be hired to work, could not get married or die [to receive the death certificate relatives had to bring the passport of the deceased to exchange for a death certificate], could not apply for a school or nursery for their children, or do very simple things such as getting a package at the post office or a book from the library. Most importantly, without the Passport the people could not freely change their place of residence, but had to be "attached to the place" with the special entry "propiska." Propiska is basically the address of the person stamped in a specified place in the Passport. In the Soviet Union, people were required to have an Internal Passport upon reaching 16 years of age.

The Internal Passport included following information:

1. Picture
2. Full name
3. Date and place of birth
4. Place of the application for the Passport
5. Nationality
6. Marital and divorce status
7. Military reserve or service status
8. Prior convictions (if any)

9. Prior citizenship (if any)
10. Some special notes, such as blood type
11. And most important, the place of their residency, propiska

Before 1974, the Passports also contained the place of work.

If someone wanted to find a job in the town of their choice they were required to show their passport. If the person resided in a different city, then their request for work was declined on the foundation that they did not have the legitimate "propiska", even if the job was available. One could seek work only in the city where they had "propiska."

Therefore, this system could be called serfdom by definition.

To clarify, "propiska" works almost like a visa. One belongs in the place where one was born and automatically gets "propiska" in their Passport when they reach age of 16. To be able to move to different city and seek a job, they had to change the "propiska" through permission of the government officials. Also, they could not reside in a different city without having an apartment, or room in a dormitory, distributed to them by their place of employment, through a different branch of bureaucrats. It's a "vicious circle."

If someone had to live someplace temporarily, they had to put this information in their passport. Temporary "propiska", for example a dorm address for students, let a person get only a temporary job for the time of studying. After that, they would be refused to have the same job, unless they managed to somehow get the permanent "propiska."

Most people could not change the place of their residency because of the difficulty of getting "propiska." That was a perfect system to discourage or stop people from migrating from one place to another.

Especially difficult, actually almost impossible, was to move to cities such as Moscow or Leningrad if one was not born there. These cities were elite cities. They were much better supplied with food and other goods than other cities in the country and too many people wished to live there. "Propiska" was a perfect tool to control "overpopulation" in the big cities.

However, there was a program called "limited." This program allowed an unmarried person get a job that Moscow residents would not do, because it involved hardship or very hazardous conditions and very little pay. This person would settle a five year labor contract, upon completion of which they would get a "propiska" in Moscow as a "reward for this hazardous work." After that, they usually would quit that job for a better one.

The Soviet people who were deprived of civil rights the most were collective farm workers. They were denied having their passports in their own hands until 1974, about 50 million people or 20% population; therefore, they could not leave their villages for more than 30 days, even for a vacation, without special permission from the director of the collective farm who had in his possession all of his farmers Passports.

The easiest way to change residency was by getting married or with the government's demand that the person should be transferred to a different place of work. Usually officials would "move" the person, and their family, either for promotion (usually connected with the Party promotion), or because of a special request for a certain needed specialist—mostly in the military industry or for scientific military research.

Three Socialist Myths

A YouTube video, made by an ex-Soviet citizen, surfaced on the Internet[103]. This citizen confronted some Wall Street protestors and asked questions.

The protester on the video wanted to replace capitalism with socialism, because she believed that socialism is a more fair system. She gave three socialistic myths believed to be true by many. She said:

1. *We won't have people unemployed*
2. *We won't have people hungry*
3. *The workers would be paid decent wages*

I would like to address these myths.

Myth Number One:

The protester said, *"We won't have people unemployed."*

Communists often attributed to <u>Lenin</u> the quote, "He who does not work shall not eat." With that saying, only productive individuals could be allowed access to the articles of <u>consumption</u> in socialist states.

Article 12 of the USSR Constitution adopted in 1936 stated,

> *"In the USSR work is a duty and a matter of honor for every able-bodied citizen, in accordance with the principle 'He who does not work shall not eat.'"*

---

[103]   http://www.youtube.com/watch?feature=player_embedded&v=8L088WJ9c98(or watch as report with Andrew Napolitano http://www.foxbusiness.com/on-air/freedom-watch/index.html#/v/1247466175001/toe-to-toe-with-the-socialists-at-wall-street/?playlist_id=158146)

"Work in the Soviet Union, however, is not so much a right as an **obligation, enforceable by Law . . . Those who avoid 'socially useful work' are liable to prosecution as 'parasites'** *(emphasis added) under Article 209 of the RSFSR (Russian Socialist Federation of Soviet Republics) Criminal Code . . ."* [104]

Unemployment was officially renounced by the Soviet government in 1930. Since then, according to the Party, there has been no unemployment of any kind. It could not be so—not under the fairest political system in the world! One would never see beggars or bums on the streets. They simply were picked by "milicia", the Soviet word for police, and put in prison or chain-gang camps.

"The Labor law was part of the Soviet Constitution and initially was characterized by the legalization and regulation of forced labor. Back in January 1918 the Soviet Congress adopted the "Declaration of Rights of Working and Exploited People," which called for universal labor service. Initially it was used for the non-laboring classes, such as the exploiters and the rich. But gradually it spread to all able-bodied citizens over 16 years old.

It is symbolic that the section one of the first Soviet Labor Codes was called **"Labor Duty,"** *and its final chapter XI—* **"Right to Work."**

After the adoption of the Decree "The Universal Labor Duty" on January, 29 1920, the labor service became mandatory for the general Soviet population without differentiation based on classes.

Adoption of specific language in the Labor Law made any court challenge useless. Transfers without the consent of the employee were not the exception but the rule. Evasion to register or turnout for labor service, absence without leave was recognized as an administrative offense, or a crime ("malicious and repeated violations").

---

[104] Social and economic rights in the Soviet bloc: a documentary review seventy By George R. Urban

The above-mentioned decree of 26 June 1940 prohibited the termination of the employment contract unilaterally, which effectively meant a working attachment to the company. Permission for leaving work could be given only by the head of the organization who, by all Soviet rules, had to be Communist members.

The Trade unions increasingly lost their function of protecting the interests of workers and in 1933 became, in essence, a federal entity.

On June 23, 1933 the merge of the USSR People's Commissariat of Labor (the department in charge of overseeing the enforcement of Labor laws) and the Trade Unions was issued by the Decree of the USSR (basically by the Soviet Constitution)."[105]

The **"Right to Work"** was a one of the other rights proclaimed by The Constitution of the USSR in 1977.

It was stated in the Article 40:

"Right to Work"—by this we mean the right for a guaranteed employment and pay in accordance with the quantity and quality and not below the state minimum,—including the right to choose a profession, occupation or work."

Reality was, as I previously mentioned about Soviet Internal Passport system, "propiska" was a perfect tool for the State to control a person's ability to change the residency and therefore an assurance that this person would not change their place of work. Most of the Soviet people have never changed their place of employment.

With so called "full employment", combined with the "command economy", the Soviet Union created a problem as bad as unemployment—"forced idleness."

---

[105] Development of Domestic Labor Laws in 20th and beginning of 21st Century http://yourlib.net/content/view/7466/88/

The Soviet Union had a planned growth for the manufacturing sector, for the sake of industry rather than public consumption, and bureaucrats were deciding what was to be manufactured rather than consumers. This system also brought great corruption.

Millions of people went to work, clocked in, and had nothing to do all day. They had a job, but their "pair of hands" was not required, was not supplied, and simply was not needed. So, people were sitting around chatting, gambling and drinking.

Because there were not enough people who wanted to work for construction or collective farms, the work was physically hard, hazardous and done without machinery and for extremely low pay; the Center required that every Soviet organization, plant, or factory would sent their workers for temporary duty to construction work or collective farms. To satisfy this requirement the bureaucrats would hire extra people with an idea to send some of them to do this type of work.

Short term farm work, such as picking potatoes, cabbage, weeding, etc., was required to be carried out by every employee of not urgent importance—students, assembly workers, engineers, and even the military. An exception was made for party elites—they had to make important decisions for the sake of the Country.

The concept of equal pay reverberated in quite low wages for everyone. There was very little reward for better performance; therefore, there was no incentive to perform. People took less pride in their work than people of other nations. The popular soviet saying was, "The fools are carrying water!"

With that said, I would like to break to the next Soviet myth:

Myth Number Two:

The protester said, *"The workers would be paid a decent wage."*

The wages of all the Soviet people were very close to being equal, and very often, it had nothing to do with their diligence, but with their job seniority and the amount of physical labor required.

The lowest pay was for workers at the collective farms. In addition, their conditions of living were extremely low. That's why almost nobody would go to live on the collective farm voluntarily. Most people who lived there were born there. The government also sent college graduates to the villages to "pay back" their free tuition, and usually these people were stuck there after they got married.

In the cities, everybody would start with the minimum wage, and then some little money was added for a college education. The intellectuals: teachers, doctors, news reporters, actors, were paid least. Their salaries were increased only by seniority and level of education, but that increase was very little. Engineers also had low pay, however those who worked at the large plants, especially military, would receive extra bonuses every month, which would add up to 20% to their monthly salary.

The next step higher in wages, were for people performing very hard physical labor: assembly-line workers, bus drivers, steel workers, miners, etc. The higher pay for these workers was connected with a very high death rate or possible trauma. For example, death rate among coal miners was very high and they were paid pretty decent monthly wages compared to others. "Each 1 million tons of coal production cost the life of 1.35 miners In Russia, and only 0.00000002 miners in USA". [106]

> "... the minimum wage in the USSR in the 80's was 70 rubles per month. The vast majority of Soviet citizens with college education started their career with a salary of 105 rubles. The salaries of the engineers, after many years of experience could reach 200-250 rubles. Highly skilled workers received 200-500 rubles. Relatively

---

[106] (translated from **Шокирующие факты о России** http://cccp-revivel. blogspot.com/2011/07/blog-post_02.html)

high salaries have always been in the military. Thus, it appears that the average wage in the USSR was about 150 rubles." [107]

The readers can calculate how much it would be in relation to the dollar; one dollar on the black market equaled 10-14 rubles in the 1980's, meaning the average monthly wage in the USSR was less than $15 per month.

The pay was so low that it was out of the question for a wife to stay home and watch the children. All women had to work. Still, it was enough for most families to sustain themselves only from payday to payday. The Soviet "apparatus" was very proud to claim that women had equal pay with men. That may be true by the Soviet Constitution, but the reality was that a great majority of women had lower qualifications than men and as a result, lower salaries. Many women performed most of the very hard physical labor, because a lot of men were alcoholics and were drinking on the job rather than working. After their hard day of work, these poor women had to stand in shopping lines, cook the food, clean the house, and take care of kids—those all were exclusively the women's chores.

The only "decent" salaries were paid to the few on the top:

Chief engineers earned around 350-450 rubles per month,

Directors of the big plants, especially military, earned up to 600-700 rubles per month. They all were required to have a Communist Party membership, and were in fact, the Communist Party elite.

The money itself did not reflect the level of prosperity. There was something that showed a person's real social order better than money—special privileges. *"The Communist Party elite shopped at special stores and had luxury cars with drivers. They owned country dachas [summer*

---

[107] (http://www.newsland.ru/news/detail/id/798929/ Soviet citizens were wealthier inhabitants of Russia)

houses] and took extravagant trips abroad."[108] The dachas and trips abroad were often "free", i.e. paid for by other people. It was considered an authorized job expense.

"The Communist Party apparatus became the most gigantic mafia the world has ever known."[109]

Because of the low salaries and lack of consumer goods, corruption in the USSR reached an unbelievably high level. It seemed as if almost every citizen was involved in some sort of corruption. Those who had access to deficit consumer goods, and basically all goods were in deficit, either exchanged them for other privileges or for bribes. "Hands wash the hands."

> *"Soviet corruption cannot be compared to corruption in the West. Corruption in western nations was optional, while most Soviet citizens would have to 'deal' a little to survive.*"[110]

Corruption was most widespread among the salespeople, autoworkers, and restaurant workers. They cheated customers in every possible way: added water or glue to the milk products, substituted bread for meat in hamburger products, under-weighed the product [food was sold by weight, not prepackaged] and cheated with the calculation of the price [there were not calculators; everything at the store was calculated by abacus]. If it was a clothes, furniture, auto parts store, etc., the salesperson would withhold the most desirable products and would not sell it to anyone, but only to the people who would pay a premium bribe or offer exchange for a different deficit product or privilege.

Myth Number Three:

The woman said, *"We won't have people hungry."*

---

[108] (http://stalingrad_1943.tripod.com/stalingrad/id19.html Eric's Soviet Collectible Page Corruption under Brezhnev)

[109] ibid

[110] ibid

I was always very skeptical when the Soviet "apparatus" told us that the USSR had much lower prices than capitalist countries, specifically the USA. Also, when American tourists would come to the USSR, with their dollars, and remark how cheap everything was, I had to smile. It is hard to compare the real differences in the costs of living and prices of different consumer goods between countries. It can be done only by contrasting the actual purchasing power.

Another difficulty is that "average" salaries between countries could not be compared equally, in my opinion. As I mentioned, in the Soviet Union the wages of all people were relatively equal. The correct comparison, between countries, could be made only between the same professions and the same qualifications. However, the doctors for example had the lowest salaries in the Soviet Union and in the USA one of the highest.

I made my own evaluation that would be visual. I wanted to be able actually see what prices of goods would be in the Soviet Union if the average salary of the Soviet worker's purchasing power would be compared to an average earnings of $2,000 per month for a U.S. worker. That way, it is easier to see the real difference in cost between Soviet and American goods.

I recalculated the prices based on the average Soviet salary 150 ruble per month for the year 1980. Why 1980's? In the beginning of 1980's there was the highest standard of living in the USSR. The previous years and did not have the inflation that happened by the beginning of 1990's, when the prices of goods were changing drastically every week. I do not claim any scientific authenticity; I just want you to have "fun" with me.

Numbers talk better than words:

Note: Everything in the USSR was weighed in kilograms (kg). To ease the conversion of the kilograms to the pounds I used the calculation of 1 kg equals 2 lb. Numbers are rounded.

Name of the product	Real price in 1980 in rubles/kg	% of the wage per 1 lb of the product	Price the USSR citizens would pay if their average salary would be $2,000 per month per 1 lb of the product
Meat (this was the official gov't store price)	1.80	0.6	about $12
Meat (real price at the market)	5.00 to 7.00	1.67%–2.33%	$33–$47
Processed meat: bologna, ham	2.38–3.50	0.80%–1.17%	$16–$23
Salami (could buy only at the market)	5.00–7.00	1.67%–2.33%	$33–$47
Fish (was very cheap)	0.75	0.25%	$5
Butter	3.60	1.2%	$24
Oil	1.56	0.52%	$10
Cheese	2.26–3.20	0.75%–1.07%	$15–$21
Eggs	1.10–1.20 per 10	0.77% per 10	$17–$19 per 12
Sugar	0.86	0.29%	$5.73 per 1 lb: 3 lb bag $17 or 5 lb bag $29
Flour	0.34	0.11%	$6.80 for 3 lb bag $11.33 for 5 lb bag
Bread	0.26	0.17% per loaf	$3.50 per loaf
Rice	0.45	0.15%	$3 per 1 lb
Macaroni	0.52	0.17%	$3.50 per 1lb

Potato	0.14	0.05%	$.93/1 lb $2.80 for 3 lb bag, $4.67 for 5 lb
Vegetables & Fruits	0.34–0.72	0.11%–0.24%	$2.26–$4.80 per 1 lb
Vodka per 0.5 liter bottle	3.62; 4.12	2.4%; 2.75%	$48–$54.90
Cigarettes (most men in USSR were smokers)	0.40 per a pack	0.27% per pack	$5.33 a pack or would be $53.33 per carton
Men's shoes	about 30 rubles	20%	$400
Women's shoes	about 40 rubles	27%	$533
Women boots	70–90	47%–60%	$947–$1,200
Pants	about 30 rubles	20%	$400
American jeans (Wrangler)	100 rubles	67%	$1,333
TV: black and white	227	151%	$3,027
TV: color not a widescreen	707	471%	$9,426
Refrigerator	250	33.33%	$3,333
Car (Fiat)	7,600	worth 4.25 years in pay of full salary	$101,330
Public transporta-tion for one way ride	0.03–0.05	0.02–0.03	$0.40–$0.67
Apartment (for 2 room with water + electric bill I paid)	23–25 rubles per month	averaged to 16%	averaged to $320 per month

In the USSR we bought almost everything by weight at the counter, and carried our own plastic bags to the store. We often bought cottage cheese, sour cream, and milk by weight. We would carry jugs to the store to buy milk and sour cream.

The quality of some products was not comparable to U.S. standards. Cooking oil, for example, was not well refined sunflower oil. One could see flakes on the bottom of the bottle which could take about 1/3 of the bottle space. We never had olive oil.

There was no meat at the store, except in Moscow and Leningrad, so the 1.80 rubles per kg price is a complete fake. We were able to buy meat only at the farm market for the price of 5-7 rubles per kg. In Novosibirsk, we had special ration cards enabling us to buy ham or meat at the store at government prices. We could buy 1 kg of processed meat or 2 kg of fresh meat for 1 person monthly.

Fruit prices that are given in the chart are for the lowest quality of apples and grapes—those from the government stores. Apples often had worms inside and half of the grapes were very rotten. People would stand in line and pinch off the rotten grapes before they would put their choice of grapes on the scale. Better choices of fruits were available at the farm market, but the price was 3.50-5.00 rubles per kg (or roughly equivalent to $23-$33 per pound).

Personal profit was a bad concept and called "speculacia"(speculation).

> From Article 13 of the USSR Constitution of 1977. ". . .
> *The private belongings or the property allocated for the use of the*
> *citizens should be used neither to derive unearned proceeds nor to*
> *the detriment of society."*

That's why a lot of people were angry at the farmers or middleman who would sell at the farm markets, just as the Wall Street woman from the video was angry at the bankers.

The farm markets were legitimate; there were special buildings for them in the cities. Food was checked by officials and farmers paid a fee for the rent of their selling place.

Many farmers were selling their product on their own, standing on the side of the road, or from their homes. My Grandma sold fresh milk to her neighbors, and they loved it because of its freshness and high quality. They knew she did not dilute it with water.

About half of the potatoes at the store were rotten, and we would have to buy the rotten potatoes with the good. Many people bought potatoes directly from the farmers by buckets, and most people grew their own.

People would grow potatoes everywhere. Some had the kitchen gardens; some just occupied a piece of land near the railway or in the outskirts of the cities, and would plant potatoes. It was a lot of work, and they had problems with looting at harvest time.

To save money, most of people would have their own kitchen gardens. Kitchen gardens in the USSR were not a hobby as in the U.S. People relied on their harvest to live through the entire winter. They spent all their weekends, and most evenings in the summer after work, taking care of their kitchen gardens. After harvest, they had to process the food into canning jars. All women performed this work after their full day at their government job.

Mushroom and berry picking in the woods were essential additions to the food supply for the families for winter.

We did not have jams at the store. We either had to buy or grow berries and then make our own preserves, or buy jams from the "old ladies" at the farm market. The most traditional were strawberry, raspberry and currant.

These berries were never sold at the stores. I remember the price of strawberries would start at the farm market at 0.50-1 ruble per cup (in my recalculation, $6.70-$13.33 per cup), and then in the peak of harvest, the price would be around 20-22 rubles per bucket. 10-15 liters would fit in the bucket, making the price around $290 per bucket (would be about $10 and higher per pound). Black currant was a little cheaper.

Oranges and bananas were not sold in the stores either. They were available exclusively in Moscow or Leningrad. I had bananas when I was 3-4 years old, and loved them, but then we did not have them for years at the stores. They reappeared again in 1990s—25 years later.

So, basically during 1970's and 1980's, the people in the USSR did not starve, but Russians had to work longer hours for their food than people did here in the U.S. However, there were instances of severe famine in the USSR during different periods of its history which I'll address in more details in the following chapters.

On a short note: The woman from the video would not have time to protest if she lived in the USSR. After work she would hurry to her kitchen garden, often in very crowded public transportation, and work until late at night if she wanted to have some food for a winter. She would then come home by bus (or whatever), "drop dead" to sleep and in the morning, go back to her low-wage work for the state and start this cycle all over.

Shopping

The Soviet people had to make daily trips to the stores. We bought only as much as we could carry. Most food stores were located a block or two from the apartment houses where we lived, and were quite small. We bought bread and milk products either daily or every other day. Other food, that kept longer, would be bought as needed or when it became available.

After work it seemed that all people were running—shopping. If they would see a line they would quickly join it and then ask "What stuff is being sold?" A line meant something desirable was sold. For Americans, it would be hard to comprehend, because it seems they always have everything in plenty. For Russians basically any desirable product, for example, window glass, toilet paper, linoleum, tile, etc., were in deficit.

There weren't any quality finishes and lacquers for the wood. Mayonnaise and ketchup were among the hardest products to find. We did not have diapers. The first time I saw diapers was in the United States. We used a piece of old cloth for the same purpose and washed it regularly. We did not have changing stations for babies anywhere, either.

Interior paint was of three colors only: brown [we used it to paint the floor], some dirty sheen of dark green [yuck!], and ivory. People preferred to paint their windows and interior doors in light blue or white, which had to be obtained from the black market.

Everything had a fixed price. Government was a monopoly. All prices were set by the Center, Moscow, and all products cost the same. Because prices were fixed, many goods, such as irons, coffeemakers, ballpoint pens, books, etc., would have preprinted prices stamped on them permanently. Even the clothes would have a sewn label with the price, similar to American labels for washing instructions.

There was no dog or cat food at the store, so we fed pets what we ate. For cats we would most often buy fish, which was much cheaper than meat or sausage. With dogs it was a little easier—they are not as picky as cats. I would always cook some extra food to give to my dog. My sister would get four ice-cream cones after school: one each for my daughter, me, herself, and my dog.

Here is something I bet Americans have never had: public drinking "vending" machines for a soda. These vending machines had a glass for public use. The machines had a special design that allowed a thirsty customer to rinse a commonly used glass prior to use. Once the glass was cleaned with the cold water, they would put it under the spout, insert the coin, and the glass would be filled with soda. For the price of 0.01 ruble, about 13 cents, it would be just water with carbon fizz. For 0.03 rubles, about 40 cents, you would receive flavored soda, somewhat reminiscent of cream-soda, but of maple color. Americans would probably find it extremely unsanitary.

Another traditional non-alcoholic summer drink was "kvas", i.e. malt. It was made out of bread [rye mostly], water, yeast, sugar, and molasses, and had a little sour-sweet bread taste. It was a favorite Russian drink in the summer.

Unlike in the United States, it was nearly impossible to return even defective products. I still feel uneasy returning goods to the store today, even though I know that in the U.S. returns are no problem. Years of "Soviet training" cannot be forgotten.

Getting an Apartment in the Soviet Union

Article 44 of the USSR Constitution adopted on October 7, 1977

"Citizens of the USSR have the right to housing. This right is ensured by the development and protection of the state-public housing; by assistance to cooperative and individual housing; by fair distribution of the residential space under public supervision, to be provided as the program for building well-appointed homes, as well as a low price to pay for rent and utilities. Citizens of the USSR have to carefully treat the housing allocated to them."

Many have heard about the long lines in the Soviet Union, but how many of you know about the long waiting lines to receive an apartment, sometimes as long as 20 years? In the Soviet Union, apartments were owned by the state, and were distributed to the people by the state, mostly through the places of their employment. Usually, a person would submit an application for an apartment at their place of work and would have to wait until an apartment became available. That could take years and years, on average ten to twenty.

A special commission of bureaucrats, which mainly consisted of the "communist elite" at the local work place, was in charge of the distribution of apartments. My father used to call them "little czars."

Micro tyrants.

Of course, there were some rules; for example, the commission would look at your marital status and whether a couple had children and how many, etc. Those who were not married or did not have children were constantly moved behind the "more worthy people" in the line. The waiting time also depended on the "bank of apartments" that was available at the particular work. For example, if one worked in the construction industry, the waiting time would be significantly shorter than for the ones who worked, for example, at a school or hospital, because government gave "privilege" to the construction industry since they always had shortages of employees. If one changed the place of his employment, they would lose their position in the waiting line for the "apartment bid" and have to start all over again with a new application at the new place of work. Another governmental tool for controlling the migration and to discourage the people from changing their work place!

However, the decision for the distribution of apartments was made on the premise, "How useful was someone to the country for this privilege to have an apartment?" That premise, together with an extreme shortage of apartments, opened the door for corruption through bribes and use of special connections. Of course, government elites, "key holders" of apartments, were the most useful members of the state and got apartments without any problem. Go figure!

For all the rest, there was the so-called "sanitary norm system":

> *"The sanitary norm system was introduced in the 1920's to ease the problem of housing shortage that was caused by urbanization and mass immigration to cities. The sanitary norm was approximately 9 square meters per person for most of the Soviet era, and a smaller living area entitled the person or family for a bigger apartment. However, the average living space usually did not meet the standard and people ended up living in highly overcrowded circumstances. For example in Moscow the average was just over four square meters per person in 1940."[111]*

We called it "meterage law." It stated that a family was entitled to 9 square meters, 81 square feet, of actual living space per person. Therefore, most families with one child could get only a one-room, not a one bedroom, apartment.

My parents and I received a one-room apartment. I slept in the kitchen until I was 14 and outgrew my child-sized bed. My parents had to move me to their room after my legs stuck far out of my bed and started touching the refrigerator.

---

[111]   Housing in Russia—Policies and Practices by Rosa Vihavainen. University of Helsinki, Department of Sociology http://blogit.helsinki.fi/respublica/ RP05_Interim_Housing.pdf

Many young families had to live with their parents while they waited for the officials to give them an apartment. My neighbors were a typical example. In a two-room apartment, one of the rooms was occupied by the two retired parents, while their son, with his wife and two children ages 12 and 7, lived in the other room. They had a fold-out couch for themselves and a bunk bed for the children. A 6.5 square meter, 58.5 sq foot, kitchen and a bathroom were shared by both families.

I remember a story about one lady, an assembly worker, who lived all her life at a dorm, which is sharing a room the size of a typical "Motel 6" room with 3-4 other people. The toilet was down the hall, and showers were in the basement of the five-floor dormitory building. This lady was constantly moved to the end of the line, because she had never been married and did not have a child. Finally, the commission decided to give her an apartment as a gift for her retirement. The old lady declined and decided to live rest of her life at the dorm. She was scared to live alone in her old age and would rather live together with the other 3 girls in the room.

Personally, I hated the dormitory. I lived in different dorms for nine years. To be stuck in the same room with 3-4 other girls, with no common interests, for years, was not enjoyable.

Soviets also had a law for upgrading an apartment. To upgrade an apartment due to the growth of the family, one had to make a request and get into the line again. To be eligible to upgrade your apartment, the family would need to occupy less than 6 square meters, 54 Sq feet, per person in their current apartment.

The quality of the new apartments left much to be desired and many new apartments would have a lot of unfinished work. People did not build it for themselves or for their own profit; they all were just on the State payroll. What difference did it make if they did a good job or bad? I've heard some horror stories, such as the drain pipe in the bathtub being plugged with cement, because the builders found it inconvenient to dispose of it in the proper place and the bathtub was closer. Whoever moved to such a newly constructed apartment would always have problems with plumbing. Also, constructors would leave behind trash, garbage, and feces that the new "lucky" tenants had to clean up.

Housing was always at an extreme deficit. In the Khrushchev period, the Soviets tried to solve the housing problem by mass producing low quality apartments into which people could "temporarily" move until better housing became available. People named them "Khrushchev Apartments" and hated them.

The Monopolistic Building and Obsolete Designs:

> "The largest share of new housing consists of widely disliked high-rise apartments. They have been produced by citywide housing kombinats[112] using obsolete, capital and energy-intensive, large-panel industrial techniques. Enjoying a monopoly position in an environment of shortage, these new kombinats are totally unresponsive to the preferences of the population. The composition of the output in terms of unit types does not match the changing composition of the urban population. The rate of design innovation is very low: fewer than two new types of apartments per decade. The quality of newly finished units is poor: upon delivery, recipients of a new unit usually must spend about 10 percent over production costs to bring their unit to a decent level. These days, due to severe shortages of industrial parts or infrastructure, housing kombinats have been known to deliver buildings in which the water supply does not always reach past the 7th or 8th floor in buildings with 9, 12, or 22 floors." [113]

I had a very poor quality of a plastering and flooring in my apartment. I tried to solve it by covering the walls with wallpaper, but it would

---

[112] Kombinats come from the word "combined" and can be thought of as a government organization which built the apartments and provided the associated services—water, electric, heat, etc.

[113] The Housing System of the Former Soviet Union: Why Do the Soviets Need Housing Markets? *By Bertrand Renaud* The World Bank http://www.knowledgeplex.org/kp/text_document_summary/scholarly_article/relfiles/hpd_0303_renaud_pt1.pdf

peel off the wall regularly because the wall was not smooth. I covered the sub-standard floor work with rugs. There were neither alternative services available to make repairs in the apartment nor supplies. Everything was done through the city "kombinat."

Right after the Revolution the Soviets came up with an idea for a "solution" to the housing shortage. Here how the University of Helsinki describe it:

> "Housing shortage remained as a constant problem in cities since the 1930s until the 1980s despite the numerous attempts for solving it over the decades. In the 1930s the housing shortage problem was responded to with a policy called "consolidation," meaning that a large apartment where the sanitary norms were exceeded was inhabited with new residents, sometimes by evicting the original ones, who usually were bourgeoisie. As a result, a new housing type was created, the communal apartment, i.e. an apartment where several unrelated people lived together sharing the common areas of the apartment, i.e. kitchen, toilet, corridor, et cetera. Communal apartments became the dominant type of urban housing in the 1930s characterizing the Soviet housing in cities until the 1990s."[114]

We called these apartments "communalka." That is one apartment, consisting of two or more rooms, where people who were not related to each other were forced, by government bureaucrats, to share the apartment. One of my ex-coworkers, a single women and a missile engineer, had a room in this type of apartment. The other room of this two-room apartment was occupied by an alcoholic. They, of course, had to share a kitchen and a bathroom as well. She complained to me that every time after she would put her clothes to soak overnight for washing, this man would urinate in the bath tub on her clothes just for fun. She finally saved a significant sum of money and "bribed" some old lady, who lived by herself in a one-room apartment, to make an

---

[114] Housing in Russia—Policies and Practices by Rosa Vihavainen. University of Helsinki, Department of Sociology http://blogit.helsinki.fi/respublica/RP05_Interim_Housing.pdf

exchange—the room in the shared "communalka" for the one room apartment.

My parents also lived for a while in "communalka" when I was a toddler. They had one room in a three-room apartment. The other two rooms were occupied by two other families. My mom stayed at home with me while my dad was at work. The husband in one of these families was constantly drunk and would beat his wife. My mom told that she was so scared that they would break the door during a fight that she would grab me and sit in a "safe corner." Finally, after one of my father's firm demands, they gave us a one-room apartment.

In the villages, small cities, or in the outskirts of big cities, people could buy or build their own houses, but the land that it was located on was owned by the state. These houses did not have showers or bathrooms and had only outhouses. All plumbing supplies were distributed by the government and only to the kombinats. My grandparents had their own house. My grandmother had to carry water to the house from the well—it was 1970's, not the 1870's. Finally, in the early 1970's, the government put in a water system on their street, and they could receive water in their house, only cold water of course, but they still did not have a sewage system. All water drained into a bucket under the sink, which my grandmother dumped in the middle of the street when it was full.

To build or buy a house was quite expensive. There were no mortgages, of course, and one could buy or build a house only after they saved enough money. Also, these houses did not have conveniences, but some people still preferred to build or buy them, because as a rule they were roomier than apartments and had their own kitchen gardens. However, laws prohibited building these houses in the large industrious cities.

Everybody in the country always complained about their cramped living conditions, but could hardly do anything about it. It was their "sacrifice" for the better life of the next generation, for their children. However, the communist elite who constantly asked people to "sacrifice" distributed to themselves the best apartments. Some apartments were modified for them as two-floor apartments. For an outsider, it looked as if they had the same apartments as other people, but if you would enter their apartment, you would realize that they had a staircase inside to the upper floor, and they had more rooms than anybody else. The elite, of course, did not advertise it too much. Everything was hidden and concealed.

Interesting statistics:

> *"In the early 1980's total area of housing accounted for 15 square meters per person in the Soviet Union. The corresponding figure in France was 30 square meters, in Germany—40 square meters, in the U.S.—50 square meters.*
>
> *Each year twice more housing was put into service in the United States than in the USSR: 260 million square meters of housing in the USA and 130 million square meters of housing in the USSR.*
>
> *The housing services in the USSR took only 6% of the average family budget, and in the USA—26.6% of the average family budget.*
>
> *The Soviet citizen worked an average of 18.2 hours to pay for housing, an American—45 hours. However payment of 1 square meter of housing required to work for 1.23 hours in the USSR, and only 0.87 hours in the USA."*[115]

---

[115] Translated by Zhanna Konetchy from <u>Советское общество второй половины 1960-х—начала 1980-х гг</u>. 1. Урбанизация и жилищная проблема http://his.1september.ru/article.php?ID=200103501

Public Transportation

A small newspaper reporter found out that I grew up in the Soviet Union and was very curious. Asking some questions he was excited that the Soviet people mostly used the public transportation and remarked, "It must be really clean in Russia." I was flabbergasted, "Are you kidding?!" I was sure that as a reporter he knew how dirty the Soviet Union was. His eyes were completely honest, no sarcasm.

No, use of public transportation does not make environment cleaner, but it does taking freedom away from the people.

The great majority of the Soviet population used buses, trolleybuses, trams, and trains.

Rush hours were the worst time to ride! As a rule, people were rude and insulting. People stormed the busses, not for a seat, but simply for a chance to ride. Sometimes bus drivers would use the "packing of the people" method to squeeze more people on. He would start the bus, and then very quickly slam on the brakes. People would be packed closer inside, and more people would jump in from outside. People were packed like "sardines in a can."

Sometimes the bus driver would yell at the passengers because they would break the doors. The opening and closing of the doors worked on water hydraulics, and in the very cold weather, they would not open—the water would freeze. People would start forcing the doors; the bus drivers lost earnings if the bus needed repair, so they were not happy.

I hated to ride in the crowded buses in the summer also, when everyone dressed lightly and was sweaty.

I remember sometime in the 1990's that Phil Donahue had a show called "Space Bridges" in cooperation with the Soviets. Some girl tried to explain to him what a communal apartment was, "communalka." I remember his face looking confused, because he could not comprehend how it was possible for completely unrelated people or families to be forced to live in the same apartment.

I suppose that I'll have the same difficulty explaining to Americans how it was to ride on the Soviet trains in second-class cars.

There were basically two classes of passenger cars for long-distance travel.

First class cars would have separate compartments with doors for privacy. There were nine compartments in the car for four people in each—two bunk beds.

The second-class cars held more people—54 passengers in the car. There were nine compartments holding six passengers in each compartment, two of which used sidelong bunk beds. To save space, there were no doors and no curtains.

The second-class cars were the crown jewel of collectivism. Everyone and everything was open to strangers for three, four, or more days. There was no privacy for changing clothes or for conversation, and no security for belongings. On hot days, many men would strip off their shirts to their bare torsos for all to see, in order to stay cool.

Every car had two washrooms with a toilet and a sink. All waste from the sink and the toilet was drained on the railway directly below. For sanitary purposes, these facilities were closed during stops at the stations. The car had no showers or air conditioners. Travel from my city in Siberia to Moscow would take about three days. The longest stretch within the Trans-Siberian Railway, Vladivostok to Moscow, would take a little over seven days by the express train.

How My Father Bought a Car in the Soviet Union

A quote from the very popular Russian book <u>Twelve Chairs,</u>[116] *"The automobile is not a luxury, but a means of transportation,"* is true in United States, but not in the USSR.

More and more people in the United States are buying into the Utopian dream about the "equality" of everyone having a Cadillac after they extort it from the "greedy rich." Let's look at the Soviet reality.

In the former Soviet Union, cars were in deficit, as were many other consumer goods: refrigerators, TVs, tape recorders, vacuum cleaners, etc. There were only four models of cars that were produced in the Soviet Union for personal use. One of the most available models was the prototype of the Fiat and put into production in the early 1970's.

> [For information: *"In 1966-1970, Fiat sponsored the building of the AvtoVAZ car factory in the Soviet Union. The factory produced an adapted version 124R of the 124 known as the Lada BA3-2101 / Zhiguli (sold as the Lada 1200 in export markets) until 1988. These cars are almost identical to the 124 apart from aluminum drum brakes on the rear wheels in place of disc brakes, modernized engine (an overhead camshaft engine, in place of the original Fiat OHV unit) and thicker steel."*[117]
>
> *"FIAT was chosen because at the time Italian communists were gaining power in Italy and it was a good chance for the USSR to show support."*[118]]

---

[116]   written in 1927 by Ilja Ilf, Evgenij Petrov

[117]   Fiat 124 From Wikipedia, the free encyclopedia http://en.wikipedia.org/wiki/Fiat_124

[118]   Automobile industry in the Soviet Union From Wikipedia, the free encyclopedia http://en.wikipedia.org/wiki/Automobile_industry_in_the_Soviet_Union

In order to buy a new car in the USSR, one had to be approved by the authorities as "worthy" and having "sacrificed" enough for the country, and therefore earned the honor of being able to purchase a car.

This person would write an application at the place of their work and wait for a certain period of time while this request would be examined and discussed by bureaucrats, "little czars", who decided if the applicant was worthy to have the opportunity to buy this car.

I was in high school when my parents wanted to buy a car. They really tried to scrape together all their savings, because they had to pay in full for the car in advance. The monopolized Soviet bank did not give loans or mortgages. My parent's salaries combined were 230-240 rubles per month. The car they applied for was a Lada (a FIAT prototype) and cost 5,500 rubles, but it was denied to them by bureaucrats. My father was not considered "worthy" to purchase the car he wanted, even though he worked for almost 20 years at the same coal mine, but he was a "surface" employee and was not a shaft man. Nevertheless, three workers, including my father, were given an opportunity to purchase a more expensive model of Lada, costing 7,500 rubles. My parents decided to take this only chance and borrowed the additional money from my grandparents.

After the "little czar's" authorization, my dad had to wait an additional time, a short period of only 6 months, until he could pay for the car in full, get his receipt, and travel over 200 km to pick up the car. The same pick-up day was appointed for other two guys.

When these three "lucky" guys, owners of their pre-paid new cars, came to the pick-up place, three cars were already selected for them, and all of these cars had defects. Even though there were many other new cars on the lot without defects, my father's request for a car without defect was denied.

The attendant simply told them to, "take it or leave it." He explained that only these three cars were left for the current month's pick-up; the other cars would be distributed to the next month's buyers. "Leave it" meant that my father would go home without the car and would have to start the process all over again.

They decided to take what was available and then fix the cars themselves. They took the cars by their position on the list:

The first guy got a car that was missing the decorative nickel stripe on one side.

Second was my father. His car had a dent on the front bumper close to headlight.

Third guy got the car with a hole through the hood. It looked like it was cut with an ax.

The cars had barely enough gas to reach the nearest gas station, and of cause, the choice of the color was out of question. Be happy with whatever was available!

Also the Lada (Fiat) was quite a simplistic car, but was of bad quality and was not very reliable. [I couldn't believe that the Obama administration forced Chrysler to merge with Fiat.] Auto service was practically unavailable, especially in the small cities. In the big cities, one had to wait for a few months for auto service. Auto parts were hard to find and mostly were available only through the black market. Most guys spent a lot of time, almost every day in their garages, fixing their cars by themselves and consulting with each other. There was no replacement on a new car if it was defective and no new car warranty as in the U.S.

Compare my dad's situation to the service offered by the "greedy" capitalists, who want to satisfy their customer's demands in order to sell them their product. By the way, it would be a dream for many to have a pick-up truck; to be able to use it to traverse the "famous Russian bad roads", or for transporting oversized purchases, for example.

All trucks belonged to the state, and in most cases to transport furniture, or something like that, people had to "bribe" the drivers of these government trucks for that non-official "service."

On the other hand, all important government officials had private government automobiles, always black, free of charge, and supplied with drivers. Their drivers did not work regular hours and could be called any time. The "elite" often used these cars and drivers for their personal needs.

And is this a "dream of equality?" To beg the government and rely on their "generosity" for every possible necessity, for every possible product you have need of?

Soviet "Rice Fields"

A few years ago, at the age of nine or ten, our youngest son wanted to work to make some money. Nobody would hire him until he reached the age of 16, and some places wouldn't hire him until he was 18.

That reminded me of how I was taught in the Soviet schools about the "exploitation of children by capitalists." If someone hires a child and pays them money, as it used to be in the U.S., it was the "exploitation of a child." If the children were forced to work for free for the state, as in the USSR, that was not exploitation of a child, but the voluntary exchange for a common good. In socialism "everything belongs to everybody," therefore we worked for ourselves, for our own benefit.

When we were kids, we had a few chores to perform for our country for free.

The yearlong duty was a janitor job. In my school, all students from fifth grade and up had to wash the floors in the classrooms.

Every classroom at school was assigned to a group of students, about 28-30 students, and a teacher. The teacher would divide us into pairs. Every pair of students had to stay after classes were finished to clean the trash, move the desks and chairs, and to wash the floor in that classroom.

Other chores were seasonal.

One of them was work at the collective farms harvesting potatoes.

It is appears that every socialist regime comes up with their own massive program of forced labor in agriculture, i.e. symbolic "rice fields."

Soviet Union had own "rice fields"—"potato fields."

All students, starting from fifth grade and up, were excused from classes for two to three weeks to carry out their duty of greater importance and urgency—"saving the harvest."

We would board the busses at 8 a.m. and would be brought back around 5-6 p.m. Sometimes the busses were so full that over the half of students had to stand.

All the work was done by hand and we had to bring our own pitchforks, hoes, and buckets. We also had to bring our own lunch and water.

Of course, we were never paid; otherwise, it would have been an "exploitation of children." In my opinion the main idea was to condition impressionable youth to collective thinking, "From each according to his ability . . ."

When I studied at the University, first-year students were sent to work at collective farms for a month and half to help harvest the wheat. The school was, of course, suspended for that period. We got a miniscule pay for our work, since we were not children, and work for money was not an "exploitation of children" anymore.

Second-year students and up, except graduates, commuted to work daily at the potato fields during the harvest time. Again, college was suspended for 2-3 weeks in an order to send students to work at the fields.

For college students, machinery was used to bring potatoes to the surface, and the students had to pick them up and stack them into piles. The university also provided us with food.

At my regular work, all engineers also had to work at the collective farms, doing different chores, like weeding for a few weeks in the summer, which was paid by their regular work places. Some got an assignment to go for a month or two to the collective farm during summer or fall.

Another "free work for the common good" was "subbotnik."

In the new Soviet tradition every year on April 22nd the Communist Party organized "subbotniks" which commemorated Lenin's birthday. **Lenin was born on April 22, 1870.** All people were forced to "volunteer" to clean streets of garbage, plant trees, etc.—again, for the common good, to "improve the environment", and to prove that the "common property" is more important and essential then individual property.

April, 22 of 1970 was a jubilee which celebrated the 100th anniversary of Lenin's birth. I don't want to sound conspiratorial but . . . does this date sound familiar . . . the first Earth Day?

"Subbotnik" was a symbol of the ideological war against individual property and property owners. Lenin's own words about the first "subbotnik" are following:

> "*the ground is being cleared for the actual building of socialism, for the development of new social links, a new discipline of work in common and a new national (and later an international) system of economy of world-historic importance.*" [119]

Lenin's entire premise was that individuals were not capable of maintaining their own property, were driven by greed, and would exhaust all resources for their petty profit. For that reason all property must be converted from private to public property for the benefit of all people. *This man was a covetous PIG.*

> "*This is a matter of transforming the very habits of the people, habits which, for a long time to come, have been defiled and debased by the accursed private ownership of the means of production . . . For hundreds of years, freedom of trade and of exchange has been to millions of people the supreme gospel of economic wisdom,*

---

[119] *V.I. Lenin* From The First Subbotnik On The Moscow–Kazan Railway To The All-Russia May Day Subbotnik http://www.marxists.org/archive/lenin/works/1920/may/02.htm

the most deep-rooted habit of hundreds and hundreds of millions of people. This freedom is just as utterly false, serving to mask capitalist deception, coercion and exploitation, as are the other 'freedoms' proclaimed and implemented by the bourgeoisie, such as the 'freedom to work', (actually the freedom to starve), and so on.

In the main we have broken irrevocably with this 'freedom' of the property-owner to be a property-owner, with this 'freedom' of capital to exploit labor, and we shall finish the job. We are combating its remnants ruthlessly, with all our might . . .

Let us build a new society! . . .

We shall work for years and decades practicing subbotniks, developing them, spreading them, improving them and converting them into a habit. We shall achieve the victory of communist labor." [120]

[120]   ibid

Insider Look at the "Perestroika"

Many people who lived outside of Russia and received their information from enthusiastic reports of the mainstream media, learned about Democracy growing in Russia, but this was quite a distorted picture. Americans knew, and could recite, the famous word "perestroika." The worldwide media said that Russia is on the road to a "free-market economy" and even called it "capitalism." I have only one question: Could it be a free-market economy, or capitalism, without ownership of private property? As I remember, the Communist Party allowed people to start their own small business, but it did not let people own the property.

By the middle of the 1980's, after 70 years of the Soviet "command" policies, the economy was in such a devastated state that the Party decided to ease some principles of "pure" socialism. It was obvious that socialism did not work, but the Communist government did not want capitalism, because capitalism required freedom, and Communists did not want to lose their unlimited power. They insisted that socialism works, and that the best example is "Sweden socialism." However, they realized that there was no money in the treasury, and this was going to be a huge problem in few years. They had to do something.

> *"This is an overview of the plan [Perestroika] he [Gorbachev] presented in April of 1985 to the Plenary Meeting of the Central Committee of the Communist Party. The Communist Party then endorsed his plan of Perestroika as their general policy line."* [121]

In 1987, "perestroika" started. Gorbachev's plan in his own words:

> *"There are people in the West who would like to tell us that socialism is in a deep crisis and has brought our society to a dead end. That's how they interpret our critical analysis of the situation*

---

[121] Mikhail Gorbachev: Can Perestroika Produce Democratic Freedom? *By Jay Rogers* Published August 1991 http://www.forerunner.com/ forerunner/X0665_Gorbachev_-_Democrat.html

at the end of the seventies and beginning of the eighties. We have only one way out, they say: to adopt capitalistic methods of economic management and social patterns, to drift toward capitalism. . . .

To put an end to all the rumors and speculations that abound in the West about this, I would like to point out once again that we are conducting all our reforms in accordance with the socialist choice. We are looking within socialism, rather than outside of it, for the answers to all the questions that arise. We assess our successes and errors alike by socialist standards. Those who hope we shall move away from the socialist path will be greatly disappointed. Every part of our program of perestroika—and the program as a whole, for that matter—is fully based on the principle of more socialism and more democracy . . .

More socialism means more democracy, openness and collectivism in everyday life, more culture and humanism in production, social and personal relations among the people, more dignity and respect for the individual . . . We will proceed toward better socialism rather than away from it . . . We want more socialism and, therefore, more democracy."[122]

→ socialism 3 dignity and respect for the individual?! A complete OXYMORON!

The Party allowed the introduction of small businesses only for the craftsman and some public services. Big industries remained under the government control.

My first husband and I used this opportunity to open our small business, an agency arranging lodging for travelers.

The rules for a small business were as follows:

A small business in Russia, a "cooperative," had to operate like a collective group of people, on the same basis as a socialistic establishment. It had to be operated by no fewer than three people. We had to have regular meetings, where, as a collective group, we had to decide and document for officials who would be the head of the

---

[122] ibid

cooperative, who would be the bookkeeper, and set rules for wages, and so on. Then, we had to ask the local government officials for permission to operate.

The bookkeeper could not be related to the head of the "cooperative", for example they could not be husband and wife. A bookkeeper had to take a monthly tax report to a local government bureaucracy, who would carefully check it. Taxes did not seem too high for us in the beginning, a little over 40% on business, if I recall correctly, plus a 13% income tax. We were able to earn more money than at our government jobs.

Soon, products of small businesses started to appear and were of quite decent quality: food, clothes, shoes, etc. Government business was going into greater and greater stagnation.

Most of the people still worked for the government for the low wages, and they became increasingly envious of the improved life of the small businessmen. Many believed that this is what real capitalism looks like and thought that their hardship was caused by its unfairness. These jealous people were very happy when the Racket, or organized crime, kicked off and started to extort money from these new businesses. The Racket started growing really fast, and the government didn't do much about it. In fact they probably encouraged it.

One example almost reminds me of the movie "Godfather." Farmers were selling meat, and a mob of organized criminals came, took the best product for themselves—for free—and then made the farmers pay a "protection fee." When one farmer refused to pay, this mob openly took all his meat and threw it under the cars.

Small businessmen did not have any protection from the government and no support from the people. On the contrary, most of the people were happy to see such a travesty—punish the rich! Others did not want to get involved out of the fear of the organized crime.

The Communist Party also disliked the fast increase in the difference between the wages of the people working for a small business and government workers. Communists wanted to control this wage growth. They came with some of the most ridiculous taxes on wage increases; for example, a 3-5% increase in the wage as compared to the same month of the previous year incurred a 1 ruble tax for every 1 ruble of increase. For a 5-7% increase in wages, 2 rubles of tax was collected for every 1 ruble increase; and for wage increase over 7% there was a tax collected of 3 rubles tax for every 1 ruble increase.

Taxation of enterprises revenues used for payments to employees (effective in the fourth quarter of 1989 and in 1990)

Increase in total payments to employees, as compared to preceding period, %	Tax payments for every ruble of the increase in payments to employees, rubles
less than 3	no tax payments
3 - 5	1
5 - 7	2
more than 7	3

Source: *Izvestija*, 1989, August 11.

For fun, try to check up the calculation of this tax, especially for a newly established business, when the income for the starting year is very low but increases significantly for the next year, and you'll find out that business would need to own their own "money printing machine" to pay this kind of tax.

The repressive taxes did not bring in the expected revenue. Government needed more revenue and thought that people were hiding their money "under their mattresses."

The government decided to eliminate the 50 and 100 ruble banknotes. They required the exchange of these notes within only a 72-hour window (January 23-25, 1991). After that, all 50 and 100 ruble

---

banknotes were nullified. There were other limitations. A person could exchange not more than 1,000 rubles. Also, people could withdraw from the banks not more than 500 rubles per month.

This reform created panic and anger among the people; they did not want to lose their money. It was unbelievable. Huge lines formed at the banks as people were standing in lines for long hours to exchange a few bills. I think some were in the line all night long. People were frustrated. Some were demonstratively burning their bills in front of the banks. These pictures were all over the news. These methods were called by the government "Shock Therapy" and were supposed to stop the corruption, unfair profits, and threat of inflation.

> *"In December 1990 new Prime Minister B. S. Pavlov who insisted on eliminating the 50 and 100-ruble notes, carried a price increase. Uncontrolled devaluation of money continued. As a result, the ruble has depreciated significantly. The relationship between enterprises and regions were undermined, production continued to decline. The major cities were put on food stamps; there was a threat of famine."[123]*

All of these policies were combined with another increase of taxes. Taxes were increased retroactively every 3 months. That trick did not help to increase revenue of the government, either. The final nail in the coffin was an introduction of 25% sale tax, value added tax. The government told us that all civilized countries have this tax, and this tax will make our lives easier, because they will take the income tax of 13% off our backs. Well, we ended up with both of them.

Of course!

I remember the anger of the people at the stores when an additional 25% tax was added to the price. All stores had to cover their windows with metal protection, because during night, frustrated people would smash the windows.

---

[123]   translated by Zhanna Konetchy from: В.С. ПОЛИКАРПОВ, И.В. ЛЫСАК "ИСТОРИЯ РОССИИ В ХХ ВЕКЕ", 7.5.6. КРИЗИС ПЕРЕСТРОЙКИ И РАСПАД ССС (page 166) http://dbs.sfedu.ru/wwwdev/umr.umr_download?p_umr_id=20566

Violence was the first reaction. Then people start to learn how to avoid that tax.

A barter economy emerged. In the newspaper's advertising section, one could find all sorts of barter exchanges. One of the funniest I remember was someone exchanging a bathtub for a pig. The author of the article _Where Cash Isn't King: Barter Lines Pockets in Ex-Soviet States_ gave another comical example: _"In Altai, Siberia, two eggs buy one admission to a local showing of a Sylvester Stallone movie."_

Barter exchanges were very widespread among businesses as well to pay for their products or services, and also debts. For example, a TV company would agree to receive some product in exchange for their advertising fees.

When I was researching information on bartering in Russia, I found an incredible fact. From the year 1992 to the year 1998, bartering increased from 5% to 50%, some sources go as high as 60%. Also, I found that the Russian government dropped the rate of the sale tax to 18% in later years.

> _"People are making fortunes on barter,"_ says Alexander Bazarov, director of Credit Suisse First Boston in Kiev. _"Especially those who are in a position to control several links in the chain of transactions."_
>
> _"Flows of goods, instead of cash, are very difficult to track,"_ admits Vladimir Popov, a former banker who heads Russia's Tax Enforcement Agency. _"It's an easy way of avoiding taxes because it's hard for tax inspectors to assess profits on such deals. And besides, there is no money in the bank for accountants to seize."_[124]

EXCELLENT! Good for the people!

In the beginning of the 1990's all taxes combined totaled 80–85% or greater. The small businesses that had produced new products started to close. The "New Rich" surfaced when corrupt people bought

---

[124] Where Cash Isn't King:Barter Lines Pockets in Ex-Soviet States http://home.swipnet.se/~w-10652/barter.html

government-made products—for bribes, and sold them to the public at a great profit. Goods received from foreign charities were confiscated, before they were distributed, and were sold by the same "New Rich." People's anger and despair increased drastically.

Again, people were blaming capitalism, because all of these ideas were presented to us as "great ideas" from the West and as the "free market."

Marxist propaganda! LIES!

Hyper inflation broke out, the money significantly dropped in value every week and I, as most of the people, lost all my savings. Everywhere you went you saw depression reflected on people's faces. All food disappeared from the stores—shelves were empty. In Novosibirsk, we had ration cards for sugar, eggs, butter, meat, vodka, etc. We did not have soap, detergent, matches, salt, etc. We had a ration card for sugar, but there was no sugar at the stores. Guys could not find cigarettes. I did not cook fried or boiled eggs. With 10 eggs given for a month, it was too much of a luxury. I used eggs only for cooking other things, like pancakes. Once I accidently dropped eggs at the store right after I bought them. It was sad—here my daughter's and my month-long ration of eggs was gone!

One of my friends, a physician, told me that she did not have anything to eat except bread and tea for half of the year. She told me that she was crying every evening looking at her meager "dinner" and thinking that it was all she earned for being a doctor for 30 years.

Not long after I left Russia in 1993, the money were so much inflated that all Russians became "millionaires."

My mother told me stories that the government stopped paying salaries and pensions to the people for three, four, or six months in a row. People would go to work, but were only promised payment in the future. People did not have money to pay for rent, energy, or food.

My mother lived in a coal mining region of the city of Anzhero-Sudzhensk, where in late May of 1998 the big rebellion, "Railway War," took place.

Like everybody else in the country, miners did not get paid for their work for at least half of the year. Miners were desperate, they did not have any savings left, and their children were hungry, as well as they themselves.

Working as a school teacher that time, my mom witnessed that some of her students, most of whom were children of these miners, would start fainting from hunger in the classroom. The first time it happened she did not know why, and decide to take the child to the school nurse. When nobody was around, this kid told my mom that he did not have anything to eat for a few days. After that, she started to bring these children directly to the school cafeteria.

Out of desperation miners thought that their "silent rebellion" would attract the attention of the public and authorities. They went down the shaft and declared that they were not going to come up to the surface until they got paid what government owed them. They sat in the mine for a week.

After the director of the mine, the government's nominee, said, "Go ahead and stay there. We don't have to bring you up to bury your corpses," they understood that they were being completely ignored and their silent protest did not bring any consideration to their suffering or the suffering of their families. They decided to come to the surface and march unwashed to the local government "capitol", about 10-15 miles, to demand the pay that government owed them.

My mom was at school when someone told her to look at what was happening outside.

She saw thousands of men, covered black from coal dust, walking along on the road dressed in their miner's uniforms and helmets. They trudged in complete silence. People watching on the streets did not make a sound. Traffic stopped. My mom told that they looked like prisoners from a concentration camp, and she could not hold her tears.

When these people came to ask the local government to pay them, the government refused to face them, "We don't have any money!" was the answer.

The miners decided to block the Trans-Siberian Railway that crossed through the middle of this town and connected Vladivostok and Moscow, thereby stopping all trade from China and Japan. They sat down on the rails and told that they were not going anywhere, "Go head, squash us! We are not going to move!"

Right away special police forces, from all the major Siberian cities, were sent by the government.

The principal of my mother's school gave warning to the teachers that if they got involved in the support of miners they would be fired. The teachers said, "Screw you. Our husbands are out there and we might not see them again!"

The whole city gathered at the railway. People opened a camp and stayed in tents.

There was tension in the air! One woman told a policeman after he tried to push her, "You came here by train, you'll go back by hearse." Miners were hiding guns, pitch forks, and axes in nearby bushes and the police were very careful about confronting them. Everybody was worried about bloodshed.

Also, the government was threatening to confiscate their savings for the damage from the dysfunction of the railway. The miners answer was, "You can take everything we have. We have nothing!"

After the government agreed to pay half of their obligation to miners with the promise to pay other half later, the miners withdrew from the railway.

The miners stopped the traffic of all trains, passenger and cargo, for 248 hours.

"May 23, 1998. In the action of civil disobedience and response to the absolute inaction of the authorities, the miners decided to close the Trans-Siberian Railway. However, after people took to the rails government did not immediately respond to this unprecedented action caused by despair and mistrust. Gradually the miners were joined by doctors and teachers. Trans-Siberian highway was blocked for 248 hours. Anzhero-Sudzhensk was named "Founder of the railway war."[125]

---

[125] translated by Zhanna Konetchy from: History of Anzhero–Sudzhensk, История города Анжеро-Судженск, http://androdionov.narod.ru/ anzhero/history/new.htm

Episodes of the History: Lenin

Indoctrination does work! Use of propaganda, combined with agitation, can be found throughout all times and different nations. However, never before had the propaganda and psychological enslavement been used on such a grand scale as it was in the experiment of colossal proportion lunched by Lenin and his comrades-Bolsheviks through the forced obliteration of Christianity, the monopoly of the press, and educational system in the hands of the Soviet regime.

Living in lie became compulsory and coercive. The ideological monopoly provided control over all people and every individual. Minds and souls were assigned to the same category as things—"elements." "Discordant elements" are destroyed or isolated. Free work, free thought, free word are abolished. Truth searching is under a ban. Science, art, and history are aligned exclusively with the communist idea. Moreover, the agronomics and farmers, medicine and doctors, industries and engineers, in later years—electronics, are transferred to a rank of ideological spheres—everyone and everything.

For example, right before the WWII genetics was banned in the USSR, with the approval of "party line" scientists, because it was in contradiction to the Darwinism. "Genetics was called 'the whore of capitalism' and stigmatized as a 'fascist science.'"[126] Later, in the 1950's, cybernetics was also banned and "labeled as ideologically incorrect and as a bourgeois pseudoscience."[127]

It takes only two to three generations to raise self-censored people in complete contentment with the absolute immorality of the socialistic doctrine. Without the slightest distrust they accept their parodical existence where language is changed so that the idea of freedom became inexpressible. *"Circus dogs jump when the tamer cracks his whip, but the really well-trained dog is the one that turns his somersault when there is no whip."* (George Orwell)

---

[126] http://en.wikipedia.org/wiki/Suppressed_research_in_the_Soviet_Union
[127] ibid

These "masses" would justify incontestably the methods used by communists to institute socialism, and defend these methods as the necessity to survive in its very vulnerable state of establishment as the "fairest, most moral and only" country on the face of the earth among the hostile world, and to prevail in the triumph of the future world communist revolution.

We learned Marx and Engels's "The Communist Manifesto" at school without raising any questions of its science-based inference.

We studied Lenin's works, and reading his own words which could raise the hair of decent human beings, we did not have any, even a slight distrust, of their virtues and truth.

We read at school Lenin's words about intellectuals [*"the intellectuals, the lackeys of capital, who imagine themselves the brains of the nation. In reality they are not the brain, but 'shit'."*], and did not see cheap profanity but courage to not wrap the truth with the carefully chosen words.

After getting over the initial shock provoked by my uncle who called Lenin indecent, the murderer of the czar's family, and who blamed Lenin in the initiation of the "monstrous fratricide" of the Civil War, I started questioning Lenin's dispositions. It happened a few years before the Party revealed to the "masses" Stalin's methods of institutionalizing socialism. However Gorbachev's regime still did everything possible to keep Lenin's name as a symbol of communism and clean of atrocities. They would do anything to protect world opinion from besmirching socialism as "the most just social system."

With so many facts supporting the opposite, many liberal intellectuals still are spreading one of the greatest lies in history, which asserts that Lenin was "not as bad" as Stalin, that socialism itself is not immoral, but only Stalin's repressions gave socialism a bad reputation.

Disregarding lessons of the history some of these intellectuals, perhaps sincerely and naively, believe that socialism is the most socially just system; and if only righteous people would be in the power it could bring salvation to the people:

"I respect Lenin as a man who gave all his energy, at a total sacrifice of his personal life, to dedicating himself to the realization of socialist justice. I don't consider his methods appropriate. But one thing is certain: Men such as he are the guardians and renewers of mankind's conscience." (Albert Einstein) [128]

Others fully aware about the evil face of socialism and, either for a personal gain, or for ambition and power, use methods that George Bernard Shaw "formulated and described in the Fabian methodology: 'methods of stealth, intrigue, subversion, and *the deception of never calling socialism by its right name.*" [129]

Being very much aware about of Lenin's methods of terror and mass murder, Bernard Shaw fully approved Lenin's way as the "promised salvation and transition to higher form of civilization," so he declared in his impromptu speech honoring Lenin at a film studio in Leningrad:

"if this great communistic experiment spreads over the whole world, we shall have a new era in history. We shall not have the old collapse and failure, the beginning again, the going through the whole miserable story to the same miserable end . . . If the future is the future as Lenin foresaw it, then we may all smile and look forward to the future without fear. But if the experiment is overthrown and fails . . . then I shall have to take a very melancholy farewell of you, my friends." (Bernard Shaw) [130]

Fool

Winston Churchill revealed the true nature of Lenin and proclaimed that "neither Tamerlane nor Genghis Khan were as reckless as Lenin in expenditure of human lives."

". . . Lenin has left his mark. He has won his place . . .

---

[128] Frank and Blunt: Einstein on Others by Markkus Rovito

[129] Never Call Socialism by Its Right Name by Mary Nicholas http://www.americanthinker.com/2012/05/never_call_socialism_by_its_right_name.html#ixzz2Dp8Mm7u4

[130] George Bernard Shaw Biography https://henriksenenglish.wikispaces.com/file/view/ShawBIO.pdf

Implacable vengeance, rising from a frozen pity in a tranquil, sensible, matter of fact, good-humoured integument! His weapon logic; his mood opportunist. His sympathies cold and wide as the Arctic Ocean; his hatreds tight as a hangman's noose. His purpose to save the world: his method to blow it up. Absolute principles, but readiness to change them. Apt at once to kill or learn: dooms and afterthoughts: ruffianism and philanthropy. But a good husband; a gentle guest; happy, his biographer assures us, to wash up the dishes or dandle the baby; as mildly amused to stalk a capercailzie as to butcher an Emperor.

Lenin was the Grand Repudiator. He repudiated everything. He repudiated God, King, Country, morals, treaties, debts,[131] rent, interest, the laws and customs of centuries, all contracts written or implied, the whole structure—such as it is—of human society. In the end he repudiated himself." (W. Churchill) [132]

Churchill new the truth that the suffering of common Russian men did not start with Stalin, but Stalin was an inevitable villainous consequence of Lenin's evil socialistic experiment.

"The Russian people were left floundering in the bog. Their worst misfortune was his (Lenin's) birth—their next worst, his death."[133]

The truth is that the only difference between the "Genius of the Socialist Revolution", Lenin, and his successor and faithful disciple, Stalin, was that Lenin did not murder his fellow comrades—commissars on the same massive scale as Stalin did.

---

[131] Author's note: As soon as the Soviet Commissariat took over Russia their first decree was the "Decree of the Peace", which declared Russia's exit from the Triple Entente, and refusal to recognize and pay the imperial debts.

[132] W. Churchill PURPLE PATCH: Lenin http://www.dailytimes.com.pk/default.asp?page=story_3-11-2003_pg3_7

[133] ibid

The latest opinion of many historians claims that the October Revolution was not a revolution but a coup, organized by Lenin and a small group of Bolsheviks, in order to arrest the Provisional Government which was temporarily organized after the February Revolution, to take all power and complete control over the Russia and place it in the hands of the Bolsheviks exclusively.

> *"We must, by all means, tonight arrest the government, disarm the cadets (defeating them if they resist), etc.*
>
> *. . . by any means, leave no power into the Parliament hands before the 25th . . . Take the power today, we do not take it against the Soviets, but for them . . . It would be death or formality to wait for the oscillating vote on October 25th. The people have the right and are obliged to resolve similar issues not by vote, but by force . . ."*
> (Lenin)

On the same evening the Red Guards under the direction of Bolshevik leaders begin to capture the key points of the city: bridges, telegraph, telephone, railway stations, government buildings (especially the Winter Palace), etc.

By morning, the capital was under the control of the Military Revolutionary Committee, which announced the dissolution of the Pre-Parliament and the overthrow of the Provisional Government and so—totalitarianism arose.[134]

[The February Revolution was a spontaneous uprising started by working women on the International Women's Day, March 8, 1917, February 23rd according to Julian Calendar used in Russia at a time, which resulted in the abdication of Czar Nicholas II and the institution of the Dual Power: the Provisional Government, which was recognized internationally as Russia's legal government, and the Petrograd Soviet. The Provisional Government, which consisted of an alliance between liberals, socialists, and cadets, made plans for the formation of the

---

[134] Russia and the World XX Century. Lecture: October Coup of 1917
http://www.husain-off.ru/hb2n/h2lekc08.html

Constituent Assembly which could be elected in order to choose a more permanent government for Russia and for writing a new Constitution. The Petrograd Soviet of Workers and Soldiers Deputies was a more radical socialist group.

The First Congress of Soviets that was held in June, 1917, had 1,090 delegates representing more than 400 different Soviets. Of these, 285 were Socialist Revolutionaries, 248 Mensheviks, and 105 Bolsheviks.

By the time of the November Revolution, i.e. October coup, there were over 900 Soviets in Russia. The Bolsheviks now controlled all the Soviets in the major towns and cities. This included those in Petrograd and Moscow.

After Vladimir Lenin and the Bolsheviks took power on October 25th, corresponding to November 7th of Gregorian calendar, they initially allowed elections for the assembly to go forward as scheduled, but changed their minds after receiving less than 25 percent of the vote in those elections.

The Second Congress of Soviets was convened on the 8th of November. By using a variety of different methods, the Bolsheviks gained control and on the 14th of June 1918, Mensheviks and Socialist Revolutionaries were expelled. [135]]

Lenin's socialistic experiment brought a dictatorial regime, cruel despotism, mass terror organized by the Bolshevik government, a lack of rights, formation of hatred, lawlessness, and arbitrariness.

Yet Lenin's brutality was covered by sentimental phrases of proletarian democracy, internationalism, of "freedom, equality and fraternity."

Obsessed with the idea of building communism, with the Marx's idea "to liberate proletariat, the workers, from the Capital, to liberate the exploited from exploiters", Lenin thought mostly about achieving that goal.

---

[135] Soviets http://www.spartacus.schoolnet.co.uk/RUSsoviet.htm

Liar →

> "The first step on the path to the workers' revolution is the elevation of the proletariat to the position of ruling class . . . The proletariat will gain from its political domination by little by little tearing away from the bourgeoisie all capital, by centralizing all means of production in the hands of the State, that is to say in the hands of the proletariat itself organized as the ruling class" (Marx "The Communist Manifesto")[136]

LIES to turn the masses into his "useful idiots".

The ways and means of how to achieve this objective was of little concern to him:

> "Freedom is a bourgeois prejudice. We repudiate all morality which proceeds from supernatural ideas or ideas which are outside the class conception. In our opinion, morality is entirely subordinate to the interests of the class war. Everything is moral which is necessary for the annihilation of the old exploiting order and for uniting the proletariat. Our morality consists solely in close discipline and conscious warfare against the exploiters." (V. I. Lenin)[137]

BLM in America- 2020/21!

Lenin's strategy, with his brazen appeal to "rightly plunder what was stolen", by the eradication of religion, patriotism, family, a sense of justice, and subsequently was reduced to the tactics: "morally unbridle to become enslaved." The result of these actions was the creation of the Soviet regime, unprecedented by its foulness, the phenomenon of a biased and anti–legal mechanism which replaced law and order with fear and violence, the phenomenon of a state public slavery.

Since Marxism is "a religion of the class warfare", Lenin believed that he could "drive mankind to the communist paradise" only by a violent abolition particularly of Christianity and establishment of state atheism for all.

---

[136] Dictatorship of the Proletariat and State Socialism http://struggle.ws/berneri/dic_of_prole.html

[137] TERROR http://www.rjgeib.com/thoughts/terror/terror.html

Right after the Socialist Revolution, concurrently with the warfare on the bourgeoisie, the rich, Lenin declared warfare against the "opium of the masses", i.e. against religion and the priests:

> ". . . we must immediately put religion to an end. Priests should be arrested as counter-revolutionaries and saboteurs, shot mercilessly and everywhere, and as much as possible! Churches should be closed, sealed and converted into warehouses.

Marxists are MURDERERS.

> . . . The greater the number of representatives of the reactionary clergy and the reactionary bourgeoisie that we succeed in shooting (on this occasion), the better because this 'audience' must precisely now be taught a lesson in such a way that they will not dare to think about any resistance whatsoever for several decades." (Lenin)[138]

WoW...

According to Figes and The Black Book of Communism, 2,691 priests, 1,962 monks, and 3,447 nuns were executed as a result of Lenin's aforementioned directives.

By Marx and Lenin's teaching, *"The state is nothing but a mechanism for the oppression of one class by another. . . . As long as the proletariat needs the state, that need is not in the interests of freedom but in order to defeat their enemies [the exploiters]." (Lenin)* And "the **Dictatorship of the Proletariat** is a power not bound by any law" [by Lenin's own words] and which would (a) "forcibly take away the existing dominant capitalist state mechanism, destroy the bourgeois class, create a new, proletarian state mechanism and (b) suppress the bourgeoisie attempts to regain power."

"lawlessness will abound..." -Jesus

Matt. 24:12

> ". . . Dictatorship does not necessarily mean the destruction of democracy for the class that exercises the dictatorship over the other classes . . ." [139]

Of course not, you disgusting thieves! "Let them eat cake!" WICKED.

> "Only **Dictatorship of the Proletariat** is able to exempt mankind from the yoke of capital, from the lie, falseness, hypocrisy

---

[138] Lenin, Letter to Comrade Molotov for the Politburo (19 March 1922)

[139] V.I.Lenin Proletarian revolution and renegade Kautsky

*of bourgeois democracy, the democracy **for the rich**, and is able to establish democracy **for the poor.**"* [140]

"Democracy for the vast majority of the people, and suppression by force, i.e. exclusion from democracy, of the exploiters and oppressors of the people—that is the modification of democracy upon transition from capitalism to Communism." [141]

"This will be the replacement of freedom of assembly and the press for the minority, for the exploiters, by the freedom of assembly and the press for most people, for workers. It will be a gigantic, world-wide and historical expansion of democracy, its transformation from a lie to the truth, the liberation of humanity from the shackles of capital, which brings distortion to and curtails every, even the most "democratic" and republican, bourgeois democracy. This means replacing the bourgeois state by the proletarian state, which is the only way to the demise of the state in general." (Lenin) [142]

Lenin policies were summed up in two slogans **"Peace, Bread, Land"** and **"All power to the Soviets!"**

The Bolsheviks did not waste time—the revolution, or coup, happened on November 7, 1917. The next day, November 8, 1917 the Decree on Land was adopted which declared that all rights of private ownership of land were abolished, it was forbidden to sell, lease, and mortgage. All property of the landlords, crown, monastery, church land with all the supplies and buildings, was confiscated immediately without compensation and handed to the district land committees and the district Soviets of Peasants' deputies to be used by the proletariat and peasantry. The land was nationalized.

For economic destruction of the bourgeoisie all "well-founded classes" were imposed with a one-time "emergency tax"—consisting of a single

---

[140] V.I.Lenin About "Democracy" and Dictatorship(1918)
[141] Lenin State and Revolution (1917)
[142] ibid

contribution of 10 billion rubles. To satisfy this tax money, valuables, and objects of art were accepted.

> *"This expropriation will make it possible for the productive forces to develop to a tremendous extent. And when we see how incredibly capitalism is already retarding this development, when we see how much progress could be achieved on the basis of the level of technique already attained, we are entitled to say with the fullest confidence that the expropriation of the capitalists will inevitably result in an enormous development of the productive forces of human society."*
> (Lenin)[143] *All THIEVES have their part in the LAKE OF FIRE...*

Internal and external policies of the Bolsheviks in 1918 through the 1920's were called "War Communism" and conducted strictly "according to Marx":

1. Total expropriation of factories and land from "the rich" with the "idea" of transferring them to the workers and peasants,
2. The complete elimination of even small private property,
3. The abolition of private trade,
4. The virtual abolition of money and the transition to direct distribution of products,
5. Militarization of industries,
6. Free of charge housing, transport, social services.

In October 1918, correspondingly to the Lenin's slogan "He who does not work shall not eat", the Soviet regime issued a "Labor Books" decree by power of which all people who were falling within **Article 65** of the Constitution of 1918, in other words, those who under the Constitution were stripped of all rights, were required to obtain "Labor Books."

They had to perform "public works and duties" assigned to them, clearing streets of snow, cutting the firewood, etc., which would be recorded in their books at least once a month. These people

---

[143] V. Lenin The State and Revolution, The Economic Basis of the Withering Away of the State, Chapter 4. The Higher Phase of Communist Society

were required to visit the police once a week. Without this book these people were forbidden to move around the country, and, most importantly, without a "Labor Book", with a record of the executed work, it was impossible to get "food stamps," which in terms of "War Communism" was the equivalent of starvation.[144] Money was absolutely worthless. Hyperinflation reached a magnitude unseen before in Russian, and perhaps in worldwide history.

Because of a complete ban of free trade during "War Communism", food and commodity ration cards became the only way to get vital supplies and were issued to citizens based on their social status. For example, in 1919, in Petrograd [name for St. Petersburg during that historical period], there were 33 types of ration cards, each of which had to be updated on a monthly basis for bread, milk, footwear, etc. The population was divided into three categories: the first were the workers, the second the employees, the third—those who under the Constitution were stripped of all rights (Article 65). Ration size in the first category was four times greater than that of the third. [145]

["Does not work" means does not perform physical, "socially useful" labor. "A universal labor duty is introduced in order for the improvement of the organization of economy and for the elimination of the parasitic stratum of society.

Funny – Marx was a "parasite" to society – he never worked!

Allowing all types of work the labor law establishes only one condition—the work has to be socially useful. Any kind of activity that is not in the public benefit cannot be regarded as a performance of the universal labor duties."[146]

Article 65 gave a list of people who do not have the right to vote and be elected. On the social grounds these rights were deprived to those

---

144 A. Baiburin; Pre-history of the Soviet Passport (1917 - 1932) / / Stockpile. - 2009. - № 2 (64).
145 Valiullin, Zaripova; History of Russia, XX century
146 Source: Chistyakov The Constitution of the Russian Federation, 1918. http://constitution.garant.ru/science-work/modern/3988990/chapter/3/

who hired people in order to increase own profits, those who were living on "unearned income" in the form of interest on capital, income from business, income from property, etc., private traders, retail and commercial intermediaries, those of liberal professions if they didn't carry out socially useful function, those who didn't have an approved occupation, monks and clergymen, those who were hired by people of any of category above.

Later the "Labor Books" decree expanded to include every able-bodied worker. "Labor Books" were still in effect when I left in 1993. Every place of work would have a special bureaucratic department where they would keep these labor books for every employee and record the start and ending date of employment, reasons for the termination, the promotions, decorations, etc. The "Labor Book" would be given into the hands of the person only upon the quitting a job or being fired. The person had to find the new place of employment within 24 days; otherwise they would lose the "uninterrupted length of service," which would be reflected on that person's retirement pay and other benefits.]

At the same time period, in 1919 for the purpose of *"cleaning out" capitalists, and forcing them into a new public service"*, concentration camps were instituted by Lenin and his Bolshevik regime.

> *"Liable to confinement in them were not only individuals but also 'categories of individuals'—that is, entire classes: Dzerzhinskii (the founder of KGB) at one point proposed that special concentration camps be erected for the 'bourgeoisie.' Living in forced isolation, the inmates formed a pool of slave labor on which Soviet administrative and economic institutions could draw at no cost. The number of people in these camps according to Pipes was about 50,000 prisoners in 1920 and 70,000 in 1923; many of these did not survive the inhuman conditions."*[147]

---

[147] Lenin and the First Communist Revolutions, VII; "War Communism", the Red Terror, and Lenin's Famine http://econfaculty.gmu.edu/bcaplan/ museum/his1g.htm

Expropriation warped the spirit and accountability of people. It undermined the incentives to work and the scope of responsibility of the people for their own welfare.

"According to one estimate by 1920 the total production of Russian industry had fallen from a pre-war level of 6.059 billion gold rubles to the equivalent of just 836 million—a decline of more than 85%." [148]

The following figures show the total collapse of the economy[149]:

	1913	1921
Grain	80 million tons	37.6 million tons
Coal	29 million tons	9 million tons
Iron	4.2 million tons	1 million tons
Oil	9.2 million tons	3.8 million tons

"The only industry which thrived was that concerned with the production of paper money. The amount of currency in circulation from the beginning to the end of 1920 rose from about 225 billion rubles to 1.17 trillion. This represented a 25-fold increase over the amount of paper money in circulation in 1917."

Examples of hyper-inflation

Exchange rate of one Pound converted to Rubles:

Date	Value of £1 in rubles
1918—Quarter I	45
1918—Quarter II	60
1918—Quarter III	80
1918—Quarter IV	150

---

[148] Lancelot Lawton, _An Economic History of Soviet Russia: Volume 1_. London: Macmillan, 1932; pg. 151

[149] http://www.historyhome.co.uk/europe/russia.htm

1919—Quarter I	400
1919—Quarter II	900
1919—Quarter III	1,200
1919—Quarter IV	3,000
1920—Quarter I	6,000
1920—Quarter II	10,000
1922—Quarter I	1,650,000
1922—Quarter II	14,900,000
1922—Quarter III	18,650,000
1922—Quarter IV	71,730,000
1923—Quarter I	192,080,000
1923—Quarter II	385,000,000
1923—Quarter III	866,000,000
1923—Quarter IV	5,040,000,000

Sources: 1918-1920: M. Feitelberg, *Das Papiergelgwesen in in Räte-Russland.* (Berlin: 1920), pg. 50. Cited in S.S. Katzenellenbaum, *Russian Currency and Banking.* London: P.S. King & Son, 1925; pg. 83.

Note that during this interval the purchasing power of the pound also fell substantially so that this decline in ruble value is understated. 1922-1923: S.S. Katzenellenbaum, *Russian Currency and Banking.* London: P.S. King & Son, 1925; pg. 90.

Price is average Moscow free market price for first month of each specified quarter.

Total rubles of paper money issued by year

Year	Billions of rubles issued	Percentage increase
1916	3.5	—
1917	16.4	180.3%

1918	33.5	119.2%
1919	164.2	302.5%
1920	943.6	419.3%
1921	16,375.3	1402.0%
1922	1,976,900	11,268.2%
1923	176,505,500	8,849.6%

Source: S.S. Katzenellenbaum, *Russian Currency and Banking*. London: P.S. King & Son, 1925; pg. 59.

Peasants refused to sell their surplus products for money, which could effectively buy nothing. Facing starvation in the cities and the death of industry as peasant-workers returned to their villages, the Soviet regime "did not have any other way out to maintain its urban economy" and resorted to the use of force to expropriate "necessary" grain from peasants.

Mutual intolerance has become a "mass mental disease." The Revolution materialized not into a "just paradise," but into an "orgy" of falsehood, revenge, envy, and punishment.

Just shortly after the Revolution in 1918, the peasants for whom communism promised to give the land and bring paradise, fulfilled the "list of the State enemies."

With the completion of crushing the bourgeois, Lenin's next step was to make the same successful "class war" among the peasantry—poor peasants against "kulaks", the "rich" peasants. The precise translation of the word "kulak" is "the fist", i.e. "the greedy" because they "grab" everything in their fist.

Lenin *"despised the peasants as ignorant 'petty bourgeoisie' who stood in the way of collectivized agriculture,"*[150] who did not want to detach themselves from their "precious farmsteads," their "little petty capital" and therefore did not want to join the proletariat and stayed in the way of building communism. [Russia was an agricultural country in 1917 and over 80 percent of the Russian population were peasants. Following the logic, not the workers but peasants were "the majority," and Dictatorship of Proletariat would become a "democracy of a minority" by Lenin's own definition.] Lenin's plan was to turn all farmers into the state workers, i.e. the workers of collective farms.

> *"Based on his own statement that any 'revolution is violence,' Lenin ordered the wide use of revolutionary coercion, the 'Red Terror.' A popular poster in 1918 read: 'We shall force mankind to happiness with our iron fist!' The revolutionary coercion was used especially against the peasants"*[151]

The "Red Terror" was the device for altering "human material" for the sake of the future; and the brutal use of "Red Terror" against the peasantry would force "prodrazverstka", Lenin's new tax policy for a village—violent grain requisition, including seed grain and expropriation of other agricultural products and tools.

> *"State policy took two main forms: very low prices paid to peasants for their grain, so that the requisition essentially amounted to confiscation; or outright confiscation of all the grain possessed by the peasantry, with no payment. The policy of grain requisition was used as an instrument of class warfare in the countryside, setting poor peasants against rich peasants (and middle peasants after), so-called 'kulaks.'*

Why God says, "Thou Shalt not Covet."

---

[150] Lenin and the First Communist Revolutions, VII; "War Communism", the Red Terror, and Lenin's Famine http://econfaculty.gmu.edu/bcaplan/museum/his1g.htm

[151] translated by Zhanna Konetchy from: Политика военного коммунизма http://aleho.narod.ru/book2/ch04.htm

---

The policy of prodrazverstka was bitterly opposed by the vast majority of peasants and led to widespread violence in the countryside against the committees of poor peasants (kombedy) that worked for the Soviet state to seize grain that was being hoarded by peasant households. In response to the confiscation of their grain, peasant households drastically reduced the acreage cultivated and the amount of grain produced, which led to mass starvation and famine throughout the nation."[152]

In no circumstances was Lenin agreeable to give up the monopoly on the "bread." In <u>The Appeal to the Public for the Fight against Hunger</u> of May 29, 1918, it was proclaimed that **only the Soviet central government can distribute the grain among the hungry fairly** and deviation from the grain monopoly and violation of procurement plans produced by the Government is a serious crime against "the hungry" and the Soviet Republic.

Soviets insisted that we not believe those who say that salvation from famine would be found in the abolition of the grain monopoly and fixed prices, and in the return of the independent grain procurement, granting to the certain groups of hungry people the ability to buy their own bread in the producing provinces. The Soviets insisted that *"these groups of hungry people would compete with each other, would knock down prices and would make bread owners cling to their bread even more tightly."*

Soviets called this self-purchase *"a terrible evil"* getting in the way of the fair distribution of grain surpluses to the starving.

Lenin blamed the "rich" peasants for the famine and call *"comrades workers and starving peasants"* to engage in the war against kulaks.

"Kulaks do not want and will not allow giving bread to the hungry, no matter what concessions would be done by the State.

The bread must be taken by force from the kulaks.

---

[152] <u>Gale Encyclopedia of Russian History:</u> http://www.answers.com/topic/prodrazverstka#ixzz1dXaVfBhT

We have to go on crusade against the rural bourgeoisie.

The Government embarks this path and is calling you, comrades workers and starving peasants, to follow.

Respond immediately to a call of the Central Government!

Form militant squads from sustained and persistent workers and peasants, who are resistant to temptations and well disciplined. Send them over to work for the Central Government.

Time is short. Grain surpluses must be seized from the rich—kulaks.

Your squads, together with disciplined troops of the Red Army, under the military leadership of experienced and tested revolutionaries and specialists in the food business, will go to the expropriation of bread from the rural bourgeoisie.

Merciless war against kulaks!" (Lenin)[153]

Lenin's letter "Hanging Order"

August 11,1918
Send to Penza
To Comrades Kuraev, Bosh, Minkin
And other Penza communists

Comrades! The revolt by the five kulak volost's[154] *must be suppressed without mercy. The interest of the entire revolution demands this, because we have now before us our final decisive battle 'with the kulaks.' We need to set an example.*

_____

[153]   Lenin and other members of Soviet Commissariat; Appeal to the Public for the Fight Against Hunger
May 29,1918 http://www.hist.msu.ru/ER/Etext/DEKRET/18-05-29-4. htm

[154]   A volost' was a territorial/administrative unit consisting of a few villages and surrounding land.

1) *You need to hang (hang without fail, so that the public sees) at least 100 notorious kulaks, the rich, and the bloodsuckers.*
2) *Publish their names.*
3) *Take away all of their grain.*
4) *Execute the hostages—in accordance with yesterday's telegram.*

This has to be accomplished in such a way, that people for hundreds of miles around will see, tremble, know and scream out: let's choke and strangle those blood-sucking kulaks.

Telegraph us acknowledging receipt and execution of this.

Yours, Lenin

P.S. Use your toughest people for this. [155]

The low death estimation from this famine is about 3 million; higher death estimates reach 10 million.

OF course not!

Did Lenin sincerely believe that a grain monopoly could put famine to the end? The fact is that he knew that grain monopoly would bring "the *bourgeoisie*" to its knees; and everything that corresponds to interests of revolution, the proletariat, and communism was moral in his eyes:

It was ALL about acquiring control & power.

> "The grain monopoly, bread rationing and constrain labor service positioned in the hands of proletarian state, in the hands of sovereign Soviets, are the most powerful means of accounting and control. This means that, when extended upon capitalists and the rich in general, applied to them by the workers, unprecedented in history, will 'propel' the state apparatus in order to overcome resistance of the capitalists, for subordinating them to the proletarian state. This means of control and work coercion are more effective then criminal justice and its guillotine. The guillotine is only intimidating, and brakes down only physical resistance. Starvation breaks down mental resistance.

---

[155] http://www.loc.gov/exhibits/archives/ad2kulak.html

Peter Konetchy

That is not enough for us. We must not only 'frighten' the capitalists in the sense that they feel the omnipotence of the proletarian state and forgot to think about the active resistance. We need to break the passive, and certainly more dangerous and harmful, the resistance.

We need not only to break any sort of resistance; we need to make them work in the new organizational and governmental framework. It is not enough 'clean out' capitalists, it is necessary to force them into a new public service. This applies not only to the capitalists but as well as to the elite of the bourgeois intelligentsia, civil servants, etc.

And we have the means to do so. The very belligerent capitalist state gave this tool and weapon in our own hands. This tool is the grain monopoly, bread rationing and constrain labor service. 'Who does not work, neither shall he eat'—this is the fundamental, the first and most important rule that 'Soviet of Workers' Deputies' can introduce into the life and they will, when they become government." (V. I. Lenin)[156]

A significant part of the peasantry and the workers not only openly protested against Bolshevik political power, but also attempted to eliminate it by force.

In late 1920 through early 1921 an uprising of armed peasants swept western Siberia, Tambov, Voronezh, Middle Volga, Don, Kuban, Ukraine and Central Asia. In addition to predatory requisitions carried out by Bolsheviks, the peasants revolted against the raiding and closing of the churches.

A decree passed on January 22, 1921 called for the reduction of working rations by a third, caused strikes by the workers.

In 1921 the Kronstadt Revolt was the rising of the naval town of Kronstadt by workers, and the Navy, who initially supported the

The resistance!

---

[156]   VI Lenin. <u>Can the Bolsheviks Retain State Power?</u> Written at the end of September – 1 (14) October 1917

1917 Revolution, but now was uprising against the new Bolshevik dictatorship.

The main demands of their resolution were:

"In view of the fact that the real councils don't express the will of workers and peasants, immediately to make re-elections by secret ballots . . . Freedom of speech and the press . . . Release all political prisoners, as well as all of the workers and peasants, soldiers and sailors, imprisoned in connection with the workers and peasants' movements . . . To abolish any political departments (at the industries), as neither party can enjoy the privileges to promote their ideas and receive funds from the state for these purposes . . . To abolish Communist fighting groups in all military units, as well as different Communist duty groups dispatched at the factories . . . To grant full authority of action to peasants over all land as it is desirable for them . . . Allow owning of handicrafts work . . . We ask all military units, as well as fellow military cadets to join our resolution . . ."

 The Kronstadt rebellion was crushed by Red Army troops.

The massacre began not only on those who bore arms, but also on the entire population of the island, because Bolsheviks declared that all the inhabitants of the city were guilty of rebellion. 2,103 were sentenced to death and 6,459 people to the various prison terms. In the spring of 1922, the Bolsheviks started the mass eviction of the residents from the island of Kronstadt. In subsequent years, survivors of the Kronstadt rebellion were repressed again. [157]

"With this great day [The October Revolution] being further away from us, the value of the proletarian revolution in Russia becomes clearer to us, and we think more about of the practical experience of our work, taken in completion." (Lenin) [158]

---

[157] "Kronstadt Revolt" http://www.krugosvet.ru/enc/istoriya/ KRONSHTADTSKOE_VOSSTANIE.html?page=0, 2)

[158] Lenin; Collection of Articles, <u>Fourth Anniversary of the October Revolution</u> Complete Works, Vol II, pp. 663-669, ed. 3rd. 14/X 1921.

And what exactly was the "practical experience" of the Bolsheviks and Lenin's work?

After just seven incomplete years of Leninist tyranny Russia was unrecognizable. Russian people have been "robbed to a thread." Gold, diamonds, and currency were pocketed by the Party elites for the "world revolution", but primarily to themselves.

The nobility was physically destroyed. Merchants, businessmen, intellectuals, and officers were cleaned out. Millions of peasants were killed. The working class, on behalf of which Lenin with his comrades were leading them to the Utopia, was turned into the dust. The economy collapsed. The world's best river fleet, the pride of the Russian merchants, vanished. The railways were put into freeze and were overgrown with weeds. The banking system, one of the best in the world, was torn down and turned into ashes. The highly productive farms were looted and wiped out. The public education system, created by Czar Alexander II, was turned into a farce.

The "useful idiots," AKA, "the proletariat" literally DESTROYED THEMSELVES.

Remarkably, this new pseudo-state, from the very beginning of its establishment, developed the world program for all other countries, with a ready predatory template which to this day is imposed on all other people and nations—either by persuasion or by scheme, either by revolt or by the conquest, either by invasion or by deceit. "Everything that corresponds to interests of revolution, the proletariat, and communism is moral." *Satan's "morality" – the opposite of God's!*

Lenin never intended to stop just with the Russian proletarian revolution. It was "A Great Beginning!" and opening for a new era in world history: *"The first hundreds of millions of people in the world were freed from the imperialistic war [WW I], from the world of imperialism by the first Bolshevik revolution. The following [revolutions] shall free all mankind of these wars and yoke of the capital."* (Lenin) [159]

http://www.biografia.ru/arhiv/700.html

[159] Lenin; Collection of Articles, Fourth Anniversary of the October Revolution Complete Works, Vol II, pp. 663-669, ed. 3rd. 14/X 1921

The doctrine of the world proletarian revolution embodied in the slogan of Karl Marx's "Communist Manifesto," (published in 1848)—*"Workers of all countries, unite!"*

According to Marx and Engels, European and world proletariat alienated from the "means and tools of production" eventually would implement a socialist revolution in all countries at the same time. And any of these proletarian revolutions will automatically detonate into a continuous chain—a single world proletarian revolution.

> *"The proletariat seizes state power and turns the means of production into State property. But, in doing this, it abolishes itself as the proletariat, abolishes all class distinctions and class antagonisms, and abolishes the State as the State."* (Frederick Engels) [160]

It was also believed that the ideology of proletarian internationalism will not have anything to do with the traditional concept of the nation and national patriotism, that the proletarians do not have a motherland, *"The proletarians have nothing to lose but their chains. They have a world to win."* (Karl Marx and Frederic Engels "The Communist Manifesto")

> *"Capital is an international force. To vanquish it, an international workers' alliance, an international workers' brotherhood, is needed. We are opposed to national enmity and discord, to national exclusiveness. We are internationalists."* (Lenin, Letter to the Workers and Peasants of the Ukraine, 1919)

"All Power to the Soviets" means "All power to the government by union of proletariat and peasantry." Proletariat is the "masses" who are "free from the Capital", which means that they are "free" not just of their exploiters, the rich, but also from "the means of production", i.e. the private property of any kind.

---

[160] Frederick Engels; Socialism: Utopian and Scientific, III [Historical Materialism] http://www.marxists.org/archive/marx/works/1880/soc–utop/ch03.htm

On the other hand, the peasantry is the "petty bourgeoisie" because they would never give up their "means of production", i.e. their "petty farmsteads" unless they're forced, often violently, to become a "rural proletariat", i.e. become free of the Capital.

Therefore, "Power to the Soviets" means "ruled by the urban and rural proletariat."

> *"All citizens become employees and workers of a single countrywide state 'syndicate'. All that is required is that they should work equally, do their proper share of work, and get equal pay."* (Lenin)[161]

With the prevailing success of the socialist victory in the one country, i.e. accomplishment of "the ***first phase*** of communist society", "a society emerging out of the womb of capitalism", the next "historically preordained" phase is the victory of the communism around the world.

> *"When the **majority** of the people begin independently and everywhere to keep such accounts and exercise such control over the capitalists (now converted into employees) and over the intellectual gentry who preserve their capitalist habits, this control will really become universal, general, and popular; and there will be no getting away from it, there will be* **'nowhere to go.'** Globalism.

> *The whole of society will have become a single office and a single factory, with equality of labor and pay.* **[One World Order]**

> *. . . from this moment the need for government of any kind begins to disappear altogether.*

> *For when **all** have learned to independently administer social production, independently keep accounts and exercise control over the parasites, the sons of the wealthy, the swindlers and other 'guardians of capitalist traditions', the escape from this popular accounting and*

---

[161]   Lenin; <u>The State and Revolution, The Economic Basis of the Withering Away of the State</u>, Chapter 4. <u>The Higher Phase of Communist Society</u>

*control will inevitably become so incredibly difficult, such a rare exception, and will probably be accompanied by such swift and severe punishment (for the **armed workers**[162] are practical men and not sentimental intellectuals, and they scarcely allow anyone to trifle with them), that the **necessity** of observing the simple, fundamental rules of the community will very soon become a **habit**.*

Then the door will be thrown wide open for the transition from the first phase of communist society to its higher phase and with it to the complete withering away of the state.

The state will be able to wither away completely when society adopts the rule: 'From each according to his ability, to each according to his needs.'" (Lenin) [163]

In his pamphlet "What Is to Be Done?", Lenin outlined his strategy and tactics to be used as a blueprint for a successful revolution. Remarkably, it appears that in the United States this template is being used by our own government to force a revolution upon us, the people.

(1) ". . . there can be no revolutionary movement without a revolutionary theory." (Lenin)[164]

---

[162] **Article 19** of the Constitution of the Russian Federation of 1918 **provided workers with the right to defend the revolution with arms.** The law highlights a point – the **right to bear arms pertains to workers only**, the **"parasite elements"** (those who under **Article 65** of the constitution were stripped of all rights) **are deprived to bear arms.** Moreover, the Constitution of 1918 declared a complete disarmament of the 'wealthy classes'. (Source: Chistyakov Constitution of the Russian Federation of 1918. http://constitution.garant.ru/science–work/modern/3988990/chapter/7/ # 10037

[163] Lenin; The State and Revolution, The Economic Basis of the Withering Away of the State, Chapter 4. The Higher Phase of Communist Society

[164] All quotations to the end of this chapter are from Lenin's article 'What Is To Be Done?' (1902)

Peter Konetchy

Lenin observed that "both the working class, and an ever more diverse strata of society, produce every year increasingly large numbers of people who are dissatisfied."

His version of revolutionary theory requires class struggle, and must help the mass of the people unite to move from spontaneity, i.e. "trade union consciousness", to class warfare, i.e. "revolutionary consciousness." Without the direction of revolutionary theory, the workers inevitably slide into trying to improve their conditions within capitalism, rather than through revolt.

> (2) ". . . there will be no transformation of the capitalist system into a socialist one without a revolutionary party", which could organize the working class to play not merely a role as a stage army used by liberals, but to lead in the fight to topple capitalism. *A marxist must agitate & lead them! One of them was our president for 8 years!*

As a "practical task", he proposed a revolutionary party that acts as a guiding force, to educate and organize for revolution, not reform.

The revolutionary party has "to create an organization of revolutionaries able to guarantee the energy, stability, and continuity of the political struggle". This organization has "to understand the character of the society they live in and seek to change, they will need to study, analyze and theorize upon it in order that they can guide isolated grievances into a coherent revolutionary struggle."

Anti "Fa". "Black Lives Matter"

Political agitation must be "unified throughout [the country], illuminating all sides of life and directed to the broadest masses", i.e. influence all other "non-organized", "unsatisfied" groups and individuals to unite under the leadership of this revolutionary group under the "banner" of this "revolution theory", i.e. "class warfare."

"In order to win the cooperation of an individual, or a social group, one must appear as the champion of the cause which this person or group holds to be of paramount importance." . . . "No revolutionary movement can be durable without a stable organization of leaders which preserves continuity".

Lenin observed that "the more we narrow the membership [of the base of such a party] . . . the more difficult will it be to 'catch' such an organization." For this reason, he proposed having small, well trained groups of "professional revolutionaries at the core of the organization." He extolled the virtues of "utter centralization", and dismissed his democracy-advocating critics, pointing out that the "openness required by democracy would be suicidal for a secret organization."

Lenin's strategic principle regarding the "necessity of utilizing in the political struggle all classes, strata, or groups . . . opposed to the enemy one is fighting", was

> (1) To infiltrate into the mass labor movement.

Lenin defines this approach as the conviction of the need for "fighting against the employers, and for trying to prevail upon the government to pass laws necessary for the workers."

> (2) To control the mass media. *"A newspaper is not only a collective propagandist and a collective agitator; it is also a collective organizer."*

"Without it," he wrote, "we cannot conduct that systematic, all-around propaganda and agitation . . ."

"This newspaper [media] would become a part of the huge bellows, fanning each spark of class struggle and popular indignation into a universal combustion."

After the "Revolution" socialism could be successfully implemented in any country by three simple steps:

1. Active involvement of the government in the fiscal decisions of every enterprise. Thereafter nationalize the land, banks, and most of, or all, industries.

2. Monopolize the food production and distribution in the hands of the government by organizing state farm factories.
3. Create a famine and give to the "masses" ration cards. That would bring to their knees even the strongest malcontent. Who wants to see their children to starve?

My Family History and Accounts of Repression

My ancestors passed through the "Red Wheel" of the socialist revolution, the Civil War, the collectivization, and both World Wars. They lived through the ruthless grinder of the social experiment unseen before in its immense proportions. This experiment was driven by one purpose only, "to bring the ultimate human happiness to the masses" and the execution of this experiment showed no remorse for the brutality with which it was implemented: *"We shall force mankind to happiness with our iron fist!"*

Those methods bought all sinister instincts: lying, hatred, fear, idolatry, aspersion, defamation, falsification, denunciation (often used making children to condemn their parents), extortion, looting approved by the state and managed by the apparatus appointees, murdering those who rebel, starving those who did not want to cooperate and giving all their belongings to the looters, taking their children into the state controlled orphanages and forcing them to *"learn communism"*(Lenin), breaking the spirits of those who wanted to survive, crushing everyone into masses, into a mob who would be willing to repress individualism and submit to the communist morality, . . . but for the happiness of all of these people.

My own story would not be complete without mentioning some miscellaneous memories of my ancestors. Most of these memories were paraphrased by my parents.

My great grandparents were not "the rich," but hard-working peasants who lived decently well off. Like most others, they were crushed by the merciless "Red Wheel of the Revolution."

One of my great grandparent's families lived in the European part of Russia, nearby Pskov. They had quite a large piece of land and were farmers. Their family lived like a large commune under the same roof, working all together. Later the father of the family decided to separate every of his children's families into their own farmsteads. They built houses jointly for each of their families, and got together during holidays.

When mass collectivization started in 1928, the government took all their land and animals. Gathering what was left, they ran away from this mass collectivization to Siberia, where they were told there were no collective farms, but free land. They had to leave their already married children behind, and only my grandma, the last of their single children, joined them. She was 18 at that time. When they finally reached Siberia, after a six-month pilgrimage, there was no free land any longer, and they had to join a collective farm.

My other great grandparents were farmers who lived in Siberia. Working very hard they made a very prosperous living for themselves. Together, with four sons and their wives and children, they maintained beehives, livestock and land. They owned a black smith shop, where they made all their own equipment: harrows, plows, and mowers. They were trying to modernize their equipment to be on the cutting edge of successful farming, and buying a tractor was the next big investment in their plans. My mother told me that they were very generous people to those in need. At the beginning of the every winter they would fish and always gave away a significant part of their bounty to the widows in their village. Also, they would give grain to poor widows in need without of any expectations to be paid back. My great-grandmother would simply reply to the offer to return the grain later, "Don't worry, it's a gift for your children."

When collectivization started by the order of the Soviets, the "committees of poor peasants" were organized to requisition from the "rich" peasants what they considered to be "excessive." The village bum, who was an alcoholic and a slacker, became a head of this committee in their village. His wife and all his children barely got by because he did not have the decency and fortitude to support them.

This "committee" along with a willing mob, came to my great-grandparent's house, requisitioned all their possessions; house, animals, equipment (including a sewing machine), all their grain, seed, honey, and all their provisions. The "committee" said that they wouldn't send my great-grandparents to the GULAG only because they had never hired anybody and had all their labor done by the members of their own family; therefore, they did not exploit anyone or "suck their blood." My great-grandparents were banished from the village and did not suffer greater punishment thanks to the fact that all the other villagers loved them for their generosity. My great-grandfather could not cope with this sorrow and died of broken heart. My great-grandmother lost her mind.

A heartbreaking story was told by my father-in-law, Victor. The year of his story was around 1930 which was famous for the brutal famine, the year when millions of people died, but Stalin, with his elitist apparatus, had nightly feasts in the Kremlin.

Victor was too young then to remember clearly what happened to his family. Vaguely, he remembers that he was saved, together with his younger brother when someone, he believes it was his older sister, lowered them through a window just before she and his parents were shot by the by authorities. His sister was also a child, only about fourteen years old. He told this was first time he remembered crying. He remembered how he and his little brother were wandering around, hungry and cold. He cried a second and last time after the death of his younger brother from starvation. Victor, now in his late eighties, still blames himself for his brother's death. He thinks that he might have taken bigger portions of the scraps of food he found for himself, because he was older.

Shortly after his brother's death, a woman found him and used him to do chores in her house. For reasons unclear she dropped him at the railway station, where he was picked up and placed in an orphanage. He did not remember his name and he did not know how old he was. The orphanage authorities gave him a new first and last name and determined his approximate age by his teeth. They guessed he was about five at the time they found him and wrote down his birthday as January 1st.

Other stories I'll describe resemble the stories from the pages from "The GULAG Archipelago." Here are a few:

- One of my great uncles acquired a great work ethic on his farm prior to its confiscation. He was forced to leave the village and work at a government steel factory. Many of his co-workers were shirking and drinking on the job. Who wants to work for the government for miserable pay? In frustration my great uncle told to one of the slackers, "in the old days his butt would be kicked if he worked like that." They reported him to authorities and my great uncle's words "in the old days" were taken literally as praise of the "bourgeoisie", the enemies of Communism, and as an act of treason against the state. My great uncle was sent to the GULAG for simply mentioning the "old days" and was released after eight years on a chain gang after contracting tuberculosis. He died six month later.

- During the Great Patriotic War, or WWII, my grandfather was drafted and my mom's mother with their three children lived and worked at the collective farm. The Soviets did not pay anything to collective farmers during the war for their work. My grandma worked for check marks, one check mark per day. She had to have 365 check marks in the year. To feed themselves, they were allowed to grow some vegetables—carrots, beets, cabbage, potatoes—in their own kitchen garden, but they weren't allowed to grow wheat because of the wheat state monopoly. They had to give ¾ of their milk to the government, along with butter, wool, etc. If they did not have something, they had to produce and give it somehow.

My mother told that they found some small piece of land in the middle of the woods far away from anybody's eyes. They scavenged some grain, planted wheat, and took care of it very carefully thinking that nobody would know. At the harvest time, collective farm commissars came on their horses and trampled down all their wheat.

The collective farm held, and would not release, the internal passports of the farmers. People could not travel and would get shot on site as spies if they were caught without "paper." My grandma, having no passport, could not leave the collective farm after her husband (my grandfather) came back from the front in 1943. He wanted to bring his family to the city. My grandfather was given his passport when he went to war, and if he returned to the collective farm to work, he would need to relinquish it to the farm director, and lose the ability to ever leave the farm.

The head of the collective farm would not release my grandma's passport, and tried to put pressure on my grandfather to stay with his family in the village and return back to work at the collective farm. My grandfather's answer was, "One slave (that is my grandmother) is enough for you." I have no idea how he did not get thrown into the GULAG for his words. He stayed in the village, but worked for the railway, which was not a part of collective farm. Only after Stalin's death in 1953, was my grandmother able to get her internal passport, and their family moved to the city.

- Many people ended up going to the GULAG simply because they were trying to feed their starving children. As I just mentioned, the collective farmers did not get paid for their work during war, even with the ration cards as the people were paid in the cities. In my grandmother's village a soldier's widow was working at the grain storage, and in desperation took three kg of grain to feed her six children. She was arrested and prosecuted under the "Law of Spikelets," and sent to the GULAG. Her children were sent to an orphanage.

The "Law of Spikelets" is a common name of the law based on the decree of the Central Executive Committee and Soviet Public Commissars of the USSR "About protection of the property of state enterprises, collective farms and cooperatives, and strengthening of the public (socialist) property . . .

The common name came into use because peasants (including children) caught gleaning leftover grains, or 'spikelets,' in the collective fields after the harvest were arrested for damaging the state grain production.

Peter Konetchy

The primary punishment for theft according to this law was death by shooting (often on site). Under extenuating circumstances, the punishment was at least 10 years of imprisonment. In all cases, the convict's personal property was to be confiscated." [165]

- My father, who was a little child during WWII, told that they had a really hard time surviving on the food that his mother received on the ration cards paid for work. They lived in the city.

During the war, people had to work 12-15 hours per day and received very little pay in ration cards. Missing work was considered "desertion" and punished by GULAG. In fact, conditions were so poor that soldiers from the front would send home to their families a portion of their soldier ration. Soldier's rations were significantly enhanced by the USSR's alliance with England and the USA. Many young girls voluntarily joined the Army so that they could have enough to eat.

Being a widow, and taking care of her own old mother and her little son of six, my grandma was the only one who was supplying her family with the food ration cards.

In the beginning of the war my grandmother had a job transporting milk, from the village to the city, with a horse and carriage. Any job with access to food triggered a lot of jealousy from the neighbors. My father was about five and remembered how scarce food was. Worried about her child, my grandmother told my father to come to the certain place in the woods by the creek, where she would give him a cup of milk from the canister. Then she would replace it with a cup of water from the creek in hope that nobody would find out. Nobody knew about it but some of the neighbors reported her and authorities started interrogating my dad, deceiving him using kindness. They eventually got my dad to admit that his mother gave him a cup of milk. As soon as my father told them, he understood

---

[165]   Law of Spikelets http://www.enotes.com/topic/Law_of_Spikelets

that he said something wrong and added, "But, she did not put the water in." My grandma lost her job and started to work at digging graves.

One day she missed her work and knew that she would be punished and sent to the GULAG. She fled not telling to anyone, not her mother or my dad, where she was hiding. That day the commissar came to their home and was waiting for her all day long. He tried to please my dad, hoping that this little child would tell where she was. My father still remembers how "bacon faced" the commissar looked.

My dad told that their hunger came to the end when his cousin became older, and tried to help the family to obtain some food. My father's cousin was thirteen, and he and other teen-agers tried to help their families by getting leftover potatoes from frozen collective farm fields. Those potatoes were left un-harvested, under the snow, guarded by armed guards. In the winter, under the cover of the night, together with his teen-aged friends, he would crawl into the frozen fields to get some food for themselves and their families. Their action would fall under the "Law of Spikelets" crime. These children certainly would be shot if they were caught.

- One of the girls at my work told a similar story about WWII.

When soldiers were transferred through their city of Omsk to the front and stopped at their rail station to dine, a few people were selected to cook for these soldiers. The cooks were allowed to eat during preparation of the meal but could not take anything home. As I mentioned, soldiers were usually provided with good food and generous rations.

After dinner a great bounty of leftovers was burnt by the commissars' order. The authorities would rather have everyone equal in hunger, and destroy the food, than give it to those in need. Watching as this food was wastefully burnt; these people could not hold their tears, thinking of their starving children.

When socialists promise equality to the people they cannot promise anything but equality in misery. Misery equalizes people, whereas prosperity makes them unequal in many ways and creates "envy"—someone is always richer then someone else. There was a Soviet saying, "If I don't have a cow, I don't want that you would have two." Who would envy someone else's misery or would like to share someone else's punishment?

Conclusion and Some Facts about Soviet Constitution

My mother had an opportunity to visit us few times in the United States and was always fascinated by American wealth. She kept asking over and over again why Americans live so much better then Russian people. She told me that looking around, she saw the same people just like in Russia. She noticed that these people were not better than Russians, nor did they work harder than Russians. Why did they live so much better than Russians? Why are there no poor people in the United States?

My mother and I grew up in the culture of "perpetual struggle." According to Party speeches and media reports, everything in the USSR was a struggle, not as a struggle of a "free man" but a struggle under the authorized order—a struggle against bourgeois ideology and traditions, to increase "labor productivity", for the "party line in art", for a "new man" and against the "remnants of the past", for an endlessly waged "battle for the harvest in the conditions of the county's precarious agricultural location," for "over-planed" (i.e. above what was proposed in five-year plans) for example stocking of the wood by cutting down forests, for the "virgin soil upturned", fighting for 100% collectivization, and for "world peace." The people of the Soviet Union resignedly accepted the idea that they had to sacrifice for the future generations who would be able to reach the final goal—"the communist paradise."

I was able to live for almost an equal time period in both countries and had my own observation of both cultures. I find the biggest difference between the United States and the USSR is that in the USA, the majority of the people reach prosperity by honest deeds, using their own talent, accompanied by hard work and ingenuity, and by serving their fellow men. They keep their integrity and have clean consciences.

"America's abundance was created not by public sacrifices to "the common good," but by the productive genius of free men who pursued their own personal interests and the making of their own private fortunes. They did not starve the people to pay for America's industrialization. They gave the people better jobs,

higher wages and cheaper goods with every new machine they invented, with every scientific discovery or technological advance—and thus the whole country was moving forward and profiting, not suffering, every step of the way." Ayn Rand (Alissa Rosenbaum)

In the Soviet Union, to gain one's own wealth by honest means was virtually impossible. People had to survive and adapted to the new communist morality by cheating, stealing, and lying. They justified it by making the following excuses:

"If government takes everything from me, I will take back what is rightfully mine—at least small part of it. Nobody can out-cheat the government, anyway,"
or "If I don't take it, then somebody else will",
or "Everybody does it."

The secular morality of the Soviet citizens accepted cheating and lying as a norm. Students cheated on exams and even on computer exams. It was interpreted and justified as "ingenuity" or "cleverness." People were taking stuff from their work places for their personal use and making the excuse "that everything belongs to everybody." People were using government to pay for their personal travel expenses as a "business trip." These are only a few examples.

On the other hand, people always felt that they could be destroyed by the system, the Soviet apparatus, at any moment. My father was always saying to me that the Soviet government looked at the person as if they were a bug, and they could crush him any moment.

The Soviet apparatus trampled people's will during "Red Terror," which was focused very much on the obliteration of religion and its traditional morality, and at the same time on the forced creation of the new communist morality, through the educational strategy of raising new generations to accept the "collective breed of thinking," that is the socialistic mob mentality.

Private property was considered evil. People learned not to object to anything done by the government, because it was always done "with the best intentions and for the people's best benefit."

I was surprised to find out how many people object to the vaccination of their children in the Unites States. Parents didn't have any objections to vaccinations in the USSR. It was always done without parents' permission for the "best benefit of the children," often at schools.

"Obedient to constraint, I was compelled to submit." (Mikhail Bulgakov, *The Master and Margarita*)

The Soviets created an immoral, hypocritical society where most of the people could see and understand all of its immorality and ugliness, but could do nothing about it. They had to accept it and play along with it if they wanted some comfort in their lives.

The problem with the socialism is not just having less prosperity. A hundred years ago in the U.S., people also were poorer then now. The predicament of socialism is the feeling on the people's mind which made them think that they've done dishonest things in their life—"the sin" of accepting lying as a norm. That's why another popular saying was, "Are you sleeping peacefully at night?"

My mother's questions made me to take another look at the Soviet Constitution.

I used to think that the Constitution of the USSR was in a certain way similar to the United States Constitution. Back then I would agree with Justice Antonin Scalia who mentioned, *"The bill of rights of the former evil empire, the Union of Soviet Socialist Republics, was much better than ours. I mean it literally. It was much better. We guarantee freedom of speech and of the press, big deal! They guaranteed freedom of speech, of the press, of street demonstrations, and anyone who is caught trying to suppress criticism of the government will be called to account."* However, he mentioned that these rights were valid only on paper and called it a *"Parchment guarantee."* [166]

I used to think the same; that Soviet citizens had all these rights but only on paper, and the only reason for the "parchment guarantee" was in the hypocrisy of the government, not in the foundation of the Constitution.

Then, I read it more carefully and I noticed a stunning difference:
The premise of the U.S. Constitution is "Government by the People!"
The premise of the USSR Constitution is, "All Power to the Soviets!"

The USSR Constitution enumerates the particular rights and duties of the Soviet citizens and does not give any limitation to the power of the State (notice: All power is given to the faceless concept!). For example, the Constitution of 1977 listed the following rights to the Soviet citizens: the right to work, the right to rest, the right to health care, the right to economic security in old age, the right to housing, the right to education, the right to use cultural achievements, guaranteed freedom of religion, and the family was under state protection.

The U.S. Constitutions was adopted to restrict and limit the government to certain enumerated duties but it does not limit the rights of the people.

The USSR Constitution does not guarantee liberty to the people due to the very concept of the citizens' obligations to the state. It dictated a kind of "socialistic morality code" which could be twisted the certain way to find any citizen of the USSR guilty of harming the state and the communist ideology and therefore make them guilty of disregarding the Constitution.

For example, some of the duties of the Soviet citizens contained in the Constitution of the USSR adopted on October 7, 1977 include:

---

[166] http://thinkprogress.org/justice/2012/02/09/422358/scalia-the-soviet-unions-constitution-was-much-better-than-ours/?mobile=nc

Article 60: Diligent work and the dependable labor discipline is the duty and honor of every able bodied Soviet citizen. Evasion of socially useful work is incompatible with the principles of socialist society.

Article 65: The Soviet citizen shall respect the rights and legitimate interests of others, to be uncompromising toward anti-social behavior, and to help maintain public order.

Article 66: Citizens of the USSR are obliged to care about the education of their children, to prepare them for socially useful work, to raise worthy members of socialist society. Children are obliged to take care of their parents and help them.

Article 67: Citizens of the USSR are obliged to protect and conserve the environment.

Article 68: Concern for the preservation of historical monuments and other cultural values is the duty and obligation of citizens of the USSR.

Article 69: The International duty of citizens of the USSR is to promote friendship and cooperation with people of other countries and to maintain and promote world peace.

On the contrary, the U.S. Constitution protects the people's freedom! For this very reason it was adopted in the first place. The U.S. Constitution *"is not a charter for government power, but a charter of the citizen's protection against the government."* (Ayn Rand)

Ronald Reagan said it the best,

> *"I had a copy of the Soviet Constitution and I read it with great interest, and I saw all kinds of terms in there that sound just exactly like our own: 'freedom of assembly' and 'freedom of speech' and so forth. Of course, they don't allow them to have those things, but they're in there in the Constitution. But I began to wonder about the other constitutions, everyone has one, and our own, and why so much emphasis on ours. And then I found out, and the answer was very simple—that's why you don't notice it at first.*

But it is so great that it tells the entire difference. All those other constitutions are documents that say, 'We, the government, allow the people the following rights,' and our Constitution says 'We, the People, allow the government the following privileges and rights.'"
(Ronald Reagan)

I started to look at the Soviet Constitution more carefully when I was doing research for this book and came to conclusion that it was, in fact, a "living and breathing Constitution." You can't find a single, consistent, text of the Soviet Constitution, but rather many revised versions including the Constitution of the Russian Federation of 1918, then 1924 Soviet Constitution, the Stalin's Constitution of 1936, The Constitution of the USSR 1977, etc.

Digging deeper, the first two Constitutions emphasized the class nature of the Soviet democracy as a guarantee of democracy for the workers' majority directed against the minority of the exploiters.

The very first Constitution of the Soviet Russia was called "the Constitution of the transitional period", and proclaimed the main objective as "an establishment of the dictatorship of urban and rural proletariat and the poorest peasantry, in the form of the authoritative All-Russian Soviet Power for full suppression of the bourgeoisie . . ."[167]

The Constitution of the USSR adopted in 1924, called the formation of the Soviet Union as a State of the "dictatorship of the proletariat." The Constitution of 1936 (so-called "The Stalin's Constitution") proclaimed victory of the socialism in the USSR and that socialism was generally constructed.

The USSR Constitution of 1977 declared that the Soviet Union achieved the state of the "developed socialist society", and therefore the definition of the "dictatorship of the proletariat" was officially replaced with the "Public State under the leadership of the Communist Party."

---

[167]   The text of the Constitution of the Russian Federation of 1918

The first Constitution of 1918 along with the <u>Decrees of the Soviets</u> (1917-1918) prescribed the nationalization of the land, forests, minerals and water, livestock and equipment, estates and farms, banks, insurance companies, and one by one all industries: railways, merchant fleet, sugar industries, oil, auto, education, etc.

"In order to guarantee freedom of the press", the Soviet government closed all bourgeois newspapers and transferred printing and other necessary equipment and publishers into the hands of proletariat. Only communist newspapers could be published.

"In order to guarantee a freedom of assembly", it was necessary to provide the "masses" with the buildings. The Soviet Commissariat simply requisitioned the buildings they wanted.

> *"Freedom of the press is no longer hypocrisy, because the printing and paper are taken from the bourgeoisie. The same is true for the expropriation of the best buildings, palaces, and mansions. Soviet power insured million times greater 'democratic' rights of assembly to the masses by immediate requisition of the thousands of the best buildings which belonged to the exploiters and so gave the rights of assembly, without which democracy is a fraud . . ."*(Lenin, <u>Proletarian Revolution and Renegade Kautsky</u>)

Since the Soviet Constitution declared the separation of the church and the State[168] and therefore the Soviet people were not expected to follow the morality encouraged by the church, the Soviet Constitutions dictated Communist moral codes on the people.

Marriage and Divorce were included in the Articles of the Soviet Constitution. Before that all cases of marriage, and in the very rare occasions of divorce, were done almost exclusively through the church.

Interesting that Divorce Code was adopted by Soviet Decrees before the adoption of the "Decree of the Civil Marriage."

---

[168] Article 52 of the USSR Constitution adopted in 1977 stated: "The church in the USSR is separated from the state and school—from church."

From the "Decree of the Central Executive Committee and the Soviet Public Commissariat about Divorce" on December 29, 1917 immediately after the October Revolution,

> *"10. From now on the cases for recognition of marriages to be illegal or invalid are maintained exclusive by local court.*
>
> *11. Action of this law extends to all citizens of the Russian Republic, regardless of their belonging to a particular religious cult."*

From the <u>Decree of Civil Marriage, Children and Books about Maintaining Books of Acts of a Condition</u>. December 31, 1917

> *"From now on the Russian Republic recognizes **only civil marriages.***
>
> *Note. Church marriage, along with obligatory civil marriage, is the spouses' private affair."*

I wrote my story in the hope that Americans would take a different look at how fortunate they are to live in a free society protected by the Constitution. That they "are endowed by their Creator with certain unalienable Rights", not by the state or government, and would choose to cherish their Constitutional rights and their freedom.

It may be exciting for Americans to look at the European countries and be fascinated by their long history. Americans have to remember that their history is more fascinating than that of the Europeans. Surrounded by cultures of aristocracy, totalitarian states, imperialism, no experience or examples of freedom before in history, Americans created the first truly free society where they could keep the "fruits of their labor" without fear of being robbed by their government. They created a first and never-heard-of-before country of truly free men.

Prosperity is unachievable without Freedom. Dignity is impossible without Liberty. The Constitution protects our Freedom. We must protect our Constitution!

THE CONSTITUTION OF THE UNITED STATES

Preamble

We the People of the United States, in Order to form a more perfect Union, establish Justice, insure domestic Tranquility, provide for the common defence, promote the general Welfare, and secure the Blessings of Liberty to ourselves and our Posterity, do ordain and establish this Constitution for the United States of America.

Article. I.—The Legislative Branch

Section 1—The Legislature

All legislative Powers herein granted shall be vested in a Congress of the United States, which shall consist of a Senate and House of Representatives.

Section 2—The House

The House of Representatives shall be composed of Members chosen every second Year by the People of the several States, and the Electors in each State shall have the Qualifications requisite for Electors of the most numerous Branch of the State Legislature.

No Person shall be a Representative who shall not have attained to the Age of twenty five Years, and been seven Years a Citizen of the United States, and who shall not, when elected, be an Inhabitant of that State in which he shall be chosen.

(Representatives and direct Taxes shall be apportioned among the several States which may be included within this Union, according to their respective Numbers, which shall be determined by adding to the whole Number of free Persons, including those bound to Service for a Term of Years, and excluding Indians not taxed, three fifths of all other Persons.) **(The previous sentence in parentheses was modified by the 14th Amendment, section 2.)** The actual Enumeration shall be made within three Years after the first Meeting of the Congress of the United States, and within every subsequent Term of ten Years, in such Manner as they shall by Law direct. The Number of Representatives shall not exceed one for every thirty Thousand, but each State shall have at Least one Representative; and until such enumeration shall be made, the State of New Hampshire shall be entitled to chuse three, Massachusetts eight, Rhode Island and Providence Plantations one, Connecticut five, New York six, New Jersey four, Pennsylvania eight, Delaware one, Maryland six, Virginia ten, North Carolina five, South Carolina five and Georgia three.

When vacancies happen in the Representation from any State, the Executive Authority thereof shall issue Writs of Election to fill such Vacancies.

The House of Representatives shall chuse their Speaker and other Officers; and shall have the sole Power of Impeachment.

Section 3—The Senate

The Senate of the United States shall be composed of two Senators from each State, *(chosen by the Legislature thereof,)* **(The preceding words in parentheses superseded by 17th Amendment, section 1.)** for six Years; and each Senator shall have one Vote.

Immediately after they shall be assembled in Consequence of the first Election, they shall be divided as equally as may be into three Classes. The Seats of the Senators of the first Class shall be vacated at the Expiration of the second Year, of the second Class at the Expiration of the fourth Year, and of the third Class at the Expiration of the sixth Year, so that one third may be chosen every second Year; *(and if Vacancies happen by Resignation, or otherwise, during the Recess of the Legislature of any State, the Executive thereof may make temporary Appointments until the next Meeting of the Legislature, which shall then fill such Vacancies.)* **(The preceding words in parentheses were superseded by the 17th Amendment, section 2.)**

No person shall be a Senator who shall not have attained to the Age of thirty Years, and been nine Years a Citizen of the United States, and who shall not, when elected, be an Inhabitant of that State for which he shall be chosen.

The Vice President of the United States shall be President of the Senate, but shall have no Vote, unless they be equally divided.

The Senate shall chuse their other Officers, and also a President pro tempore, in the absence of the Vice President, or when he shall exercise the Office of President of the United States.

The Senate shall have the sole Power to try all Impeachments. When sitting for that Purpose, they shall be on Oath or Affirmation. When the President of the United States is tried, the Chief Justice shall preside: And no Person shall be convicted without the Concurrence of two thirds of the Members present.

Judgment in Cases of Impeachment shall not extend further than to removal from Office, and disqualification to hold and enjoy any Office of honor, Trust or Profit under the United States: but the Party convicted shall nevertheless be liable and subject to Indictment, Trial, Judgment and Punishment, according to Law.

Section 4—Elections, Meetings

The Times, Places and Manner of holding Elections for Senators and Representatives, shall be prescribed in each State by the Legislature thereof; but the Congress may at any time by Law make or alter such Regulations, except as to the Place of Chusing Senators.

The Congress shall assemble at least once in every Year, and such Meeting shall *(be on the first Monday in December,)* **(The preceding words in parentheses were superseded by the 20th Amendment, section 2.)** unless they shall by Law appoint a different Day.

Section 5—Membership, Rules, Journals, Adjournment

Each House shall be the Judge of the Elections, Returns and Qualifications of its own Members, and a Majority of each shall constitute a Quorum to do Business; but a smaller number may adjourn from day to day, and may be authorized to compel the Attendance of absent Members, in such Manner, and under such Penalties as each House may provide.

Each House may determine the Rules of its Proceedings, punish its Members for disorderly Behavior, and, with the Concurrence of two-thirds, expel a Member.

Each House shall keep a Journal of its Proceedings, and from time to time publish the same, excepting such Parts as may in their Judgment require Secrecy; and the Yeas and Nays of the Members of either House on any question shall, at the Desire of one fifth of those Present, be entered on the Journal.

Neither House, during the Session of Congress, shall, without the Consent of the other, adjourn for more than three days, nor to any other Place than that in which the two Houses shall be sitting.

Section 6—Compensation

(The Senators and Representatives shall receive a Compensation for their Services, to be ascertained by Law, and paid out of the Treasury of the United States.) **(The preceding words in parentheses were modified by the 27th Amendment.)** They shall in all Cases, except Treason, Felony and Breach of the Peace, be privileged from Arrest during their Attendance at the Session of their respective Houses, and in going to and returning from the same; and for any Speech or Debate in either House, they shall not be questioned in any other Place.

No Senator or Representative shall, during the Time for which he was elected, be appointed to any civil Office under the Authority of the United States which shall have been created, or the Emoluments whereof shall have been increased during such time; and no Person holding any Office under the United States, shall be a Member of either House during his Continuance in Office.

Section 7—Revenue Bills, Legislative Process, Presidential Veto

All bills for raising Revenue shall originate in the House of Representatives; but the Senate may propose or concur with Amendments as on other Bills.

Every Bill which shall have passed the House of Representatives and the Senate, shall, before it become a Law, be presented to the President of the United States; If he approve he shall sign it, but if not he shall return it, with his Objections to that House in which it shall have originated, who shall enter the Objections at large on their Journal, and proceed to reconsider it. If after such Reconsideration two thirds of that House shall agree to pass the Bill, it shall be sent, together with the Objections, to the other House, by which it shall likewise be reconsidered, and if approved by two thirds of that House, it shall become a Law. But in all such Cases the Votes of both Houses shall be determined by Yeas and Nays, and the Names of the Persons voting for and against the Bill shall be entered on the Journal of each House respectively. If any Bill shall not be returned by the President within ten Days (Sundays excepted) after it shall have been presented to him, the Same shall be a Law, in like Manner as if he had signed it, unless the Congress by their Adjournment prevent its Return, in which Case it shall not be a Law.

Every Order, Resolution, or Vote to which the Concurrence of the Senate and House of Representatives may be necessary (except on a question of Adjournment) shall be presented to the President of the United States; and before the Same shall take Effect, shall be approved by him, or being disapproved by him, shall be repassed by two thirds of the Senate and House of Representatives, according to the Rules and Limitations prescribed in the Case of a Bill.

Section 8—Powers of Congress

The Congress shall have Power To lay and collect Taxes, Duties, Imposts and Excises, to pay the Debts and provide for the common Defense and general Welfare of the United States; but all Duties, Imposts and Excises shall be uniform throughout the United States;

To borrow money on the credit of the United States;

To regulate Commerce with foreign Nations, and among the several States, and with the Indian Tribes;

To establish an uniform Rule of Naturalization, and uniform Laws on the subject of Bankruptcies throughout the United States;

To coin Money, regulate the Value thereof, and of foreign Coin, and fix the Standard of Weights and Measures;

To provide for the Punishment of counterfeiting the Securities and current Coin of the United States;

To establish Post Offices and Post Roads;

To promote the Progress of Science and useful Arts, by securing for limited Times to Authors and Inventors the exclusive Right to their respective Writings and Discoveries;

To constitute Tribunals inferior to the supreme Court;

To define and punish Piracies and Felonies committed on the high Seas, and Offenses against the Law of Nations;

To declare War, grant Letters of Marque and Reprisal, and make Rules concerning Captures on Land and Water;

To raise and support Armies, but no Appropriation of Money to that Use shall be for a longer Term than two Years;

To provide and maintain a Navy;

To make Rules for the Government and Regulation of the land and naval Forces;

To provide for calling forth the Militia to execute the Laws of the Union, suppress Insurrections and repel Invasions;

To provide for organizing, arming, and disciplining the Militia, and for governing such Part of them as may be employed in the Service of the United States, reserving to the States respectively, the Appointment of the Officers, and the Authority of training the Militia according to the discipline prescribed by Congress;

To exercise exclusive Legislation in all Cases whatsoever, over such District (not exceeding ten Miles square) as may, by Cession of particular States, and the acceptance of Congress, become the Seat of the Government of the United States, and to exercise like Authority over all Places purchased by the Consent of the Legislature of the State in which the Same shall be, for the Erection of Forts, Magazines, Arsenals, dock-Yards, and other needful Buildings; And

To make all Laws which shall be necessary and proper for carrying into Execution the foregoing Powers, and all other Powers vested by this Constitution in the Government of the United States, or in any Department or Officer thereof.

Section 9—Limits on Congress

The Migration or Importation of such Persons as any of the States now existing shall think proper to admit, shall not be prohibited by the Congress prior to the Year one thousand eight hundred and eight, but a tax or duty may be imposed on such Importation, not exceeding ten dollars for each Person.

The privilege of the Writ of Habeas Corpus shall not be suspended, unless when in Cases of Rebellion or Invasion the public Safety may require it.

No Bill of Attainder or ex post facto Law shall be passed.

(No capitation, or other direct, Tax shall be laid, unless in Proportion to the Census or Enumeration herein before directed to be taken.) **(Section in parentheses clarified by the 16th Amendment.)**

No Tax or Duty shall be laid on Articles exported from any State.

No Preference shall be given by any Regulation of Commerce or Revenue to the Ports of one State over those of another: nor shall Vessels bound to, or from, one State, be obliged to enter, clear, or pay Duties in another.

No Money shall be drawn from the Treasury, but in Consequence of Appropriations made by Law; and a regular Statement and Account of the Receipts and Expenditures of all public Money shall be published from time to time.

No Title of Nobility shall be granted by the United States: And no Person holding any Office of Profit or Trust under them, shall, without the Consent of the Congress, accept of any present,

Emolument, Office, or Title, of any kind whatever, from any King, Prince or foreign State.

Section 10—Powers prohibited of States

No State shall enter into any Treaty, Alliance, or Confederation; grant Letters of Marque and Reprisal; coin Money; emit Bills of Credit; make any Thing but gold and silver Coin a Tender in Payment of Debts; pass any Bill of Attainder, ex post facto Law, or Law impairing the Obligation of Contracts, or grant any Title of Nobility.

No State shall, without the Consent of the Congress, lay any Imposts or Duties on Imports or Exports, except what may be absolutely necessary for executing it's inspection Laws: and the net Produce of all Duties and Imposts, laid by any State on Imports or Exports, shall be for the Use of the Treasury of the United States; and all such Laws shall be subject to the Revision and Controul of the Congress.

No State shall, without the Consent of Congress, lay any duty of Tonnage, keep Troops, or Ships of War in time of Peace, enter into any Agreement or Compact with another State, or with a foreign Power, or engage in War, unless actually invaded, or in such imminent Danger as will not admit of delay.

Article. II.—The Executive Branch

Section 1—The President

The executive Power shall be vested in a President of the United States of America. He shall hold his Office during the Term of four Years, and, together with the Vice-President chosen for the same Term, be elected, as follows:

Each State shall appoint, in such Manner as the Legislature thereof may direct, a Number of Electors, equal to the whole Number of Senators and Representatives to which the State may be entitled in the Congress: but no Senator or Representative, or Person holding an Office of Trust or Profit under the United States, shall be appointed an Elector.

(The Electors shall meet in their respective States, and vote by Ballot for two persons, of whom one at least shall not lie an Inhabitant of the same State with themselves. And they shall make a List of all the Persons voted for, and of the Number of Votes for each; which List they shall sign and certify, and transmit sealed to the Seat of the Government of the United States, directed to the President of the Senate. The President of the Senate shall, in the Presence of the Senate and House of Representatives, open all the Certificates, and the Votes shall then be counted. The Person having the greatest Number of Votes shall be the President, if such Number be a Majority of the whole Number of Electors appointed; and if there be more than one who have such Majority, and have an equal Number of Votes, then the House of Representatives shall immediately chuse by Ballot one of them for President; and if no Person have a Majority, then from the five highest on the List the said House shall in like Manner chuse the President. But in chusing the President, the Votes shall be taken by States, the Representation from each State having one Vote; a quorum for this Purpose shall consist of a Member or Members from two-thirds of the States, and a Majority of all the States shall be necessary to a Choice. In every Case, after the Choice of the President, the Person having the greatest Number of Votes of the Electors shall be the Vice President. But if there should remain two or more who have equal Votes, the Senate shall chuse from them by Ballot the Vice-President.) **(This clause in parentheses was superseded by the 12th Amendment.)**

The Congress may determine the Time of chusing the Electors, and the Day on which they shall give their Votes; which Day shall be the same throughout the United States.

No person except a natural born Citizen, or a Citizen of the United States, at the time of the Adoption of this Constitution, shall be eligible to the Office of President; neither shall any Person be eligible to that Office who shall not have attained to the Age of thirty-five Years, and been fourteen Years a Resident within the United States.

(In Case of the Removal of the President from Office, or of his Death, Resignation, or Inability to discharge the Powers and Duties of the said Office, the same shall devolve on the Vice President, and the Congress may by Law provide for the Case of Removal, Death, Resignation or Inability, both of the President and Vice President, declaring what Officer shall then act as President, and such Officer shall act accordingly, until the Disability be removed, or a President shall be elected.) **(This clause in parentheses has been modified by the 20th and 25th Amendments.)**

The President shall, at stated Times, receive for his Services, a Compensation, which shall neither be increased nor diminished during the Period for which he shall have been elected, and he shall not receive within that Period any other Emolument from the United States, or any of them.

Before he enter on the Execution of his Office, he shall take the following Oath or Affirmation:

"I do solemnly swear (or affirm) that I will faithfully execute the Office of President of the United States, and will to the best of my Ability, preserve, protect and defend the Constitution of the United States."

Section 2—Civilian Power over Military, Cabinet, Pardon Power, Appointments

The President shall be Commander in Chief of the Army and Navy of the United States, and of the Militia of the several States, when called into the actual Service of the United States; he may require the Opinion, in writing, of the principal Officer in each of the executive Departments, upon any subject relating to the Duties of their respective Offices, and he shall have Power to Grant

Reprieves and Pardons for Offenses against the United States, except in Cases of Impeachment.

He shall have Power, by and with the Advice and Consent of the Senate, to make Treaties, provided two thirds of the Senators present concur; and he shall nominate, and by and with the Advice and Consent of the Senate, shall appoint Ambassadors, other public Ministers and Consuls, Judges of the supreme Court, and all other Officers of the United States, whose Appointments are not herein otherwise provided for, and which shall be established by Law: but the Congress may by Law vest the Appointment of such inferior Officers, as they think proper, in the President alone, in the Courts of Law, or in the Heads of Departments.

The President shall have Power to fill up all Vacancies that may happen during the Recess of the Senate, by granting Commissions which shall expire at the End of their next Session.

Section 3—State of the Union, Convening Congress

He shall from time to time give to the Congress Information of the State of the Union, and recommend to their Consideration such Measures as he shall judge necessary and expedient; he may, on extraordinary Occasions, convene both Houses, or either of them, and in Case of Disagreement between them, with Respect to the Time of Adjournment, he may adjourn them to such Time as he shall think proper; he shall receive Ambassadors and other public Ministers; he shall take Care that the Laws be faithfully executed, and shall Commission all the Officers of the United States.

Section 4—Disqualification

The President, Vice President and all civil Officers of the United States, shall be removed from Office on Impeachment for, and Conviction of, Treason, Bribery, or other high Crimes and Misdemeanors.

Article III.—The Judicial Branch

Section 1—Judicial powers

The judicial Power of the United States, shall be vested in one supreme Court, and in such inferior Courts as the Congress may from time to time ordain and establish. The Judges, both of the supreme and inferior Courts, shall hold their Offices during good Behavior, and shall, at stated Times, receive for their Services a Compensation which shall not be diminished during their Continuance in Office.

Section 2—Trial by Jury, Original Jurisdiction, Jury Trials

(The judicial Power shall extend to all Cases, in Law and Equity, arising under this Constitution, the Laws of the United States, and Treaties made, or which shall be made, under their Authority; to all Cases affecting Ambassadors, other public Ministers and Consuls; to all Cases of admiralty and maritime Jurisdiction; to Controversies to which the United States shall be a Party; to Controversies between two or more States; between a State and Citizens of another State; between Citizens of different States; between Citizens of the same State claiming Lands under Grants of different States, and between a State, or the Citizens thereof, and foreign States, Citizens or Subjects.) **(This section in parentheses is modified by the 11ᵗʰ Amendment.)**

In all Cases affecting Ambassadors, other public Ministers and Consuls, and those in which a State shall be Party, the supreme Court shall have original Jurisdiction. In all the other Cases before mentioned, the supreme Court shall have appellate Jurisdiction, both as to Law and Fact, with such Exceptions, and under such Regulations as the Congress shall make.

The Trial of all Crimes, except in Cases of Impeachment, shall be by Jury; and such Trial shall be held in the State where the said Crimes shall have been committed; but when not committed within any State, the Trial shall be at such Place or Places as the Congress may by Law have directed.

Section 3—Treason

Treason against the United States, shall consist only in levying War against them, or in adhering to their Enemies, giving them Aid and Comfort. No Person shall be convicted of Treason unless on the Testimony of two Witnesses to the same overt Act, or on Confession in open Court.

The Congress shall have power to declare the Punishment of Treason, but no Attainder of Treason shall work Corruption of Blood, or Forfeiture except during the Life of the Person attainted.

Article. IV.—The States

Section 1—Each State to Honor all others

Full Faith and Credit shall be given in each State to the public Acts, Records, and judicial Proceedings of every other State. And the Congress may by general Laws prescribe the Manner in which such Acts, Records and Proceedings shall be proved, and the Effect thereof.

Section 2—State citizens, Extradition

The Citizens of each State shall be entitled to all Privileges and Immunities of Citizens in the several States.

A Person charged in any State with Treason, Felony, or other Crime, who shall flee from Justice, and be found in another State, shall on demand of the executive Authority of the State from which he fled, be delivered up, to be removed to the State having Jurisdiction of the Crime.

Peter Konetchy

(No Person held to Service or Labour in one State, under the Laws thereof, escaping into another, shall, in Consequence of any Law or Regulation therein, be discharged from such Service or Labour, But shall be delivered up on Claim of the Party to whom such Service or Labour may be due.) **(This clause in parentheses is superseded by the 13th Amendment.)**

Section 3—New States

New States may be admitted by the Congress into this Union; but no new States shall be formed or erected within the Jurisdiction of any other State; nor any State be formed by the Junction of two or more States, or parts of States, without the Consent of the Legislatures of the States concerned as well as of the Congress.

The Congress shall have Power to dispose of and make all needful Rules and Regulations respecting the Territory or other Property belonging to the United States; and nothing in this Constitution shall be so construed as to Prejudice any Claims of the United States, or of any particular State.

Section 4—Republican government

The United States shall guarantee to every State in this Union a Republican Form of Government, and shall protect each of them against Invasion; and on Application of the Legislature, or of the Executive (when the Legislature cannot be convened) against domestic Violence.

Article. V.—Amendment

The Congress, whenever two thirds of both Houses shall deem it necessary, shall propose Amendments to this Constitution, or, on the Application of the Legislatures of two thirds of the several States, shall call a Convention for proposing Amendments, which, in either Case, shall be valid to all Intents and Purposes, as part of this Constitution, when ratified by the Legislatures of three fourths of the several States, or by Conventions in three fourths thereof, as the one or the other Mode of Ratification may be proposed by the Congress; Provided that no Amendment which may be made prior to the Year One thousand eight hundred and eight shall in any Manner affect the first and fourth Clauses in the Ninth Section of the first Article; and that no State, without its Consent, shall be deprived of its equal Suffrage in the Senate.

Article. VI.—Debts, Supremacy, Oaths

All Debts contracted and Engagements entered into, before the Adoption of this Constitution, shall be as valid against the United States under this Constitution, as under the Confederation.

This Constitution, and the Laws of the United States which shall be made in Pursuance thereof; and all Treaties made, or which shall be made, under the Authority of the United States, shall be the supreme Law of the Land; and the Judges in every State shall be bound thereby, any Thing in the Constitution or Laws of any State to the Contrary notwithstanding.

The Senators and Representatives before mentioned, and the Members of the several State Legislatures, and all executive and judicial Officers, both of the United States and of the several States, shall be bound by Oath or Affirmation, to support this Constitution; but no religious Test shall ever be required as a Qualification to any Office or public Trust under the United States.

Article. VII.—Ratification *Documents*

The Ratification of the Conventions of nine States, shall be sufficient for the Establishment of this Constitution between the States so ratifying the Same.

Done in Convention by the Unanimous Consent of the States present the Seventeenth Day of September in the Year of our Lord one thousand seven hundred and Eighty seven and of the Independence of the United States of America the Twelfth. In Witness whereof We have hereunto subscribed our Names.

Go Washington—President and deputy from Virginia

New Hampshire—John Langdon, Nicholas Gilman

Massachusetts—Nathaniel Gorham, Rufus King

Connecticut—Wm Saml Johnson, Roger Sherman

New York—Alexander Hamilton

New Jersey—Wil Livingston, David Brearley, Wm Paterson, Jona. Dayton

Pensylvania—B Franklin, Thomas Mifflin, Robt Morris, Geo. Clymer, Thos FitzSimons, Jared Ingersoll, James Wilson, Gouv Morris

Delaware—Geo. Read, Gunning Bedford jun, John Dickinson, Richard Bassett, Jaco. Broom

Maryland—James McHenry, Dan of St Tho Jenifer, Danl Carroll

Virginia—John Blair, James Madison Jr.

North Carolina—Wm Blount, Richd Dobbs Spaight, Hu Williamson

South Carolina—J. Rutledge, Charles Cotesworth Pinckney, Charles Pinckney, Pierce Butler

Georgia—William Few, Abr Baldwin

Attest: William Jackson, Secretary

The Amendments

The following are the Amendments to the Constitution. The first ten Amendments collectively are commonly known as the Bill of Rights.

Amendment 1—Freedom of Religion, Press, Expression. Ratified 12/15/1791.

Congress shall make no law respecting an establishment of religion, or prohibiting the free exercise thereof; or abridging the freedom of speech, or of the press; or the right of the people peaceably to assemble, and to petition the Government for a redress of grievances.

Amendment 2—Right to Bear Arms. Ratified 12/15/1791.

A well regulated Militia, being necessary to the security of a free State, the right of the people to keep and bear Arms, shall not be infringed.

Amendment 3—Quartering of Soldiers. Ratified 12/15/1791.

No Soldier shall, in time of peace be quartered in any house, without the consent of the Owner, nor in time of war, but in a manner to be prescribed by law.

Amendment 4—Search and Seizure. Ratified 12/15/1791.

The right of the people to be secure in their persons, houses, papers, and effects, against unreasonable searches and seizures, shall not be violated, and no Warrants shall issue, but upon probable cause, supported by Oath or affirmation, and particularly describing the place to be searched, and the persons or things to be seized.

Amendment 5—Trial and Punishment, Compensation for Takings. Ratified 12/15/1791.

No person shall be held to answer for a capital, or otherwise infamous crime, unless on a presentment or indictment of a Grand Jury, except in cases arising in the land or naval forces, or in the Militia, when in actual service in time of War or public danger; nor shall any person be subject for the same offense to be twice put in jeopardy of life or limb; nor shall be compelled in any criminal case to be a witness against himself, nor be deprived of life, liberty, or property, without due process of law; nor shall private property be taken for public use, without just compensation.

Amendment 6—Right to Speedy Trial, Confrontation of Witnesses. Ratified 12/15/1791.

In all criminal prosecutions, the accused shall enjoy the right to a speedy and public trial, by an impartial jury of the State and district wherein the crime shall have been committed, which district shall have been previously ascertained by law, and to be informed of the nature and cause of the accusation; to be confronted with the witnesses against him; to have compulsory process for obtaining witnesses in his favor, and to have the Assistance of Counsel for his defence.

Amendment 7—Trial by Jury in Civil Cases. Ratified 12/15/1791.

In Suits at common law, where the value in controversy shall exceed twenty dollars, the right of trial by jury shall be preserved, and no fact tried by a jury, shall be otherwise re-examined in any Court of the United States, than according to the rules of the common law.

Amendment 8—Cruel and Unusual Punishment. Ratified 12/15/1791.

Excessive bail shall not be required, nor excessive fines imposed, nor cruel and unusual punishments inflicted.

Amendment 9—Construction of Constitution. Ratified 12/15/1791.

The enumeration in the Constitution, of certain rights, shall not be construed to deny or disparage others retained by the people.

Amendment 10—Powers of the States and People. Ratified 12/15/1791.

The powers not delegated to the United States by the Constitution, nor prohibited by it to the States, are reserved to the States respectively, or to the people.

Amendment 11—Judicial Limits. Ratified 2/7/1795.

The Judicial power of the United States shall not be construed to extend to any suit in law or equity, commenced or prosecuted against one of the United States by Citizens of another State, or by Citizens or Subjects of any Foreign State.

Amendment 12—Choosing the President, Vice-President. Ratified 6/15/1804. *The Electoral College*

The Electors shall meet in their respective states, and vote by ballot for President and Vice-President, one of whom, at least, shall not be an inhabitant of the same state with themselves; they shall name in their ballots the person voted for as President, and in distinct ballots the person voted for as Vice-President, and they shall make distinct lists of all persons voted for as President, and of all persons voted for as Vice-President and of the number of votes for each, which lists they shall sign and certify, and transmit sealed to the seat of the government of the United States, directed to the President of the Senate;

The President of the Senate shall, in the presence of the Senate and House of Representatives, open all the certificates and the votes shall then be counted;

The person having the greatest Number of votes for President, shall be the President, if such number be a majority of the whole number of Electors appointed; and if no person have such majority, then from the persons having the highest numbers not exceeding three on the list of those voted for as President, the House of Representatives shall choose immediately, by ballot, the President. But in choosing the President, the votes shall be taken by states, the representation from each state having one vote; a quorum for this purpose shall consist of a member or members from two-thirds of the states, and a majority of all the states shall be necessary to a choice. And if the House of Representatives shall not choose a President whenever the right of choice shall devolve upon them, before the fourth day of March next following, then the Vice-President shall act as President, as in the case of the death or other constitutional disability of the President.

The person having the greatest number of votes as Vice-President, shall be the Vice-President, if such number be a majority of the whole number of Electors appointed, and if no person have a majority, then from the two highest numbers on the list, the Senate shall choose the Vice-President; a quorum for the purpose shall consist of two-thirds of the whole number of Senators, and a majority of the whole number shall be necessary to a choice. But no person constitutionally ineligible to the office of President shall be eligible to that of Vice-President of the United States.

Amendment 13—Slavery Abolished. Ratified 12/6/1865.

1. Neither slavery nor involuntary servitude, except as a punishment for crime whereof the party shall have been duly convicted, shall exist within the United States, or any place subject to their jurisdiction.
2. Congress shall have power to enforce this article by appropriate legislation.

Amendment 14—Citizenship Rights. Ratified 7/9/1868.

1. All persons born or naturalized in the United States, and subject to the jurisdiction thereof, are citizens of the United States and of the State wherein they reside. No State shall make or enforce any law which shall abridge the privileges or immunities of citizens of the United States; nor shall any State deprive any person of life, liberty, or property, without due

process of law; nor deny to any person within its jurisdiction the equal protection of the laws.

2. Representatives shall be apportioned among the several States according to their respective numbers, counting the whole number of persons in each State, excluding Indians not taxed. But when the right to vote at any election for the choice of electors for President and Vice-President of the United States, Representatives in Congress, the Executive and Judicial officers of a State, or the members of the Legislature thereof, is denied to any of the male inhabitants of such State, being twenty-one years of age, and citizens of the United States, or in any way abridged, except for participation in rebellion, or other crime, the basis of representation therein shall be reduced in the proportion which the number of such male citizens shall bear to the whole number of male citizens twenty-one years of age in such State.

3. No person shall be a Senator or Representative in Congress, or elector of President and Vice-President, or hold any office, civil or military, under the United States, or under any State, who, having previously taken an oath, as a member of Congress, or as an officer of the United States, or as a member of any State legislature, or as an executive or judicial officer of any State, to support the Constitution of the United States, shall have engaged in insurrection or rebellion against the same, or given aid or comfort to the enemies thereof. But Congress may by a vote of two-thirds of each House, remove such disability.

4. The validity of the public debt of the United States, authorized by law, including debts incurred for payment of pensions and bounties for services in suppressing insurrection or rebellion, shall not be questioned. But neither the United States nor any State shall assume or pay any debt or obligation incurred in aid of insurrection or rebellion against the United States, or any claim for the loss or emancipation of any slave; but all such debts, obligations and claims shall be held illegal and void.

5. The Congress shall have power to enforce, by appropriate legislation, the provisions of this article.

Amendment 15—Race No Bar to Vote. Ratified 2/3/1870.

1. The right of citizens of the United States to vote shall not be denied or abridged by the United States or by any State on account of race, color, or previous condition of servitude.
2. The Congress shall have power to enforce this article by appropriate legislation.

Amendment 16—Status of Income Tax Clarified. Ratified 2/3/1913.

The Congress shall have power to lay and collect taxes on incomes, from whatever source derived, without apportionment among the several States, and without regard to any census or enumeration.

Amendment 17—Senators Elected by Popular Vote. Ratified 4/8/1913.

The Senate of the United States shall be composed of two Senators from each State, elected by the people thereof, for six years; and each Senator shall have one vote. The electors in each State shall have the qualifications requisite for electors of the most numerous branch of the State legislatures.

When vacancies happen in the representation of any State in the Senate, the executive authority of such State shall issue writs of election to fill such vacancies: Provided, That the legislature of any State may empower the executive thereof to make temporary appointments until the people fill the vacancies by election as the legislature may direct.

This amendment shall not be so construed as to affect the election or term of any Senator chosen before it becomes valid as part of the Constitution.

Amendment 18—Liquor Abolished. Ratified 1/16/1919. Repealed by Amendment 21, 12/5/1933.

1. After one year from the ratification of this article the manufacture, sale, or transportation of intoxicating liquors within, the importation thereof into, or the exportation thereof from the United States and all territory subject to the jurisdiction thereof for beverage purposes is hereby prohibited.
2. The Congress and the several States shall have concurrent power to enforce this article by appropriate legislation.
3. This article shall be inoperative unless it shall have been ratified as an amendment to the Constitution by the legislatures of the several States, as provided in the Constitution, within seven years from the date of the submission hereof to the States by the Congress.

Amendment 19—Women's Suffrage. Ratified 8/18/1920.

The right of citizens of the United States to vote shall not be denied or abridged by the United States or by any State on account of sex.

Congress shall have power to enforce this article by appropriate legislation.

Amendment 20—Presidential, Congressional Terms. Ratified 1/23/1933.

1. The terms of the President and Vice President shall end at noon on the 20ᵗʰ day of January, and the terms of Senators and Representatives at noon on the 3d day of January, of the years in which such terms would have ended if this article had not been ratified; and the terms of their successors shall then begin.
2. The Congress shall assemble at least once in every year, and such meeting shall begin at noon on the 3d day of January, unless they shall by law appoint a different day.
3. If, at the time fixed for the beginning of the term of the President, the President elect shall have died, the Vice President elect shall become President. If a President shall not have been chosen before the time fixed for the beginning of his term, or if the President elect shall have failed to qualify, then the Vice President elect shall act as President until a President shall have qualified; and the Congress may by law provide for the case wherein neither a President elect nor a Vice President elect shall have qualified, declaring who shall then act as President, or the manner in which one who is to act shall be selected, and such person shall act accordingly until a President or Vice President shall have qualified.
4. The Congress may by law provide for the case of the death of any of the persons from whom the House of Representatives may choose a President whenever the right of choice shall have devolved upon them, and for the case of the death of any of the persons from whom the Senate may choose a Vice President whenever the right of choice shall have devolved upon them.
5. Sections 1 and 2 shall take effect on the 15ᵗʰ day of October following the ratification of this article.
6. This article shall be inoperative unless it shall have been ratified as an amendment to the Constitution by the legislatures of three-fourths of the several States within seven years from the date of its submission.

Amendment 21—Amendment 18 Repealed. Ratified 12/5/1933.

1. The eighteenth article of amendment to the Constitution of the United States is hereby repealed.
2. The transportation or importation into any State, Territory, or possession of the United States for delivery or use therein of intoxicating liquors, in violation of the laws thereof, is hereby prohibited.
3. The article shall be inoperative unless it shall have been ratified as an amendment to the Constitution by conventions in the several States, as provided in the Constitution, within seven years from the date of the submission hereof to the States by the Congress.

Amendment 22—Presidential Term Limits. Ratified 2/27/1951.

1. No person shall be elected to the office of the President more than twice, and no person who has held the office of President, or acted as President, for more than two years of a term to which some other person was elected President shall be elected to the office of the President more than once. But this Article shall not apply to any person holding the office of President, when this Article was proposed by the Congress, and shall not prevent any person who may be holding the office of President, or acting as President, during the term within which this Article becomes operative from holding the office of President or acting as President during the remainder of such term.
2. This article shall be inoperative unless it shall have been ratified as an amendment to the Constitution by the legislatures of three-fourths of the several States within seven years from the date of its submission to the States by the Congress.

Amendment 23—Presidential Vote for District of Columbia. Ratified 3/29/1961.

1. The District constituting the seat of Government of the United States shall appoint in such manner as the Congress may direct: A number of electors of President and Vice President equal to the whole number of Senators and Representatives in Congress to which the District would be entitled if it were a State, but in no event more than the least populous State; they shall be in addition to those appointed by the States, but they shall be considered, for the purposes of the election of President and Vice President, to be electors appointed by a State; and they shall meet in the District and perform such duties as provided by the twelfth article of amendment.
2. The Congress shall have power to enforce this article by appropriate legislation.

Amendment 24—Poll Tax Barred. Ratified 1/23/1964.

1. The right of citizens of the United States to vote in any primary or other election for President or Vice President, for electors for President or Vice President, or for Senator or Representative in Congress, shall not be denied or abridged by the United States or any State by reason of failure to pay any poll tax or other tax.
2. The Congress shall have power to enforce this article by appropriate legislation.

Amendment 25—Presidential Disability and Succession. Ratified 2/10/1967.

1. In case of the removal of the President from office or of his death or resignation, the Vice President shall become President.
2. Whenever there is a vacancy in the office of the Vice President, the President shall nominate a Vice President who shall take office upon confirmation by a majority vote of both Houses of Congress.
3. Whenever the President transmits to the President pro tempore of the Senate and the Speaker of the House of Representatives his written declaration that he is unable to discharge the powers and duties of his office, and until he transmits to them a written declaration to the contrary, such powers and duties shall be discharged by the Vice President as Acting President.
4. Whenever the Vice President and a majority of either the principal officers of the executive departments or of such other body as Congress may by law provide, transmit to the President pro tempore of the Senate and the Speaker of the House of Representatives their written declaration that the President is unable to discharge the powers and duties of his office, the Vice President shall immediately assume the powers and duties of the office as Acting President.

Thereafter, when the President transmits to the President pro tempore of the Senate and the Speaker of the House of Representatives his written declaration that no inability exists, he shall resume the powers and duties of his office unless the Vice President and a majority of either the principal officers of the executive department or of such other body as Congress may by law provide, transmit within four days to the President pro tempore of the Senate and the Speaker of the House of Representatives their written declaration that the President is unable to discharge the powers and duties of his office. Thereupon Congress shall decide the issue, assembling within forty eight hours for that purpose if not in session. If the Congress, within twenty one days after receipt of the latter written declaration, or, if Congress is not in session, within twenty one days after Congress is required to assemble, determines by two thirds vote of both Houses that the President is unable to discharge the powers and duties of his office, the Vice President shall continue to discharge the same as Acting President; otherwise, the President shall resume the powers and duties of his office.

Amendment 26—Voting Age Set to 18 Years. Ratified 7/1/1971.

1. The right of citizens of the United States, who are eighteen years of age or older, to vote shall not be denied or abridged by the United States or by any State on account of age.
2. The Congress shall have power to enforce this article by appropriate legislation.

Amendment 27—Limiting Congressional Pay Increases. Ratified 5/7/1992.

No law, varying the compensation for the services of the Senators and Representatives, shall take effect, until an election of Representatives shall have intervened.

The Kentucky Resolutions of 1798

The following resolutions were proposed to the Kentucky Legislature, and this version was adopted on November 10, 1798, as a protest against the Alien and Sedition Acts passed by Congress. They were authored by Thomas Jefferson, but he did not make public the fact until years later. This represents one of the clearest expressions of his views on how the Constitution was supposed to be interpreted.[169]

1. *Resolved*, That the several States composing, the United States of America, are not united on the principle of unlimited submission to their general government; but that, by a compact under the style and title of a Constitution for the United States, and of amendments thereto, they constituted a general government for special purposes—delegated to that government certain definite powers, reserving, each State to itself, the residuary mass of right to their own self-government; and that whensoever the general government assumes undelegated powers, its acts are unauthoritative, void, and of no force: that to this compact each State acceded as a State, and is an integral part, its co-States forming, as to itself, the other party: that the government created by this compact was not made the exclusive or final judge of the extent of the powers delegated to itself; since that would have made its discretion, and not the Constitution, the measure of its powers; but that, as in all other cases of compact among powers having no common judge, each party has an equal right to judge for itself, as well of infractions as of the mode and measure of redress.

2. *Resolved*, That the Constitution of the United States, having delegated to Congress a power to punish treason, counterfeiting the securities and current coin of the United States, piracies, and felonies committed on the high seas, and offenses against the law of nations, and no other crimes, whatsoever; and it being true as a general principle, and one of the amendments

---

[169] Original   URL: http://www.constitution.org/cons/kent1798.htm Maintained: Jon Roland of the Constitution Society

to the Constitution having also declared, that "the powers not delegated to the United States by the Constitution, not prohibited by it to the States, are reserved to the States respectively, or to the people," therefore the act of Congress, passed on the 14th day of July, 1798, and intituled "An Act in addition to the act intituled An Act for the punishment of certain crimes against the United States," as also the act passed by them on the—day of June, 1798, intituled "An Act to punish frauds committed on the bank of the United States," (and all their other acts which assume to create, define, or punish crimes, other than those so enumerated in the Constitution,) are altogether void, and of no force; and that the power to create, define, and punish such other crimes is reserved, and, of right, appertains solely and exclusively to the respective States, each within its own territory.

3. *Resolved*, That it is true as a general principle, and is also expressly declared by one of the amendments to the Constitutions, that "the powers not delegated to the United States by the Constitution, our prohibited by it to the States, are reserved to the States respectively, or to the people"; and that no power over the freedom of religion, freedom of speech, or freedom of the press being delegated to the United States by the Constitution, nor prohibited by it to the States, all lawful powers respecting the same did of right remain, and were reserved to the States or the people: that thus was manifested their determination to retain to themselves the right of judging how far the licentiousness of speech and of the press may be abridged without lessening their useful freedom, and how far those abuses which cannot be separated from their use should be tolerated, rather than the use be destroyed. And thus also they guarded against all abridgment by the United States of the freedom of religious opinions and exercises, and retained to themselves the right of protecting the same, as this State, by a law passed on the general demand of its citizens, had already protected them from all human restraint or interference. And that in addition to this general principle and express declaration, another and more special provision has been made by one of the amendments to the Constitution, which expressly declares,

that "Congress shall make no law respecting an establishment of religion, or prohibiting the free exercise thereof, or abridging the freedom of speech or of the press": thereby guarding in the same sentence, and under the same words, the freedom of religion, of speech, and of the press: insomuch, that whatever violated either, throws down the sanctuary which covers the others, arid that libels, falsehood, and defamation, equally with heresy and false religion, are withheld from the cognizance of federal tribunals. That, therefore, the act of Congress of the United States, passed on the 14th day of July, 1798, intituled "An Act in addition to the act intituled An Act for the punishment of certain crimes against the United States," which does abridge the freedom of the press, is not law, but is altogether void, and of no force.

4. *Resolved*, That alien friends are under the jurisdiction and protection of the laws of the State wherein they are: that no power over them has been delegated to the United States, nor prohibited to the individual States, distinct from their power over citizens. And it being true as a general principle, and one of the amendments to the Constitution having also declared, that "the powers not delegated to the United States by the Constitution, nor prohibited by it to the States, are reserved to the States respectively, or to the people," the act of the Congress of the United States, passed on the—day of July, 1798, intituled "An Act concerning aliens," which assumes powers over alien friends, not delegated by the Constitution, is not law, but is altogether void, and of no force.

5. *Resolved*. That in addition to the general principle, as well as the express declaration, that powers not delegated are reserved, another and more special provision, inserted in the Constitution from abundant caution, has declared that "the migration or importation of such persons as any of the States now existing shall think proper to admit, shall not be prohibited by the Congress prior to the year 1808" that this commonwealth does admit the migration of alien friends, described as the subject of the said act concerning aliens: that a provision against prohibiting their migration, is a provision against all acts equivalent thereto, or it would be nugatory: that to remove

them when migrated, is equivalent to a prohibition of their migration, and is, therefore, contrary to the said provision of the Constitution, and void.

6. *Resolved*, That the imprisonment of a person under the protection of the laws of this commonwealth, on his failure to obey the simple order of the President to depart out of the United States, as is undertaken by said act intituled "An Act concerning aliens" is contrary to the Constitution, one amendment to which has provided that "no person shalt be deprived of liberty without due progress of law"; and that another having provided that "in all criminal prosecutions the accused shall enjoy the right to public trial by an impartial jury, to be informed of the nature and cause of the accusation, to be confronted with the witnesses against him, to have compulsory process for obtaining witnesses in his favor, and to have the assistance of counsel for his defense;" the same act, undertaking to authorize the President to remove a person out of the United States, who is under the protection of the law, on his own suspicion, without accusation, without jury, without public trial, without confrontation of the witnesses against him, without heating witnesses in his favor, without defense, without counsel, is contrary to the provision also of the Constitution, is therefore not law, but utterly void, and of no force: that transferring the power of judging any person, who is under the protection of the laws from the courts, to the President of the United States, as is undertaken by the same act concerning aliens, is against the article of the Constitution which provides that "the judicial power of the United States shall be vested in courts, the judges of which shall hold their offices during good behavior"; and that the said act is void for that reason also. And it is further to be noted, that this transfer of judiciary power is to that magistrate of the general government who already possesses all the Executive, and a negative on all Legislative powers.

7. *Resolved*, That the construction applied by the General Government (as is evidenced by sundry of their proceedings) to those parts of the Constitution of the United States which delegate to Congress a power "to lay and collect taxes, duties,

imports, and excises, to pay the debts, and provide for the common defense and general welfare of the United States," and "to make all laws which shall be necessary and proper for carrying into execution, the powers vested by the Constitution in the government of the United States, or in any department or officer thereof," goes to the destruction of all limits prescribed to their powers by the Constitution: that words meant by the instrument to be subsidiary only to the execution of limited powers, ought not to be so construed as themselves to give unlimited powers, nor a part to be so taken as to destroy the whole residue of that instrument: that the proceedings of the General Government under color of these articles, will be a fit and necessary subject of revisal and correction, at a time of greater tranquillity, while those specified in the preceding resolutions call for immediate redress.

8th. *Resolved*, That a committee of conference and correspondence be appointed, who shall have in charge to communicate the preceding resolutions to the Legislatures of the several States: to assure them that this commonwealth continues in the same esteem of their friendship and union which it has manifested from that moment at which a common danger first suggested a common union: that it considers union, for specified national purposes, and particularly to those specified in their late federal compact, to be friendly, to the peace, happiness and prosperity of all the States: that faithful to that compact, according to the plain intent and meaning in which it was understood and acceded to by the several parties, it is sincerely anxious for its preservation: that it does also believe, that to take from the States all the powers of self-government and transfer them to a general and consolidated government, without regard to the special delegations and reservations solemnly agreed to in that compact, is not for the peace, happiness or prosperity of these States; and that therefore this commonwealth is determined, as it doubts not its co-States are, to submit to undelegated, and consequently unlimited powers in no man, or body of men on earth: that in cases of an abuse of the delegated powers, the members of the general government, being chosen by the people, a change by the people would be the constitutional remedy; but, where powers are assumed which have not been delegated, a nullification of the act is the rightful remedy: that every State has a natural right in cases not within the compact, (*casus non fœderis*) to nullify of their own authority all assumptions of power by others within their limits: that without this right, they would be under the dominion, absolute and unlimited, of whosoever might exercise this right of judgment for them: that nevertheless, this commonwealth, from motives of regard and respect for its co States, has wished to communicate with them on the subject: that with them alone it is proper to communicate, they alone being parties to the compact, and solely authorized to judge in the last resort of the powers exercised under it, Congress being not a party, but merely the creature of the compact, and subject as to its assumptions of power to the final judgment of those by whom, and for whose use itself and its powers were all created and modified: that if the acts before specified should stand, these conclusions would flow from them; that the general government may place any act they think proper on the list of crimes and punish it themselves whether enumerated or not enumerated by the constitution as cognizable by them: that they may transfer its cognizance to the President, or any other person, who may himself be the accuser, counsel, judge and jury, whose suspicions may be the evidence, his order the sentence, his officer the executioner, and his breast the sole record of the transaction: that a very numerous and valuable description of the inhabitants of these States being, by this precedent, reduced, as outlaws, to the absolute dominion of one man, and the barrier of the Constitution thus swept away from us all, no ramparts now remains against the passions and the powers of a majority in Congress to protect from a like exportation, or other more grievous punishment, the minority of the same body, the legislatures, judges, governors and counsellors of the States, nor their other peaceable inhabitants, who may venture to reclaim the constitutional rights and liberties of the States and people, or who for other causes, good or bad, may be obnoxious to the views, or marked by the suspicions of the President, or be thought dangerous to his or their election, or other interests, public or personal; that the friendless alien has indeed been selected as the safest subject of a first experiment; but the citizen will soon follow, or rather, has already followed, for already has a sedition act marked him as its prey: that these and successive acts of the same character, unless arrested at the threshold, necessarily drive these States into revolution and blood and will furnish new calumnies against republican government, and new pretexts for those who wish it to be believed that man cannot be governed but by a rod of iron: that it would be a dangerous delusion were a confidence in the men of our choice to silence our fears for the safety of our rights: that confidence is everywhere the parent of despotism—free government is founded in jealousy, and not in confidence; it is jealousy and not confidence which prescribes limited constitutions, to bind down those whom we are obliged to trust with power: that our Constitution has accordingly fixed the limits to which, and no further, our confidence may go; and let the honest advocate of confidence read the Alien and Sedition acts, and say if the Constitution has not been wise in fixing limits to the government it created, and whether we should be wise in destroying those limits, Let him say what the government is, if it be not a tyranny, which the men of our choice have con erred on our President, and the President of our choice has assented to, and accepted over the friendly stranger to whom the mild spirit of our country and its law have pledged hospitality and protection: that the men of our choice have more respected the bare suspicion of the President, than the solid right of innocence, the claims of justification, the sacred force of truth, and the forms and substance of law and justice. In questions of powers, then, let no more be heard of confidence in man, but bind him down from mischief by the chains of the Constitution. That this commonwealth does therefore call on its co-States for an expression of their sentiments on the acts concerning aliens and for the punishment of certain crimes herein before specified, plainly declaring whether these acts are or are not authorized by the federal compact. And it doubts not that their sense will be so announced as to prove their attachment unaltered to limited government, weather general or particular. And that the rights and liberties of their co–States will be exposed to no dangers by remaining embarked in a common bottom with their own. That they will concur with this commonwealth in considering the said acts as so palpably against the Constitution as to amount to an undisguised declaration that that compact is not meant to be the measure of the powers of the General Government, but that it will proceed in the exercise over these States, of all powers whatsoever: that they will view this as seizing the rights of the States, and consolidating them in the hands of the General Government, with a power assumed to bind the States (not merely as the cases made federal, casus fœderis but), in all cases whatsoever, by laws made, not with their consent, but by others against their consent: that this would be to surrender the form of government we have chosen, and live under one deriving its powers from its own will, and not from our authority; and that the co–States, recurring to their natural right in cases not made federal, will concur in declaring these acts void, and of no force, and will each take measures of its own for providing that neither these acts, nor any others of the General Government not plainly and intentionally authorized by the Constitution, shalt be exercised within their respective territories.

9th. *Resolved*, That the said committee be authorized to communicate by writing or personal conference, at any times or places whatever, with any person or persons who may be appointed by any one or more co–States to correspond or confer with them; and that they lay their proceedings before the next session of Assembly.

CPSIA information can be obtained at www.ICGtesting.com
Printed in the USA
BVOW081128140313

315509BV00001B/2/P